THE
ZIONIST
REVOLUTION

THE
ZIONIST
REVOLUTION

A New Perspective

Harold Fisch

ST. MARTIN'S PRESS
NEW YORK

For information, write:
St. Martin's Press, Inc., 175 Fifth Avenue, New York, N.Y. 10010
Printed in Great Britain
First published in the United States of America in 1978

Library of Congress Cataloging in Publication Data

Fisch, Harold.
    The Zionist revolution.

    Includes bibliographical references and index.
    1. Zionism—History. 2. Jews—Identity. I. Title.
DS149.F497   956.94'001   78–424

Contents

For Joyce
for everything

Acknowledgments

ELEMENTS of the chapters which follow, now much revised and rounded out, first appeared in various journals, among them: *Midstream, Mitzpeh, The American Zionist, Forum, The South African Jewish Observer, Commentary,* and *The New Leader.* Acknowledgment is hereby made to the editors and proprietors of these journals. To my friend E. Addy Cohen of Savyon I owe a sincere debt of gratitude for his help and encouragement at all times. Miss Rhea Magnes, a former pupil and now an experienced columnist and editor, was the first to suggest how this material could be shaped into a book.

Finally the author wishes to acknowledge the support of the World Zionist Organization which helped to make this publication possible.

H.F.
Jerusalem
January, 1978

I

Introduction

I

THE HISTORY OF ZIONISM in the nineteenth century is rooted in paradox. On the one hand Zionism was an expression of the desire to abolish the difference sensed by Jews between themselves and other men, a difference which has led, in varying degree, to isolation on the part of the Jew and emotions ranging from distrust to brutal intolerance on the part of the non-Jew. On the other hand the Zionist Movement constituted the ultimate affirmation of this difference, a courageous, even defiant, gesture against all attempts at assimilation by Jews in exile.

Zionism can be regarded – and was regarded by many of its early exponents – as the final step in the process of Jewish emancipation. From the time of the French Revolution on, the great themes of Jewish striving had been liberation, equal rights, admission to the wider society of enlightened men. In western Europe the ghetto walls had fallen down at the sound of the trumpet of emancipation, and the Jew had stepped abroad into a freedom which his forbears had scarcely known. Jews were on the way to equality. In eastern Europe, of course, the story was different. As the Jews of France and Britain advanced into the light, those of Russia seemed to move into greater darkness. 'As long as I am Czar,' said Nicholas II – and he remained czar until his reign came to a bloody end in 1917 – 'the Jews of Russia shall not receive equal rights.' But even if pogrom and repression constituted the climate of their lives, the Russian Jews, no less than their fellow Jews in the West, dreamed of emancipation, equal rights, fraternity, enlightenment. But what was one to do if the reality outside so rudely contradicted the dream and the promise? For a man like Leo Pinsker, writing in 1882, there was an answer to this. If the Jews, as citizens, could not attain those equal rights to which they aspired, then they must strive for what he called 'auto-emancipation', i.e. self-emancipation as a group, admission to the family of nations on an equal footing with other national groups.[1]

Pinsker's aim was thus not essentially different from that of the enlightened Jews of the West who had striven for equal rights during the nineteenth century. It was merely that he transposed the idea to the national level. By becoming a nation like other nations Jews would become normal. They would no longer carry the burden of peculiarity. The Jewish problem, in the sense of the problem of discrimination levelled at Jews as Jews, would disappear. A little later on many sensitive men from the Jewish communities of western and central Europe were to arrive at conclusions similar to Pinsker's, as a result of their disillusionment with the process of liberation in the context of European society. True, Jews had attained, or were on their way to attaining, equal rights as citizens, but subtler discrimination still continued. John Galsworthy was to show in his play *Loyalties* (1922) that the Jew was still the outsider, and that in a moment of stress the upper class would band together against him much as they did in the Middle Ages. And if this was evident to Galsworthy, how much more evident must it have been to the Jews themselves, who were striving to break free from the constraints of their status as eternal outsiders? American society, though supposedly more open and liberal, was hardly different in this respect from British society. Ludwig Lewisohn, who grew up in North America in the first two decades of the twentieth century, recorded in his autobiography how he had gradually been made to realize that, as a Jew, he would never be able to compete on terms of equality with his non-Jewish friends and colleagues in the universities and in the arts. His solution lay in one concept: Zionism.[2]

Theodor Herzl had established the nature of the illness and its remedy at the time of the trial of Captain Albert Dreyfus, who was charged with treason in Paris in 1894. The ordinary laws of evidence and the principle of judicial impartiality did not seem to

apply to Dreyfus because he was a Jew – and this in a land where
the banner of liberty and equality had first been unfurled! The
logical conclusion was that emancipation, in the sense of the grant
of civil rights, was not enough. There had to be a further decisive
phase – national liberation. Only when Jews achieved a national
status comparable with that of other peoples would the scandal of
otherness be removed. Here East and West joined hands. The
lesson that Herzl learned from the Dreyfus trial was to be confirmed by the trial of Mendel Beilis in Kiev in 1913, when,
incredibly, the medieval blood libel was revived (in the Middle
Ages Christians often perpetrated murderous assaults on Jews,
who were accused of having killed Christian children in order to
use their blood in the baking of Passover bread) in the form of a
charge of ritual murder – though if anything the Russian judiciary
worked more rapidly and more efficiently than the French for the
vindication of the innocent. For many this had only one meaning:
the problem of Jewish suffering and of gross (or more muted)
anti-Jewish prejudice called urgently for a national-territorial
solution. This and this alone would enable the Jewish people to
pluck the golden fruit of emancipation with its promise of liberty,
fraternity and equality. This, basically, is the Zionism of Pinsker,
Herzl and Nordau.

But this is only one side of the history of Zionism. Its other
aspect, its celebration of the unique quality, the separateness, of
the Jewish people was an equally compelling, if contradictory,
motive for the foundation of the Movement. The Return to Zion
made its appeal to the Jewish soul – and here the more visionary
apostles of modern Zionism, Moses Hess, Ahad Ha'am and Rabbi
A. I. Kook, are our spokesmen – precisely because it appeared to
provide a means of stemming the tide of emancipation and assimilation. Zionism was quintessentially a Jewish phenomenon; it
would serve to foster all that was unique in Jewish memory and
experience. In an era in which Jewish identity was threatened on
all sides, it would provide a means of deepening and strengthening
that identity. Instead of the languages of the non-Jewish environment, the Hebrew language would become the language of the
Jew, and through that language the Jewish soul would be redeemed.
Zionism would thus become an instrument not primarily for
normalizing the Jewish condition, but for emphasizing the specific

inwardness of Jewish existence *in spite of* the equalizing processes of the new liberalism.

In respect of this counter-theme, too, Zionism represents a natural extension of Jewish striving in eastern and western Europe throughout the nineteenth century. For along with the struggle for equal rights which we have noted, a major effort was in progress on the part of the Jew to defend his separate existence as a covenant people, a people, in Balaam's words, 'who dwells alone' (*Numbers* 23:9). Here was a centripetal movement to match the centrifugal movement of emancipation. During the nineteenth century Jewish communities had devised various mechanisms for preserving themselves against social and cultural symbiosis, against the pressure, that is, of the new liberal atmosphere. These had included the establishment of voluntary ghettos in various localities and there were also the various religious compromises, such as Reform and Conservative Judaism, which were intended to preserve Jewish life from total erosion. In the East the traditional fabric of rabbinic Judaism remained largely intact, but pressures were mounting there also, and the story of Jewish life in the east European *shtetl* at the turn of the century is very much the story of a younger generation abandoning the life-style of its ancestors and seeking what the poet Chaim Nahman Bialik called 'the wind and the light' of emancipation.

In this situation the most powerful instrument devised to preserve Jewish singularity was undoubtedly Zionism. Not only the Return to Zion itself; almost equally the organizational and social activity accompanying the theme of the Return was to constitute a bulwark against assimilation. S. Y. Agnon in his depiction of the Jewish township in decline (for instance, in *A Simple Tale* (1935)) gives us frequent glimpses of the Zionist clubhouse which for many had taken the place of the old *Bet Midrash* (House of Study) by the beginning of the century. There the young men and women could meet to read the Hebrew and Yiddish newspapers and talk endlessly about the doings of their people in the new 'colonies' of Palestine. The zeal and fervour of these 'Lovers of Zion' were bound up inevitably with a deep desire for self-authentication. The Jew in the land of Israel could be, at last, himself, and that meant to be unique, defined by his special history and his special role in the world. Thrice daily the pious Jew repeats the declaration of unity: 'Hear, O Israel, the Lord our God, the Lord is One' (*Deuteronomy* 6:4). And, to correspond with this, God is said to make his own declaration of unity, the text of which is: 'Who is like thy people Israel, a singular nation in the land . . . ?' (2 *Samuel* 7:23).

Here, then, are two interwoven themes; nor is it always possible to disentangle them. Chaim Weizmann's posture was essentially that of a Western liberal come to demand equal rights for the Jewish people. This was the source of his charm, and it was this that made his case unanswerable. But he was also responding to a call by no means explicable in terms of liberal politics. Thus he describes his early Zionist stirrings as a boy:

The obstinacy and persistence of the movement cannot be understood except in terms of faith. This faith was part of our make-up; our Jewishness and our Zionism were interchangeable; you could not destroy the second without destroying the first. We did not need to listen to propaganda. When Zvi Hirsch Masliansky, the famous folk-orator, came to preach Zionism to us, he addressed the convinced . . . he invariably drew on texts from the book of Isaiah, which all of us knew by heart. But we heard in his moving orations only the echo of our innermost feelings.[3]

Weizmann here pays tribute to the force of the Jewish prophetic idea as the spring of Zionist endeavour. No doubt the orator whom he mentions quoted to his young auditors the verse from Isaiah which says:

And it shall come to pass in the last days, that the mountain of the Lord's house shall be established on the top of the mountains, and shall be exalted above the hills, and all the nations shall flow unto it. And many people shall go and say, Come and let us go up to the mountain of the Lord, to the house of the God of Jacob; and he will teach us of his ways, and we will walk in his paths; for out of Zion shall go forth the law, and the word of the Lord from Jerusalem. (*Isaiah* 2:2, 3)

This is the 'Zionism of Zion'. These are the dreams and metaphors which even the more practical Zionists carry somewhere in their baggage. Of course they don't bother to analyse them. If they did they would find that these verses imply a history for the Jewish people significantly different from other kinds of history, a destiny more agonizing (think of chapter 53, the 'Servant' chapter, of

Isaiah) but also more exalted. Zionists have always had some intuition of this, and yet the logic of the Basle Programme accepted by the Zionist Movement in 1897 was that not of Isaiah but of the other national movements of the nineteenth century which had brought independence to Italy, to Greece and to many smaller countries. The theme was the political enfranchisement of the Jewish people: 'Zionism seeks to establish a home for the Jewish People in Palestine secured under public law,' it declared.[4] What the linguists would call the 'deep structure' of this sentence is the same as that of all the liberal declarations of the nineteenth century. Change a word or two and it might be a motto for Mazzini or Garibaldi in their striving for Italian unity. Transpose it into the private sphere and you can read it as: 'Emancipation seeks to establish equality for the Jewish citizen secured under public law.' At work in this sentence – in all its possible transformations – is a meliorative view of human relations. Man is finally advancing towards freedom. National liberation is of a piece with the emancipation of the slaves in America, the Italians in Italy or the Jews in Europe. All these manifestations are part of the same tide of progress which began with the French Revolution and will reach its climax when men became tolerant, rational and free. The Jewish problem is a little less tractable than most, but even that will prove amenable in time to a liberal-rational solution. Theodor Herzl based his plan for the creation of a Jewish state on what he called 'the theory of rationality',[5] for it seemed to him to make excellent sense and to be perfectly in accord with the normally accepted laws of political behaviour.

Herzl and Weizmann were fortunate in making these claims at the period of maximal liberal optimism. 'Bliss was it in that dawn to be alive', and to be a Zionist meant to have a claim on men of goodwill all over Europe and America. It was not only that the Zionist argument was just, but its justice gave it political force and validity. The men to whom the Zionist argument appealed, high-minded liberals and Christians like Lord Balfour, Jan Smuts and C. P. Scott, were also the men who seemed to have the future in their hands.

But, sadly, the expectation of those years has not been realized. The great age of liberalism is clearly over, and a harsher political climate prevails. The Western powers at Helsinki in 1975, America at their head, spent no time whatever bemoaning the fate of Estonia, or Latvia or Lithuania – states which have been swallowed up in the new Russian empire. It was taken for granted that great powers have imperative interests which transcend the rights of small nations. In these circumstances, does not the Zionism of Herzl and Weizmann begin to look a trifle old-fashioned? Does not Israel's appeal for justice, for security and independence guaranteed 'under public law' begin to have a slightly quaint flavour in an age when even lip-service to such ideals is becoming increasingly rare? If it was only a matter of political rhetoric this would not be so serious, but Israel takes its commitment to Western liberalism seriously (more seriously than do the Western powers themselves) and this can have grave practical consequences. In 1973, forewarned by a few hours of the coming Arab onslaught, Israel studiously avoided taking any preventive action, hoping thereby to win the sympathy of the world by ceding the opprobrium of aggression to the other party. The result was not encouraging. The adroit use of the oil weapon by Israel's enemies rendered every other kind of claim nugatory, and in the aftermath of that war Israel's political isolation became extreme.

II

What I shall argue in this book is that Israel's ideological link with a Western liberal tradition is rooted in a fallacy. Zionism is only partially the offspring of the Enlightenment. It is also, and indeed primarily, the offspring of the Jewish myth.[6] And it is the language of that myth which must be studied if Zionism is to be correctly understood by Jew and gentile alike. What occurred in the nineteenth century was a linguistic deception, or, perhaps more correctly, self-deception. Zionism was presented as a movement parallel with all the other movements of national liberation, and the rhetoric of the *Risorgimento* was borrowed and applied to the situation of the Jewish people, whose problems were now to yield to a rational solution. This linguistic delusion had at the time important and valuable results. It made Zionism comprehensible to a great many people whose goodwill and support proved vital to the success of the endeavour. More important, it also made Zionism comprehensible to a great many alienated Jews, who were unconscious of the real nature of the force to which they were responding. They were able to persuade themselves that they were doing what all other peoples were doing in their generation – returning home to seek their independence; although the truth is that not one single people in the nineteenth century ever 'returned home'. The Italians and the Greeks were at home already, and those who weren't (like the American negroes) had not the slightest intention of ever returning.

But in spite of valuable gains, the employment of this rhetoric in place of the Jewish language of Zionism has created problems which now beset the state of Israel. The main such problem is an educational one. The young Israeli has been brought up to believe that Israel is a state like other states; to be an Israeli is, basically, very much like being a Frenchman or a Dutchman. But he quickly comes to realize that this is not so: existentially he is set apart from others. He discovers at the age of eighteen that henceforward his personal life will be conditioned by the fact that he lives in a country surrounded by implacable enemies. If he goes abroad, the shock will be even greater: he quickly becomes aware that he belongs to a 'peculiar people', in the sense that he is either peculiarly interesting or peculiarly troublesome to other people. For this experience he is not morally prepared, for he has been taught that Israel is a 'normal' state, or at least is rapidly on the way to becoming one. The result is bewilderment and frustration.

Our ancestors in the ghetto had no such difficulties. They knew that they carried the special burdens of Jewish history and they could either rejoice in or lament this, as the case might be. As a matter of fact they did both. Their descendants, however, were given to believe that all that was needed for a solution of the 'Jewish problem' was freedom and statehood. But freedom, it appears, is not enough, and statehood, while propelling the Jew into the centre of world attention, has only rendered the Jewish problem more acute. As for the Jews of the Diaspora, it is now obvious to them that Israel is not a state like other states. It may be a source of pride but it is also a source of new and profound anxiety. Either way it belongs to a special Jewish dimension.

At the political level, in avoiding recognition of the special charge at work in the Return to Zion, we have also placed ourselves at a disadvantage. Zionism, basing itself on abstract right and justice, has often let more forceful arguments go by default. The question of to whom the Land belongs has often been answered by vague references to justice for the homeless Jew, an ethical argument which hardly touches on the claim to sovereignty over a particular territory, especially when that sovereignty is contested by another people also claiming to be homeless. Similarly when, as a result of the Six Day War in June 1967, Israel came into possession of the whole biblical land of Canaan, including Jerusalem itself – 'the mountain of the Lord's house' of which Isaiah had spoken – Israeli spokesmen had difficulty in giving expression to the special nature of this moment of liberation. Everyone felt it and everyone was uplifted by it. There was, as Maurice Samuel termed it, a 'shock of self-identification'.[7] It was not only a home-coming but a meeting with a deeper, forgotten self. And yet when it came to drawing conclusions and justifying those conclusions before the world, Israel tended to fumble and to look for formulae which seemed liberal and logical but, in fact, convinced no one: 'We wish to remain in Jerusalem because it is not right that the city should be divided again' – as though it is somehow the physical integrity of Jerusalem that is at stake rather than the inalienable bond between the Jewish people and the 'holy hill' of Zion. With regard to Hebron, Jericho, Shechem and Beth-El, the so-called West Bank, we have recourse to all manner of formulae, the commonest of which is that we are not legally obliged to part with them unless a peace treaty is agreed; or that if those areas are handed over to the Palestinian Arabs they are liable to be used as a base for terrorist attacks on Israel. Both of these arguments are manifestly true but they leave out the main issue, which is that the Jewish people has always regarded these areas as its homeland, and that its connection with them is what Zionism is all about.

When pressed, as he was on his appearance before the Peel Commission which visited Palestine in 1936, the late David Ben-Gurion would say, 'The Bible is our mandate' – meaning that it constitutes the basis of the Jewish claim to the land of Israel. We may imagine that this brought a polite smile to the faces of the members of that august Commission, who were not in the habit of connecting the Bible with real, everyday politics. The point is that Ben-Gurion, Bible-conscious though he was, was not capable of convincing the sceptic that he was talking about something as potent, say, as Mao's Little Red Book. No one scoffs at that because we can see what mighty forces it has released in the world, whereas the Bible suggests to the twentieth-century Western conscience nothing politically more dangerous than the musical banks in Samuel Butler's *Erewhon*.

For the Arabs it is clear that Zionism is a force as potent as any other great modern revolution. But they have no means of tracing that force to its origin, since the Jews have not really thought out that matter either. Sometimes it seems as if the Arabs dimly understand the Jewish purpose in the land of Israel better than the Jews do themselves. Throughout the years since the Arab conquest in the seventh century they have been uneasy about their title and have betrayed nervousness about the Jews who were there and might still come back. Thus it is said that they bricked up the 'Gate of Mercy' in the eastern wall of the Temple Mount to prevent the Jewish Messiah from gaining entry when he came to claim his own. They took care to erect a mosque on the site of the Temple itself, after determining its exact location according to Jewish tradition. In this way they hoped to establish successor rights and thus obviate the reversion of the title to the Jews: in the Middle East politics and religion go very much together. Even the dead are mobilized for political purposes. The Arabs have been at pains to obliterate signs of continued Jewish residence in Jerusalem by removing thousands of tombstones from the great Jewish necropolis on the Mount of Olives and building mosques and other structures over the graves themselves. The dead are powerful witnesses, especially when we are dealing with a cemetery which has been in almost continuous use for Jewish burial since biblical times.

Oddly enough modern Zionism, seeing itself primarily as the child of the Enlightenment, has tended to play down the history of Jewish settlement before the end of the nineteenth century, since the earlier settlement was manifestly unconnected with socialism, liberalism or any other Western rational motive. But the fact is that Jews had come to live in Palestine in greater or lesser numbers throughout the centuries. There was never a time when the Jews were completely absent; Jewish settlement in the Galilee, for instance, had been continuous during the whole period of the Exile. From the early eighteenth century on Jewish immigrants began to arrive in groups of several hundreds at a time, among them a large group of the followers of the Hassidic rabbi, Menahem Mendel of Vitebsk. Clearly the motivation for this type of immigration and settlement was messianic, biblical; it had little to do with the politics of the *Risorgimento*. The same applies to the creation of the first modern Jewish agricultural village of Petah Tikva in 1878. The settlers, who came chiefly from the Old City of Jerusalem, were moved by a desire to fulfil a biblical command by restoring glory and fertility to the Holy Land. It was this faith which enabled them to lay the foundations of modern Jewish agricultural settlement in Palestine.[8] It is true that their initiative was later to be strengthened mightily by the arrival of the socialists of the so-called Second *Aliyah* (or wave of immigration) in the early years of the twentieth century. These young men and women were largely in revolt against the faith of their ancestors. Nevertheless the original impulse was neither socialist nor liberal: it was a Jewish impulse which had little or nothing to do with contemporary movements in Europe.

The tensions between these two kinds of ideology and the resultant distortions and confusion over the real nature of Zionism are the subject of this book. The implication for our time is obvious. Until the Jew understands himself and acknowledges his own identity and motives, he will scarcely be in a position to present his case to others.[9] Worse than that, he will be the subject of fantasies and delusions which will rob him of his confidence and faith, that faith which enabled his ancestors to remove mountains – for the very terracing of the Judean hills is a mute witness to Jewish faith and love for the land of Israel – and his less remote ancestors to settle in the inhospitable and malaria-infested dust of Petah Tikva, to create there the beginnings of modern Jewish independence.

2

The Covenant

I

THE EARLY ZIONISTS started with a very keen sense of the radical abnormality of Jewish existence as they found it in the Diaspora. They perceived the presence of some peculiar irritant in Jewish experience, the grain of sand, so to speak, in the oyster. For Theodor Herzl, Max Nordau and Leo Pinsker, that irritant was, in one word: anti-semitism. In so far as the Jew had peculiar obsessions, peculiar difficulties with his surroundings and with himself, this was the consequence of anti-semitism. But anti-semitism was something extrinsic to the Jew. It was a condition of his environment rather than of his soul. Moreover it was essentially negative. It represented the external pressure which made Zionism necessary, but with the accomplishment of the Zionist programme it would disappear. Unlike the sand in the oyster, it would become no part of the resultant pearl. With the creation of the Jewish state, anti-semitism, having done its work, would be no more. Herzl is very clear about this. In the final section of *The Jewish State* he remarks, 'When once we begin to carry out the plan, anti-semitism would stop at once and for ever. For it is the conclusion of peace.'[1] A strange prognosis, surely, for a man who had otherwise so remarkable a grasp of the future!

Herzl, therefore, does not recognize any deep, abiding and intrinsic ground of Jewish abnormality, nor does he prepare us for the possibility that such abnormality, even narrowly defined as the external pressure on the Jew, would continue after the foundation of that Jewish state which he had so amazingly envisioned.

From this point of view we would do better to start not with the
visionary Herzl, but with the existentialist philosopher, Jean-Paul
Sartre, writing in the sad aftermath of the Nazi Holocaust. He, too,
recognizes the fundamental abnormality of Jewish existence but he
sees this in more positive terms as a challenge, a gateway to liberty.
The inauthentic Jew fools himself that he can melt away into his
environment, that he can be accepted as an equal, that he can
become both within and without like everyone else, but the truly
liberated, the authentic Jew, says Sartre, is the one who learns to
live with his abnormal condition, who:

> knows that he is one who stands apart, untouchable, scorned, pro-
> scribed – and it is as such that he asserts his being. At once he gives up
> his rationalistic optimism; he sees that the world is fragmented by
> irrational divisions . . . and in proclaiming himself a Jew he makes some
> of these values and these divisions his.[2]

Sartre has here abandoned the optimism of the late nineteenth
century and has adopted a more realistic standard. Like Herzl he
believes that it is anti-semitism which has created the Jewish
problem, the problem of Jewish separatism. But he sees that
separation as something that can lead to positive self-respect and
as a deep and permanent feature of Jewish life.

Jews who accept their isolation, their difference, are better off
than those who don't. This represents a remarkable psychological
and historical insight on Sartre's part. Nevertheless Sartre, too,
was capable of extraordinary error, as we can see from our present
point of vantage. For his thesis, hardly less than Herzl's, has been
disproved by subsequent events. Sartre claimed that the ground of
the existential uniqueness, the isolation of the Jews, is the bourgeois society of the West. False economic and social values have
corrupted our civilization and the middle class, consisting as it
does of employers, distributors and parasites, has consequently
become the fertile soil of anti-semitism. Jews will be different as
long as society is dominated by the bourgeoisie, with its unsolved
problems, its frustrations and fears; but in a revolutionary society
upheld by radical Marxism there would be no Jewish problem and
consequently no barriers between Jew and non-Jew.

It is ironical to note, only thirty years after the publication of
Sartre's book, that anti-semitism, in the sense of the refusal to

recognize the right of the Jew to national sovereign existence, flourishes among the radical, revolutionary circles of the New Left which count themselves the followers of Sartre and other left-wing intellectuals like himself. It is not that they oppose nationalism as such. On the contrary, they are, for the most part, uncritical supporters of Arab nationalism and the new nationalisms of Asia and Africa, but for them Jewish nationalism is *ipso facto* inadmissible, a Fascist reversion, a stain on the world community. Why should this irrational discrimination against the Jew (for that is what it surely is) continue to manifest itself precisely in those circles which have set themselves the task of destroying the old bourgeoisie and bringing about the classless society of a Marxist paradise?

The question becomes even more exigent when we consider that even within the Soviet Union where, according to Marxist theory, anti-semitism ought long ago to have been overcome, the abnormality of the Jewish condition continues to be strikingly evident. The Jews are, in fact, the focus of a new revolutionary ferment; they do not become assimilated into the structure of a socialist society, nor does the socialist society any longer desire to assimilate them. In the past few years we have seen amongst Jews of the Soviet Union a remarkable revival of Jewish identity, even of Jewish religious identity, and it is the more remarkable because it has affected a generation almost completely alienated from the sources of Jewish historical experience.

II

What did both Herzl and Sartre overlook? Where did they go wrong? We may suggest that what they disregarded was the aspect of mystery. They treated anti-semitism as a social and political problem, capable of solution on fairly simple, rational lines. They neglected the possibility that Jewish history might be different in some significant way from other kinds of history, governed by specific laws which were not exactly those of dialectical materialism or the politics of the *Risorgimento*. They saw that the Jew was isolated, that his situation was anomalous, so they sought to normalize his status. National self-determination according to the model of Italy or Greece was Herzl's remedy; world socialism was

Sartre's. What was ignored was the possibility that anti-semitism is the result of a spiritual tension, of a resistance to the Jewish myth of salvation. 'It is the vocation of Israel that the world execrates,'[3] says Jacques Maritain.

Israel, which is not of the world, is to be found at the very heart of the world's structure, stimulating it, exasperating it, moving it. Like an alien body, like an activating leaven injected into the mass, it gives the world no peace, it bars slumber, it teaches the world to be discontented and restless as long as the world has not God; it stimulates the movement of history.[4]

From this point of view anti-semitism, with its dreadful and violent rejection of the Jew and his role in the world, is a way of paying tribute to the mystery of Israel,[5] and so is the philo-semitism of a man like Maritain himself. Either way a neutral reaction to the Jew seems to be impossible. But it is not only the world's passionate reaction to the Jew which reveals the mystery of Israel. There is also the Jew's reaction to himself; there is his awareness, however obscure and unconscious, of his own vocation. Here is a source of spiritual tension which both Sartre and Herzl ignored. They ignored the possibility that within the Jew himself there could be a root of restlessness, a burden of otherness which is the result not of anti-semitism but of an inner need, an urge, a positive impulse working within Jewish life and history. Many millions of Jewish bodies have been burnt in the fire over the centuries – the only kind of fire most observers have recognized – but there is also, as the prophet said, an unextinguished flame within which conditions Jewish existence.

It is remarkable how insensitive both these great men, Herzl and Sartre, were to the religious charge within Jewish history. Herzl, as is well known, insisted that when the Jewish state came into existence the rabbis would be kept in their synagogues. The Jewish problem was a secular phenomenon and its solution would likewise be secular. Sartre categorically denied that the Jews constituted either a religious or a national community. 'Jews,' he said, 'have only a ceremonial and polite contact with their religion.'

It is *neither their past, their religion, nor their soil that unites the sons of Israel.* If they have a common bond, if all of them deserve the name of Jew, it is because they have in common the situation of a Jew, *that is, they live in a community which takes them for Jews.*[6]

Sartre discovered – and this is the most important insight in his book – that Jews could live in dignity only when they accepted and affirmed this special situation, when they took the burden of otherness on themselves instead of trying to ignore or escape it. But for Sartre even these authentic Jews are really only making a virtue of necessity. It would be better for them and better for the world, it is implied, if their differences could disappear and they could be like everyone else. It is precisely in this respect that the experience of the most sensitive Jews who have achieved authenticity contradicts Sartre's thesis. One such Jew, for instance, was the American Jewish writer, Ludwig Lewisohn. We have already mentioned how the social pressure, the covert anti-semitism that he found in America, drove him towards Zionism. But there was another side to the story. In meditating on his own identity and on that of his people, he became aware of a root of discontent within himself. This was not occasioned solely or chiefly by the world's rejection of him; on the contrary, it was he who felt impelled to reject the world around him as inadequate and unsuited to his spiritual needs:

I had come to the conclusion, then, that the greater part of my sore discontent with life had arisen for me not from my likeness to my American friends but from my special unlikeness to them. . . . Both our written and our oral tradition reach back to the dawn of human history; they are the expression of what we have always been and essentially still are.[7]

The content that he needed he found in Judaism and Zionism. He felt the need to liberate himself *as a Jew* from the false standards of the society around him. This Sartre would recognize as the reaction of an authentic Jew, but the authentication in Lewisohn's case sprang not primarily from outside pressure but rather from that within, and it took the form of a recognition that he belonged to a people with its *own* history, its *own* traditions and its *own* homeland. And one may add that Lewisohn's experience was not unique, although his expression of it was unusually articulate; the same spiritual pilgrimage has been made by countless assimilated

Jews in the West who have acquired a positive sense of their
identity as Jews in the past few decades.

III

What is the nature of this force working within Jewish life and
history which makes for separation, which urges the Jew forward
in ways that put him at odds with his environment? We have
spoken of self-identification; but what is the nature of the identity
that he feels must be his? If, as Sartre says, it is his special
situation which differentiates the Jew, what is the true nature of
that situation? We are not asking here what Judaism requires
Jews to believe; we are asking, rather, what terms classical Judaism
has to offer which can help them to understand their unique situation in the world as Jews. This is an existential question which now
presses hard on Israelis today – harder even than on Jews in
the past. Why, they ask, is this nation different from other
nations?

In theological terms – terms which both Herzl and Sartre avoid
– Israel's strange existence is defined by the Covenant or *Berit*.
This Covenant is the central experience of Israel recorded in the
Scriptures. But though it is located in certain specific historical
contexts (the promises to the patriarchs and, later, the solemn
treaty entered into at Mount Sinai with the whole people, assembled
there under the leadership of Moses), the Covenant is felt to
underly the existence of Israel at all times. As Martin Buber puts
it, 'They [the tribes] became Israel only when they became
partners in the Covenant of the God.'[8] It became, for Israel, the
key to the understanding of all reality: political, social, historical.
It entered into all departments of life.[9] It also endowed the whole
people with a common task, a sense of unity and purpose, which
was the foundation of its communal life. Even the order of Nature
can only be conceived of as based on a primeval covenant between
God and his creation (cf. *Genesis* 8, 9). It is thus Israel's central
myth.

The Covenant has a bearing on the moral history of the world
as a whole, proceeding as it does under divine providence from the
beginning to the end of days. God is engaged: Man is tested. But
within that universal drama Israel has its unique role. 'And I will

walk among you, and will be your God, and you shall be my people' (*Leviticus* 26:12). Israel becomes the covenant people *par excellence*, summoned to bear witness to the purposes of creation, to endure the messianic tensions of history, to undertake the task of building a sanctuary out of the materials of this world. In the most comprehensive of all covenant formulae Israel receives its vocation: that of becoming 'a kingdom of priests and a holy nation' (*Exodus* 19:6). If all this suggests a sublime call, it also suggests a crippling burden. No wonder the rabbis pictured Mount Sinai as hanging over the people, ready to crush them! If Israel is the mediator of a divine blessing – 'in thee shall all families of the earth be blessed' (*Genesis* 12:3) – Israel is also the 'suffering servant' marked out in Sinai for peculiar trials, made the object of a strange hostility. The Covenant is made up of promise and obligation, terror and fulfilment.

We have spoken of the Covenant as Israel's central myth. But this should not be taken as implying that it is a mere subjective phenomenon, a kind of collective notion or fantasy which Jews are free to subscribe to or abandon if they choose. The Covenant is not one possible interpretation of reality: it is reality itself as Israel experiences it. There are millions of Jews who try to escape it, but it seems that it is impossible for them wholly to do so. It belongs to the existential condition which Israel endures; it is as much an aspect of the environment of the Jew, of his situation, as it is of his soul. Jews all over the world discovered this at the time of the Holocaust; they discovered it again in 1967 and in 1973. They are in a manner coerced, subject, willy-nilly, to the strange destiny which is its theme. 'I will cause you to pass under the rod,' declared the prophet, 'and bring you into the discipline of the Covenant' (*Ezekiel* 20:37).

A modern Jewish thinker, Rabbi Joseph B. Soloveichik, has distinguished between two Covenants.[10] The first, which he terms 'the covenant of ineluctable destiny', is marked by constraint, isolation, terror. It is Jonah trying to escape 'from the presence of the Lord' but being rudely awakened and forced to declare his identity. It is Israel in Egypt, set apart, oppressed, but also united in a common fate. The second Covenant, which Soloveichik calls 'the covenant of vocation' is different. According to this bond the people voluntarily undertake a mission in full consciousness of the responsibilities and privileges involved: it is an expression of loving care on the part of God and voluntary self-dedication on the part of the people. At Sinai, which is the archtypal source of this version of the Covenant, we have, in effect, an arrangement freely undertaken by the contracting parties, the people of Israel meeting God, as it were, on equal ground. The rabbis dramatized this by predicating that God had offered the Torah to each of the nations in turn. One refused because it found it impossible to observe the prohibition forbidding stealing, another because of the prohibition forbidding murder and so forth. In the end the people of Israel alone accepted the offer, saying, 'We will do and we will hearken' (*Exodus* 24:7). Unconditional freedom is joined with unconditional obligation.

Having freely accepted the terms, Israel is now inescapably governed by them. From one point of view the life of the Covenant is a fearful burden, a pressure thrusting us apart from others, but from another it is a liberating vision, a challenge, an opportunity. To be 'a people that dwells alone and that shall not be reckoned among the nations' (*Numbers* 23:9) is a fearful thing, as every Jew has felt at one time or another, but seen in a positive light, it is to be a nation immune to the Spenglerian laws of decline and dissolution, a nation joined to the laws of life. For the Covenant claims to be a programme for an undying people, one linked by divine promise with both the beginning and the end of time. Israel functions in the unconsciousness of the human race (so Freud has taught us) as a symbol of the authority of the Father and, as such, is both loved and hated – Israel calls ancestral matters to mind; but Israel also symbolizes the bright hope for the future. For if the Covenant is rooted in the memory of the past, it also points to the future with its promise of redemption; it endures as long as the world endures. This is the remarkable claim which lies at the heart of Judaism. We can, of course, scorn it or ignore it. But the question is, will it ignore us, will it let us alone? Even if we do not choose, may we not be chosen just the same?

The faithful Jew – or if we use Sartre's term, the 'authentic' Jew – is the Jew who accepts the vocation that is implied in the Covenant, with its burden of uniqueness, of suffering as well as joy. He is not simply coerced by the bond of 'ineluctable destiny'; he wishes, like Lewisohn, to fulfil himself as a Jew. He does not really expect to enjoy a normal status; he expects to meet as well as he can the terms of his contract and, in so doing, to advance the divine plan a little further. This is his extraordinary privilege. He takes part in a historical adventure than which there is nothing more momentous, more significant and valuable.

Now it is here that the bond between the Jewish people and the land of Israel is located. In every one of the Covenants with the patriarchs the promise of the land is included.

And I will establish my covenant between me and thee and thy seed after thee in their generations for an everlasting covenant, to be a God to thee and to thy seed after thee. And I will give to thee and thy seed after thee the land in which thou dost sojourn, all the land of Canaan for an everlasting possession; and I will be their God. (*Genesis* 17:7, 8)

The Jew is driven by a force as old as history itself to reunite himself with his land. It is the Holy Land where the Sanctuary is to be constructed. There and there alone can Israel perform its service as 'a kingdom of priests and a holy nation'. If the vocation of Israel is a mystery, then the vocation of the land is no less mysterious. 'Zion,' says Buber,'is the heart of the renewed world.'[11] It is the 'city of the Great King' (*Psalms* 48:3), chosen to be the physical setting for the fulfilment of the covenant drama. It is by reunion with its land that Israel is redeemed. For if the Covenant roots itself in time, it also roots itself in space. If history becomes the history of salvation, then geography, too, is touched with promise.

Much has been said of the beauty of Jerusalem and of the fragments of ancient glory which it contains, but neither its beauty nor its monuments are of the essence; the bond between Israel and its land belongs more to the province of that which is unseen, more to the future than to the past. It beckons to its exiles, 'the dreamers of Zion', a promise veiling itself in hills and rocks, a trembling image of regeneration. This does not make Israel's love affair with the land less passionate: if anything, it is intensified by the added dimension of the transcendental. The Covenant, in fact, rests on a triad of relationships: God, land and people. The land is holy only because God chooses to dwell in it and chooses that we should dwell in it with him. Take away the theological dimension and Zionism itself turns to ashes.[12] For the land does not satisfy as an end in itself but only as a means to salvation, that intimated, for instance, in the final verses of Ezekiel's great vision of renewal:

They shall dwell in the land where your fathers dwelt that I gave to my servant Jacob; they and their children and their children's children shall dwell there for ever, and my servant David shall be their prince for ever. I will make a covenant of peace with them; it shall be an everlasting covenant with them; and I will bless them and multiply them, and will set my sanctuary in the midst of them for evermore. My dwelling place shall be with them; and I will be their God, and they shall be my people. (*Ezekiel* 37:25–7)

It is thus no mere lust for conquest that ultimately drives Israel towards Zion. The American pioneers of the eighteenth and nineteenth centuries who rushed westwards to seize the riches of the new land were also driven, to some extent, by the concept of a covenant which had become a part of their Protestant heritage. They believed they were responding to a divine call, fulfilling a divine destiny. Nevertheless some ethical dimension was missing; it was not a sense of the sacredness of the land which chiefly drew them on; it was not a case, for them, of a non-material bond linking people with land and both with that God who had chosen to dwell in it from the beginning of time – that would be a distortion of American history. For Israel, on the other hand, the Return cannot really be understood in any other terms.

The two dominant impulses in the Return to Zion are, in fact, obligation and love; an obligation which holds one even when the land appears bleak and inhospitable and when hostile strangers dwell in it, and a love for which the only proper analogy is the love of the bridegroom for the bride. That was how the Jew felt in 1967, when he was reunited with the Holy City and with the ruined walls of his Temple. It was a moment in which the story of Israel suddenly acquired meaning, a moment of truth for every one. What was revealed then was the truth of the Covenant as a continuing reality comprising divine promise and human achievement. 'God has a dream,' said the American Jewish philosopher, Abraham Heschel, commenting eloquently on the events of June 1967. 'The task of Israel is to interpret the dream.' And he added: 'In the upbuilding of the Land we are aware of responding to the biblical Covenant, to an imperative that kept on speaking to us throughout the ages, and which never became obsolete or stale.'[13]

IV

Sartre, who knew mainly the assimilated Jews of France, may be forgiven for failing to acknowledge the covenant bond which unites the people of Israel as a whole with the land of Israel. Here is a factor which certainly does not fit in with his thesis. Yet without it how is one to understand the Jew today? How is one to understand the solidarity of the Jews of the Diaspora with their brethren in the land and with the land itself, their incredible efforts, both material and immaterial, on its behalf? How is one to understand the sense of an unfolding identity which the Jew experiences when returning to his land – a land which he has not personally known, of which all his knowledge is derived from religious and literary traditions but which holds and draws him nonetheless? When the secular Jew found himself at the Western Wall at the climax of the Six Day War he found within himself religious echoes of which he had been unaware till then. Here was the core of his Jewish identity. We should not blame Sartre for failing to understand this. Even Herzl was taken by surprise when he was made conscious of the full force of the love of Zion as it exploded at the Sixth Zionist Congress in 1903. An offer had been made by the British Government of a portion of territory in Uganda for a national home for the Jewish people. It was passionately rejected by the 'Zionists of Zion', for whom the stones of the Holy Land were better than the bread of an alien shore. For Herzl this was an offer that should have been taken seriously; it went far towards satisfying a normal desire for national independence. But Jewish history was evidently not normal history, and Jewish nationalism, not normal nationalism.

The Irish Americans will not return to Ireland, but many Jews will return to Israel, from lands of freedom as well as from lands of servitude. Jews, even when they have long forgotten the accents of biblical Hebrew and have adopted the language of their environment, have not forgotten the imperatives of the love of Zion – a mystery, if you like, but one which has in our time found expression in the most surprisingly practical forms. From this point of view Zionism is a unique movement of liberation for the Jewish soil and body and a movement, too, which includes in itself the theme of redemption on a universal scale. The prophetic finale of the vision of renewal, 'For out of Zion shall go forth the Law, and the word of the Lord from Jerusalem' (*Isaiah* 2:3), is no mere rhetorical adornment of Zionism: it is of its essence.

Progressive Westerners in our time are understandably suspicious of myths which unite elements of religion and nationalism. The truth is, however, that the underlying motive of Zionism, whether consciously acknowledged by Zionists or not, is utterly different from that of other nationalisms – different, certainly, from the perverted forms of nationalism which have plagued Europe in our century. The Covenant is what gives it meaning, and the Covenant is at bottom a moral passion, an urge for self-discovery and an attempt to establish the divine kingdom. The sceptics may smile, but the passion we are speaking of is too real, has endured too long, has expressed itself in forms too vital to be lightly dismissed.

Political ideologies of the nineteenth-century type are no longer in fashion. Zionism disguised itself for a time as one of these, and for this reason it now shares in the general disparagement of historicism and ideology.[14] Neither communism, nor liberalism have fulfilled the great hopes reposed in them at the beginning of this century. Is Zionism not simply like these, one more grandiose, doctrinaire programme of human improvement, even less impressive than the others on account of its narrower national base, and less convincing because of its quaintly biblical authority? The answer is that Zionism is both more and less than a political ideology. If it is borne aloft by vision, it is also rooted in experience. It is not a pattern which Jews have tried to impose upon history; for many of them it is rather the history from which they try to escape. 'Whither shall I flee from thy face?' asks the Psalmist (*Psalm* 139:7). The Covenant is not a mental construct: it is remorselessly empirical; it is the experience of a command, of an overwhelming love which seizes on the willing and unwilling alike. God will pursue Israel, says the prophet Hosea, like a roaring lion; and they will come back trembling from Egypt and from Assyria to return to their homes in Zion, led there by the inexorable bonds of love (*Hosea* 11:4, 10, 11). If we require an accurate definition of Zionist experience in our time, we shall find it in these august and dialectical images.

3

Alienation

I

THE FATHERS of the Zionist Revolution stressed the healing power of the Return; it was to be the cure of a sickness, the name of which was *Galut* (Exile). For *Galut* signified not only the geographical dispersion of the Jewish people, but also a psychological state of disorientation. Jews, said Leo Pinsker in 1882, are sick, the more so because they no longer understand what it is they need to make them whole. Everywhere an alien, the Jew presents a 'tragi-comic figure . . . with distorted countenance and maimed limbs'.[1] Ahad Ha'am, writing a few years later, affirmed that the emancipated Jews of the West were more sick than their persecuted brethren in the East. Their emancipation was only external; within they were slaves. By contrast the Jews of the East were outwardly confined but inwardly free.[2] The moral and intellectual slavery of the so-called emancipated Jews was the more acute because it was unconscious: they sought to become inconspicuous, to become absorbed into the surrounding culture, but they were not aware of how this marked them out for scorn and derision. Having renounced their inner Jewish identity, they suffered from 'spiritual emptiness'.[3] Max Nordau, probably the most brilliant of the early Zionist leaders, was, amongst his other accomplishments, a trained psychologist. This may have helped him to diagnose the Jewish condition. He described the Jews of the West as enjoying an illusory emancipation. In their desire to disappear, they gave up both their self-respect and their sense of reality. They became *Luftmenschen* – 'dangling men' – lacking any firm anchorage either in society or in the economic structure of their countries of residence.[4] Spiritually enfeebled, they were not even capable of defending their own vital interests as Diaspora Jews when these were threatened. He cites the Dreyfus affair in Paris in the 1890s. What shocked Nordau chiefly at the time was not the eruption of anti-semitism within the supposedly liberal French upper and middle classes, but the moral paralysis and cowardice of the Jewish community which, on the whole, remained silent, hoping that the storm would somehow blow over. It was not the official Jewish leadership which raised its voice on behalf of Captain Dreyfus, but Picquart, Clemenceau and Zola.[5] The Jews of the Exile, said Nordau, were like the Lacedaemonian helots of Antiquity, degrading themselves for the benefit of their contemptuous oppressors, the Spartans, and silently swallowing every manner of insult.[6]

This, then, was a sickness of the soul, for which the modern term is 'alienation'. The early Zionists discerned – and this was their most profound insight – that the effect of granting the Jews civil rights in their countries of dispersion was merely to interiorize their alienation; for the subtler forms of discrimination remained, whilst the inner strength that came from a sense of spiritual and national identity was gradually eroded. But how was alienation to be cured and, above all, what were the components of that true identity of which the alienated *Galut* Jew had been deprived? It is here that the confusions and contradictions of classical Zionism emerge once again. Pinsker, Nordau and Herzl all recognized in their different ways that the sickness of the *Galut* was a psychological state involving an absence of wholeness, of authenticity. As such it was not curable by the granting of mere political rights. On the contrary, they recognized that alienation in its sharpest form occurred among those who had, in fact, achieved such rights. Nevertheless they based their remedy for alienation on the simple formula of political restoration; that is to say, the granting of national rights to the collectivity of the Jewish people. Here was the panacea. Restore the Jewish people to its land and all would be well. All that was needed was the integrity and strength that come from a corporate national existence on native soil; to become a nation like the other nations. Alienation was, after all, nothing more than homesickness, and the cure for homesickness was home!

The failure to understand the full nature of the crisis which the Jewish people was suffering can be expressed theologically; the political Zionists overlooked what is termed in the rabbinic tradition *Galut HaShekhina* – the exile of the Divine Presence itself.[7] God is said to accompany the Jewish people into exile, and this is in one sense a source of comfort and strength. But in another sense the exile of the *Shekhina* implies that, corresponding to the physical separation of Israel from its land, there is a kind of metaphysical exile, a homelessness which affects the very ground of reality as a result of which Israel confronts a universe emptied of meaning. Israel's condition becomes the outward symptom of a deeper disorder, the universal forfeiture of wholeness and unity. And just as this exile is a particularized image of the archetypal exile of man from the Garden of Eden, so the Return takes on a wider meaning also. It does not exhaust itself in the setting up of one more nation-state among others: it signifies ultimately a movement designed to restore harmony to a world radically in need of healing. This is the burden of the teaching, for instance, of Rabbi Abraham Isaac Kook, one of the great spiritual leaders of the *Yishuv* in Palestine before the foundation of the state of Israel.[8] Nor is this at bottom a matter of an eccentric or mystical reading of Zionism. The fact is that such words as *Galut* and *Shivah-Teshuvah* (Return-Repentance) are semantically charged in this way. They have inevitable overtones, like the word 'Zion' itself. They do not signify merely physical or political states. The pain of exile is not the pain simply of the separation from one's land: it is a metaphysical ache. The yearning for return is not simply a hunger for national rights: it is a hunger for renewal, as in the plea 'Restore us to thyself, O Lord, that we may return (*nashuvah*): renew our days as of old' (*Lamentations* 5:21). Such renewal is a phenomenon associated with the Covenant: it involves the fundamental re-ordering of relations between man and man, and between man and God. These are, of course, literary metaphors, but they are the metaphors with which Zionism is nourished and without which it cannot be understood.

But alienation or *Galut* and its antitype, Return, are not private myths confined to the literary imagination of Israel. It may be claimed that *Galut*, in the sense in which it was understood by Rabbi Kook and others, is a phenomenon which sensitive men have long recognized and grieved over, and never more so than in our own century. If the Jew is alienated and in search of his true home, then the experience of our time has made us aware that mankind is in need of a cure for its universal homelessness. Alienation was the emotional starting point for nineteenth-century Zionism; in the twentieth century it has become the manifest sign of a general crisis. Modern literature is haunted by images of exile and loss, starting with Proust's attempted recovery of the lost world of his childhood and T. S. Eliot's memory of the children at play in the sunlight of the rose garden. Saul Bellow's hero, Moses Herzog, meditates in mid-century on his childhood in the Montreal ghetto before he and his generation were sucked up in the feverish and unstable life of the great cities. Nor is this merely a question of alienation from one's past, from the tradition; there is the deeper alienation of man from himself. In a famous short story by Kafka we witness the metamorphosis of a man into a cockroach, a vulnerable and short-lived insect. Such symbolism goes deep into man's sense of his condition in the twentieth century. Interestingly the Jew often comes to typify this universal condition. We have mentioned Bellow's alienated hero, Moses Herzog. But he was, in fact, anticipated by Leopold Bloom, the Jewish pro- tagonist of James Joyce's famous novel *Ulysses* (1922).[9] The Jew, outcast and victim, seeking love in a world from which love is largely absent, becomes a representative of Everyman.

There is thus a profound sense in which the exile of the Jew is a symbol for the human condition in our day. For a long time men placed their hopes – Jews perhaps more than others – in the values of Western liberalism with its commitment to life, liberty and the pursuit of happiness. But the outcome has not been consonant with these great aims. Fear and violence are often more characteristic of the life of the great cities than happiness and prosperity. In many cases these cities have been all but abandoned by their inhabitants. The drug culture is for many what is left of the pur- suit of happiness, a phantom which still eludes its pursuers. Jews, who are all, in a sense, survivors of the Nazi Holocaust, are peculiarly well placed to measure the failure of the technological civilization of the West: in the very heart of Europe in the mid- twentieth century residual Christianity and humanism have proved inadequate to withstand the upsurge of barbarism. Our help, it seems, will not come from the 'secular city' in which Western man has invested so much of his spiritual capital from the days of Spinoza and earlier.[10] This has been sadly noted by many. But in pondering the meaning of our discontents, observers have generally pointed to the more superficial factors. Too much affluence, too little affluence or else the widespread chemical contamination of the environment – each of these has been designated the root cause of our maladies. But what clearly besets the West is something more than the problem of ecology; it is the problem of a lost identity, of the need for a more stable relationship with oneself, with one's past and with one's future.

Now if we view the Zionist answer to the *Galut* narrowly and on its own terms, as an outgrowth of nineteenth-century nationalism and populism, it would seem to be only marginally relevant to this universal twentieth-century problem. But if we view it in biblical terms as essentially a movement of spiritual return – a 'going up to the mountain of the Lord' – then it becomes possible to see its relevance to the *Galut* of mankind in our troubled century. The return of the Jew to his land and to his origins becomes the concrete symbolization of a wider search for meaning, with Israel in its classical role of mediator, bearing the sicknesses of all but also extending salvation and cure through the processes of its own liberation. And all this has the most direct and practical bearing on the policies, internal and external, of the Jewish state in our own time. Are we a part of Western civilization, subject to the same currents of nihilism, permissiveness and revolt against authority? Or are we called upon to stand apart, to confront the West in the name of values peculiar to the Jewish tradition?[11] And if so, what are those values and to what extent do they constitute an answer to alienation?

The biblical paradigms are helpful here. Lot, we may remember, has to be forcibly persuaded to leave the doomed cities of the Plain (*Genesis* 19:15, 16). The land which he thinks will provide him with wealth, security and a home turns out to be an environmental hazard. He does not leave it easily, and perhaps this is the measure of his own inner contamination. Leaving Sodom is for him, in fact, rather like going into exile, for he has become attached to its comforts and he has come to tolerate even its sexual perversions. To that extent he is alienated from his truer self. But the

composite biblical image for alienation, with its accompanying loss
of true identity, is the exile of the Children of Israel in Egypt.
There are wealth, power and influence in Egypt for Israelites such
as Joseph and Moses who have 'made it' in a sophisticated and
enlightened society, but there is also a lack of authenticity, a sense
of homelessness and bondage which even the wealthy and influential experience. The Bible speaks (*Exodus* 15:26) of the 'sicknesses of Egypt' which the liberated slaves will no longer suffer –
sicknesses, presumably, of the soul as well as the body. But still,
liberation is not easy and the 'mixed multitude' of exiles often
relapses, hankering after the world it has left behind, with its
comforting mind-drugs, its easy idolatries, its lack of responsibility. If they have to leave Egypt it is out of necessity rather than
choice. And yet, like the Jews who followed the Zionist call at the
beginning of the twentieth century, their motives are confused.
Many of them are looking simply for another Egypt, where they
can enjoy all that Egypt has to offer without being physically
enslaved. Others, we may suppose, remain true to the vestigial
memories of the Covenant, its promise and obligations. The
rabbis noted that, in spite of a radical assimilation with their
environment, the Israelites in Egypt held on stubbornly to their
Israelite identity – 'they changed neither their names nor their
tongue'.[12]

Egypt, then, is a state of mind as well as a geographical location.
Over against it stands the Promised Land with its pledge of liberation, but before one can enter it a movement must take place –
from the Covenant of necessity to the Covenant of vocation. There
must be commitment, self-dedication, for the answer to alienation
is not unbounded freedom. Indeed unrestricted freedom resulting
in social and moral anarchy is itself a sign of alienation. It is not
by giving a licence to everyone to pursue his own wayward instincts
that we shall achieve a cure for the Egyptian sickness, but by
defining social and national objectives to which the individual may
willingly commit himself. The liberated slaves must take upon
themselves covenant obligations. No longer is the individual the
measure of all things: he thinks in terms of family, nation and
community. The community living in accordance with its covenant
bonds becomes in Hebrew a 'holy community', for the community
itself is holy once it finds the true path. Each man seeks his own

personal satisfaction, but the community reaches out to something better and higher. It becomes a priesthood and, as a priesthood, it offers healing to all. In the new land there will be cities of refuge for the unintentional murderer; there will be humane laws; the rights of property will be controlled. There will be a task for the individual within the framework of the community; he will devote his tithes to the maintenance of the scholars and the poor; he will consecrate his fields, his days, his family life, by symbolic offering, by abstinence at set seasons, by feast and fast. There will be no room for libertinism either in sex, society or economics. In short alienation will be cured by commitment: 'For unto me the Children of Israel are servants: they are my servants whom I brought forth out of the land of Egypt' (*Leviticus* 25:55).

II

All this takes us some way from Zionism and its achievements as reflected in the state of Israel today. The Israeli leadership does not call for the establishment of the 'holy community'; their language is not that of the Covenant. And the result is that they have little to offer as palliatives for the deeper *Galut*, the alienation of the spirit for which Zionism was to have been the cure. The question is: how much longer can the real spiritual motive of Zionism be ignored? In the early years of state-building the ingathering of Jews and the establishment of state institutions provided fulfilment and a sense of purpose in and of themselves. But this is no longer so. If Zionism is no more than a movement to bring about the physical return of the Jews to their land, then the growing Israeli generation have no further use for it. They are no longer dispersed and statehood as such no longer excites them. Their problem is deeper: it is the problem of a wounded self-respect, of a doubtful identity, of a purpose that seems to have been lost with the passing of the first generation of pioneers and liberators. In a word, aliena-tion has become part of the inheritance of the young Israeli himself, and what he unconsciously asks of Zionism is a cure for this condition.

It is hardly necessary to stress the gravity of Israel's political and military situation at the present time; it is perhaps not quite so evident, however, that Israelis, especially younger Israelis, are undergoing a moral crisis of almost equal gravity. Of course the one is bound up with the other. It is the external threat which raises the urgent question of the essential values and purposes for which the state was called into existence. The young Israeli requires to know for what *cause* he is fighting. At one time the Zionist Revolution was clearly on the side of progress: one fought for freedom and one fought against tyranny; it was as simple as that. But now the Israeli finds himself unexpectedly cast in the role of reactionary. How is one to maintain one's moral faith and integrity when faced, for instance, with the charge of imperialism? What is the answer to that? It is of course a *canard*. The young Israeli knows very well from his father and grandfather that they fought in the underground or the *Haganah* in order to free their land from the yoke of British imperialism. In the thirties and forties they were members of a national liberation movement, with all that that implied in terms of self-respect and the respect of lovers of freedom everywhere. But their children now find themselves assailed on all sides as the representatives of imperialism, while 'progressive' forces everywhere proclaim the members of the Palestinian Liberation Organization (and similar bodies) as the freedom fighters of the Middle East! When the PLO come to kill his family or blow up his school, the young Israeli reacts with spontaneous fury and generally wins the battle. He has evidently a bond with the future and the past stronger than the politics of the so-called 'liberation movements' – which are, in any case, not quite so pure and liberating as they used to be. But the switching of roles as between liberators and imperialists compounds the moral crisis for the young Israeli. His confusion becomes deeper, eating away at the source of his self-respect and threatening to convert his idealism and virtue into cynicism. In extreme cases he will decide to quit a country which seems to provide so little rest for his body or spirit. For, let us remember, 'Zionism' also requires him to serve for anything up to a hundred days a year in the reserves, even when there are no wars to keep him away from home for longer periods!

The majority will no doubt remain to build their future in Israel, but they will be constantly beset by doubts. Where do we go from here? Who are we? What are we doing here? To what are we bidden? And above all: what is it that others hate and distrust in us? Why can we not achieve normalcy like other national communities? The last two questions were precisely those asked by the Jews of the Diaspora in the nineteenth century, when they became aware of the failure of mere political and civil emancipation. Zionism, as normally presented, does not seem to have answers to these questions and as a result Israelis often find its rhetoric disturbing. Statehood, its crowning achievement, has brought with it problems and difficulties which the authors of the Basle Programme of 1897 or of the Declaration of Independence of 1948 hardly provided for. Zionism, in short, has removed the obvious cause of Jewish homelessness, but it has not allayed the sense of belonging to a community of whom it might be said: 'He was despised and rejected of men; a man of pain and acquainted with sickness' (*Isaiah* 53:3). The early Zionist spokesmen had somehow not taken this prophecy of Isaiah into account, or if they had, they had treated it as part of that condition which would be automatically cured once Jewish independence had been achieved.

In other words, the new Israeli experiences just a little of that sickness unto death which his ancestors in the Diaspora knew. Pinsker's 'auto-emancipation' has proved no more successful as a remedy for this than the earlier emancipation. The creation of the state of Israel is a mighty fact and, most of us would add, an irreversible one; but then so was the breaking down of the walls of the ghetto in the eighteenth and nineteenth centuries. But neither of these epoch-making events has cured the Jew of the malady of alienation. The Israeli is no longer a *Luftmensch* like the emancipated Jews observed by Nordau at the end of the nineteenth century, but he nevertheless feels acutely that he lacks a firm anchorage and a safe future. In this sense alienation is still with him in the deeper consciousness of a spiritual vacuum which mere statehood cannot fill. The new Israeli is in search of a further meaning for his existence. This search is rendered the keener, as we have said, by Israel's political isolation, which presses down on each and every sensitive person, but it is at bottom not so much a political phenomenon as an aspect of a spiritual crisis. The fathers have eaten sour grapes and the children's teeth are set on edge.

The founders had, by and large, given up the faith of their ancestors and had adopted instead alternative ideologies, such as the Tolstoyan ethic of work (purveyed by A. D. Gordon), the Marxist dialectic or high-minded Western liberalism. Most of these once-hopeful doctrines have since proved bankrupt. The final blow for many of the Marxists came with the revelations of the Twentieth Party Congress in 1956; the disillusionment with the West has been nourished by the West's own disillusionment with itself – what, after all, has happened to the American dream? And as for the high idealism of the doctrine of salvation through work, the young Israeli is now unhappily aware that most of the corruption in his society centres on a privileged class which has grown rich on the profits of monopoly socialism and state-owned corporations. It is difficult to uphold the original image of the *kibbutz* as the symbol of the ethic of work and service, when the *kibbutzim* have now, owing to the exigencies of market realities, become large-scale employers of labour, and the members themselves have tended more and more to become a class of business executives and skilled managers. All this is, no doubt, a necessary development and, in economic terms, is probably good for the country, but it has inevitably meant a cooling-off of idealistic fervour amongst the *kibbutz* members themselves, as well as a check on the unstinted admiration which their pioneering endeavours once aroused.

The earlier gods have failed (or at least have become somewhat tarnished with age) but the need for a sustaining faith remains as strong as ever. But where is that faith to come from? The majority will not look to the synagogue, for if secular Zionism has failed to provide them with positive aims of its own, it has nevertheless succeeded effectively in alienating many of them from the traditional religion of the past. The new Jew has been deprived of the sabbath without being granted any alternative source of spiritual power to replace it. What he has been granted instead is a state, a flag and a new annual festival, Independence Day, which tends to lose much of its original exaltation as the years go by. Ironically Independence Day is now most actively celebrated in the synagogues, where the rabbis have devised for the faithful an order of service of sorts to give content and permanence to the occasion. The majority who do not visit the synagogue remain untouched in their deeper selves as the bright memory of the original Independence Day of 1948 grows ever fainter.

III

Statehood, of itself, has not brought salvation. And if this is true for the native-born Israeli, it is even truer for the young Jews of the Diaspora who come to seek a haven for their spirit in the land of Israel. In the years immediately following the foundation of the state, the Ingathering of the Exiles brought to Israel in their tens of thousands the oppressed Jewish populations of Morocco, Algeria, Iraq and Yemen. For them the magic of Jewish independence and political emancipation was sufficient in itself. This was the dream of deliverance come true. They had been brought to the Promised Land on eagles' wings in fulfilment of the prophecy, and they could ask no further blessing. This kind of liberation the Zionism of the time, as embodied in the nascent state, was well equipped to supply. If for the Jews of Italy and Germany in the eighteenth century it was Napoleon who acted the part of Joshua and blew the trumpet of liberation, then for the Yemenites of 1949 and 1950 David Ben-Gurion was the deliverer. It was a messianic moment. The situation was relatively unproblematical; the trouble only began later.[13]

The situation has been very different, however, in the sixties and seventies. During this period the chief candidates for ingathering have come from the free world (chiefly the USA and South America) or from the Soviet Union. And for many thousands of those Jews the starting point for the Return has been not exactly physical oppression, or even political disabilities, but a powerful desire to affirm or discover anew their Jewish identity. They have looked to Israel for a spiritual rather than simply a physical liberation. They have not been in flight but in search! True, the young Jews of the Soviet Union have found themselves increasingly restricted in the last twenty years. The path for their advancement in many of the professions and in the universities has been blocked by a discriminatory policy. But this was not really the cause of the great wave of emigration to Israel which began around 1969. It was, to some extent, the other way round. The discriminatory policies were themselves, to a considerable degree, a reaction on the part of the authorities to signs of independence and discontent on the part of Soviet Jewry. Those who had survived the Holo-

caust and the Stalin purges were no longer quite so ready to become
assimilated into the communist system as their fathers and grand-
fathers had been in the immediate aftermath of the Revolution.
There was, as all observers have noted, a Jewish awakening,
spurred on by the rise and consolidation of the state of Israel and
culminating in the Six Day War. Soviet Jews wanted above all to
join their brothers and share their fate. Such a spiritual and
national awakening is not really provided for in the communist
system. In Stalin's time it would have been brutally suppressed.
His successors chose the path of compromise: they introduced
oppressive measures but they also permitted selective emigration,
giving priority to the chief trouble-makers.

Israel naturally received the new arrivals with open arms. But it
rapidly became clear that this was not a repeat of the North
African and Yemenite experience. For these Jews from Russia the
open society of Israel was of course a liberation, as was the physical
reunion with their people and their land, but they could not rest
content with that. Half a century of communist education had
conditioned Soviet Jews to assume that societies need collective
aims to make them function. They had, on the whole, rejected
communism, but where was the alternative Jewish-Israeli doctrine
that was going to take its place? Communism had taught them that
behind every work of man there is politics, and behind every
political idea there is a myth, a hope. The communist myth had
proved false, but what was to replace it? After all, man does not
live by bread alone.

The new Soviet immigrants did not, therefore, accept the system
they found in Israel in the uncritical fashion of earlier immigrants
from North Africa. Many of them have shown impatience with the
socialist establishment, especially some of its outworn rituals. The
red flag on May Day in Israel is a symbol which survives from an
earlier time. Only a small minority of those who display it really
identify themselves with the ideals of international socialism. But
for a great many of the new Russian immigrants to see the flag in
Israel is strange and disturbing: it represents for them the auto-
cratic system from which Israel was to be a refuge and to which it
was to provide an answer. It is useless to tell them that Israel is
doctrinally free, like the West, and that each man chooses to
believe as he wishes. They know very well that communist totali-

tarianism is not the answer, but the free-for-all, *laissez-faire* system of the West is not the solution either. Such tolerance may seem to some the source of democracy; to others it is the progenitor of moral anarchy and spiritual void. They have been schooled to recognize the signs of inner disintegration in Western-style democracy and they see too many of these in Israel.

A trivial but revealing instance is provided by the story of a skilled lathe worker from Leningrad who, on arrival in Israel, was placed in a small factory in the Tel-Aviv area. His employer was more than satisfied with him and all went well for some weeks; then one day he turned up at the labour-exchange to ask for another job. On inquiry it transpired that he had worked too hard and too well. His fellow workers in the factory had gradually become tired of his excessive industry and his constant pleas to them to work harder and not to take off unauthorized time for lounging and malingering. Finally they had gone in a body to the owner and threatened to walk out if the new Russian worker was not fired. It seems sometimes that all that is left of classical socialist ideology in Israel is the belief in the absolute right to strike in all circumstances.

The other type of immigrant in the sixties and seventies has come from the West, the largest annual group being from North America. These people are fleeing from oppression even less than their Soviet brethren. Israel's offer of political enfranchisement does not impress them greatly. They have not come to Israel in search of political freedom and the right to vote – they have had all that back home. Nor are they going to be won over by a duty-free automobile and a shining new apartment. These perquisites are, of course, an expected minimum, but they are not what the American Jew fundamentally seeks. He seeks above all an idea, a purpose, some content beyond the ideals of a consumer society. All is not well in the American city-jungle, and the American immigrant is not necessarily heartened by the poor imitations of the urban life-style of the West that he finds in Tel-Aviv. He has seen enough night clubs and vulgar American films; what he needs is a more satisfying use of leisure and a deeper love between men. He seeks to preserve the Jewish family bond threatened with erosion in the 'other-directed' society of the West.[14] And above all he seeks a society in which he can bring up his children free from the fear of urban violence, a society enriched with a sense of the Jewish past and the Jewish future.

It is no secret that a large proportion of the new American immigration is neo-orthodox in religious outlook and practice. They have been through the full experience of emancipation but they have been left with their Judaism relatively intact. They thus represent an implicit challenge to the majority culture in Israel, which holds that Jewish traditional faith and observance belong to a backward and outworn society. The computer expert from Boston or the Orthodox lawyer from New York have nothing to learn of modernity or the blessings of emancipation from Israel's secularist majority. Indeed, ironical to relate, they often find the atheism, the heroic rationalism of the second-generation Israelis a trifle quaint and old-fashioned, as though these innocent children of the early socialist pioneers were still living in the age of Comte, Feuerbach or the Fabian Society! The situation, therefore, is very different from that which the Zionist establishment encountered in the forties and fifties, when they had to deal with the religious scruples of the Yemenite and Iraqi immigrants. The children of those immigrants had their pious ear-locks summarily removed by the barber and in many instances were transferred in spite of the protests of their parents to non-religious schools and institutions to be turned into good Israelis.[15] The rough-and-ready methods worked and, as a result, a large proportion of the younger generation of the oriental communities lost their faith in the God of their ancestors and gained nothing in return.[16] The new American Israeli is less amenable to this kind of treatment.

There is a second type of young American immigrant. He belongs to the radically disillusioned generation and his problem, which is indeed the problem of Western civilization generally, is the problem of a lost identity. He has come to Israel with a combination of motives – general discontent, a desire to find something newer and better and a kind of residual Jewish consciousness which represents his last hope in the search for values and a meaningful aim in life. Israel is not particularly well geared to help this kind of young immigrant, the truly alienated youth of our time, some of whom have already experimented with the drug culture and other manifestations of enlightenment. Zionism, which was to have provided an answer to the alienation from which these young people suffer, has, seemingly, little to offer them. Some, but very few, will find their way to the *kibbutzim* and will make their future there; others, to some of the more unconventional talmudical academies which have grown up in Jerusalem and elsewhere in the past few years to cater for the rootless wanderers from the West. But, on the whole, Israel will be one more stopping-place in their unrequited search for meaning.

Zionism, we must remind ourselves, was to have been the answer to the Exile. And exile is still with us in a different but no less acute form than in the past. Dispersion does not press on the modern American or even Russian Jew in the same way that it pressed on the east European Jew at the end of the last century. It is not because he is deprived of a living by a vicious czarist regime, or because his daughters are threatened by the Cossacks, that the modern Jew desires liberation. His problem is deeper; it is the problem of a lost identity, a problem which he shares with Western man generally but which he feels more acutely both in his exposed position as victim and scapegoat and because his sense of a true identity has not been completely erased. It is still with him in fleeting images, in haunting memories. The garden gate may have been shut and the cherubim stationed there with their revolving swords, but he can still see over the fence and behold a better, more sunlit place within. Zionism has stressed the concept of statehood and, indeed, statehood is its basis. The 'holy community' seeks a holy land in which to fulfil itself. But Zionism has scarcely begun, as yet, to define the society that it will attempt to create in its liberated land. Will it be simply a reflection of the alienated society of the West? If so, what will it have to offer to the young Jew of today who looks to Israel for spiritual enfranchisement, for a word of power, a healing touch?

Israel rightly dedicates itself first and foremost to survival. But it may well be that survival itself is bound up with the affirmation of aims and values which give meaning to survival and which alone make all the agony and sacrifice worthwhile.

4

Moses Hess

In this and the following chapter I shall attempt to present the ideas of four major Zionist philosophers, each of whom showed an awareness of Zionism as a revolutionary salvation myth, combining spiritual and political elements in a dynamic synthesis. The first of these visionary philosophers is Moses Hess (1812–75), who had the unusual distinction of being one of the fathers of the Communist Revolution and the Jewish Revolution at one and the same time.

I

Hess has an assured place in the annals of Zionism but he has rarely been taken completely seriously either by Zionists or by their opponents. For one thing he has generally been overshadowed by the politically more resourceful Theodor Herzl and, as a consequence of this, his *Rome and Jerusalem* (1862), which appeared twenty-three years before Herzl's *Judenstaat*, has been regarded as a sort of chance inspiration, a happy stroke of eccentric genius, a mere premonition of greater things to come. But this assessment fails to do justice to Hess's political vision and insight. Karl Marx spoke of Hess as 'an enthusiast and a fantast', yet communist historians have testified to the fact that both he and Engels were influenced by Hess to a considerable degree. If they finally saw him as a deviant and an eccentric, it was because the 'Communist Rabbi Moses' (as his friend Arnold Ruge called him)[1] had been outrageous enough to espouse the idea of the national regeneration of the Jewish people. Jewish survival was for orthodox communists an irrelevance, a quirk of history with no significance beside that of the dialectical processes which were to usher in the socialist paradise. If nationality in general was a crime, Jewish nationality was an absurdity; and if religion was an opiate for the people, Judaism was no longer even a successful opiate since it was the mere fossil of a religion! Hess thought differently, not because he was an enthusiast, but because he had in him something of the prophet. At a time when the Jewish people was thought to be a mere collection of flotsam on the shores of history, a non-people, a tribe whose race was run, Hess spoke of the day when the Jews would establish settlements by the Suez Canal (at that time incomplete) and on the banks of the Jordan river. It was rather like the discovery by Lowell of the perihelion of the planet Pluto thirty years before that planet was actually observed. Prophecy means, among other things, perceiving the true drift of history, hearing the challenge it addresses to us and articulating the response. Moses Hess was in this respect not unlike his more famous namesake: though not himself privileged to enter the Promised Land, he nevertheless saw it from afar and beckoned us towards it.

Moses Hess was like the biblical Moses in another respect also. Moses of old, we may remember, was able to compete with, and even to give lessons to, the 'wise men' of Egypt. He was, shall we say, philosophically and scientifically emancipated and was even not averse, at one point, to adopting some of the Midianite state-craft of his father-in-law, Jethro! Nevertheless, learned though he was in the wisdom of the Egyptians, he rejected Egyptian philosophy and science in the end and opted for Jewish exclusivity. In Hess there was a similar ambivalence. He was a man of stature among European *savants*, occupying a position somewhere near the fountainhead of the great revolutions which have changed the world in the last century and a half. A latter-day Hegelian, he believed that through the historical process man would achieve salvation. Nevertheless he found that ultimately salvation is of the Jews. Zionism (although the term had not yet been coined) was for him both the culmination of the liberal revolutions of the nineteenth century and also, in a way, their antithesis. In Zionism religion and history would be made one; the seen and the unseen joined together in ideal unity. Nationalism would be gratified and simultaneously fused with a larger theme, that of world salvation.

Hess offered a dual perspective. He was, as we have said, a European, a man of the Enlightenment, and yet his strong sense of Jewish identity and of the absolute claims of Jewish history enabled him to achieve a critical distance from the fashionable ideologies of the Enlightenment. *Rome and Jerusalem* has two fundamental premises. One of these is that Jews must participate in the 'great regeneration of nations' which started with the French Revolution.

Springtime in the life of nations began with the French Revolution. The year 1789 marks the Spring equinox in the life of historical peoples. Resurrection of nations becomes a natural phenomenon at a time when Greece and Rome are being regenerated. Poland breathes the air of liberty anew, and Hungary is preparing itself for the final struggle of liberation. . . . Among the nations believed to be dead and which, when they become conscious of their historic mission, will struggle for their national rights, is also Israel. . . .[2]

From this point of view his argument is based on a strict analogy between the fate of Israel and that of Italy, between 'the eternal city on the banks of the Tiber' and 'the eternal city on the slopes of Moriah'. Jews and Italians are, so to speak, connected to the same power supply – that of the politics of the *Risorgimento*. Their fates are harmonized. But his second premise concerns the absolute *unlikeness* of Israel to those nations. After many years of attempted assimilation, he tells us, he was moved to write *Rome and Jerusalem* as a testimony to the unappeasable uniqueness of Judaism and of the Jewish people:

After an estrangement of twenty years, I am back with my people. I have come to be one of them again, to participate in the celebration of the holy days, to share the memories and hopes of the nation, to take part in the spiritual and intellectual warfare going on within the House of Israel, on the one hand, and between our people and the surrounding civilized nations, on the other; for though the Jews have lived among the nations for almost two thousand years, they cannot, after all, become a part of the organic whole.[3]

Emancipation so eagerly sought by the assimilated Jews of the West had failed because Jews had special drives within them which required for their expression a national framework and national autonomy:

they cannot assimilate with the peoples among whom they live without at the same time denying their national religion and tradition.[4]

Those of our brethren who, for purposes of obtaining emancipation, endeavour to persuade themselves, as well as others, that modern Jews possess no trace of a national feeling, have really lost their heads.[5]

He speaks with contempt of the German Reform rabbis of his time who, in their anxiety to assimilate with the surrounding German culture and to live like Germans, had dropped all those differentiating customs of dress, diet, calendar and daily life which the Jewish religion has laid upon the Jew. The Jew, according to Hess, has a redemptive task in the world, and in order to perform it he has to preserve his separate nationality.

Here, then, are the two contradictory starting points for Hess's Zionist programme. It may, of course, be argued that both lead to the same practical conclusion. Whether he starts from Jewish uniqueness or from the notion of a pre-stabilized harmony between Israel and the new liberated nations of Europe, he is driven to argue that Jews are a nation and are destined to return to Palestine. But there is an emotional incongruity between the two positions. The one is fundamentally optimistic: the world is progressing towards fulfilment and the Jews will have a normal and natural share in this fulfilment. The other position is far less optimistic: the world is riven with hatred and prejudice; it is deeply in need of salvation and the supreme evidence for this lies in the special status of the Jew and in the irrational hatred which he arouses. This he finds to be especially the case in Germany. Nothing, not even conversion to Christianity, can relieve the Jew of what he calls 'the enormous pressure of German Anti-semitism':[6] 'To our German Jews, the feeling of hatred towards the Jews displayed by the Germans has always remained an unsolved puzzle.' He adds: 'It is impossible for a man to be at the same time a Teutomaniac and a friend of the Jews.'[7]

In these circumstances Zionism constitutes a kind of moral witness. It is a voice crying in the wilderness. In the face of reactionary patriotism and the desire for racial dominance which he finds in Germany (in this how remarkably prescient he is of later developments), Jews are called upon to exhibit nationalism in its ideal form, the form in which the love of land and people are linked with the highest ethical obligations. The German model, he says, is based on dualism: it is marked by 'theoretical cosmopolitanism' or abstract idealism on the one hand, and by narrow racial antipathies on the other.[8] The two do not combine. By contrast the Jewish model is based on unity: it roots love of land and people in the holiest of the heart's affections, namely, the love of family growing out towards the disinterested love of man.[9]

Without clearly realizing it Hess has here seized upon a central feature of the Covenant, its atomic nucleus, so to speak. The family is not merely the symbol of that covenant love (*hesed*) which binds man and God, it is also for Judaism the very material embodiment of the Covenant, its indispensable framework. In the covenant bond between husband and wife (see *Malachi* 2:14), in the respect for parents (*Leviticus* 19:3) and in the love for children (*Psalms* 103:13) the larger Covenant is not only intimated, but actually enacted, preserved and taught.[10] Hence the enormous importance which Jews traditionally attach to family relations. The family is not for Jews simply a convenient social and biological arrangement. It has always been more than that – an ideal in itself, an expression of the lonely spirit of man in his striving for community. And, of course, the bonds within the family unit are reproduced on a larger scale for the people as a whole. The relations of mutuality between the scattered members of the 'House of Israel' are marked by the same covenant love and covenant responsibility as those within the family itself. 'All Israelites are responsible for one another,' say the rabbis.[11] The Passover feast or *Seder* is essentially a family occasion when every member has his allotted role in the celebration and yet, in keeping with its national character as the day on which the 'people of Israel' virtually came into existence, the neighbour, the stranger and the poor are invariably bidden to the feast. They participate as members of the wider family of Israel.

Hess has a strong intuition of this dimension of Judaism, even if he does not employ the terminology of the Covenant. Jewish nationalism, he says, combines the natural solidarity of the tribe with the highest ideals and strivings of the spirit in an ideal unity (he is indebted here to Spinoza for some concepts). And in even more elevated words he pays tribute at this point to the Jewish

belief in immortality, which he claims is likewise an integral part
of its national myth:

> The Jewish belief in immortality is the product of our remarkable
> family love. Our immortality extends back into the past as far as the
> Patriarchs, and in the future to the Messiah's reign. It is the Jewish
> conception of the family which gave rise to the vivid belief in the
> continuity of the spirit in human history.[12]

This sentence (which is, incidentally, echoed along with other
portions of Hess's book in George Eliot's novel, *Daniel Deronda*)
endows the Hegelian theme of historical development with an ideal,
almost transcendent value. History is the reality in which we exist,
but what gives it meaning is the immaterial power of love, binding
past, present and future together. For Hess the symbol of Jewish
nationalism, and perhaps the source of his own Jewish national
sentiments, was the sight of his pious grandfather weeping, as he
tells us, for the ruined Temple at Jerusalem on the Fast of the
Ninth of Av, and praying with utter conviction for its restoration.

It follows that the national revival of Israel which the world so
desperately needs is something *sui generis*. Christianity, according
to Hess, has not mediated true salvation. It has even accentuated
the dualism of spirit and matter and has located the theme of
salvation within the individual soul instead of within the life of
the community where it truly belongs. But the Christian era is
nearing its end, Christianity having failed to influence developments in Europe following the French Revolution. Christianity
has no answer, for instance, to 'Teutomania', nor does it provide
an antidote to false social theories (such as those of Hess's fellow
communists) based on 'anti-national humanitarianism'.[13] But
Judaism, with its ideal of community and nation based on the
ethic of love, can now come into its own. Through Jewish literature,
art and science – as these will blossom in its regenerated land –
Judaism will yet exert an immense influence on modern history;
and he concludes that, 'Once more the Torah will go forth from
Zion and the Word of the Lord from Jerusalem.'[14] Thus we are
back with the prophet Isaiah and his messianic view of Israel's
restoration as a source of universal blessing. Hess took this quite
seriously. He was, after all, the contemporary and friend of Marx
and Engels, whose vision was no less messianic than his and who –

so Hess might have claimed – had simply secularized Isaiah's metaphors, substituting the classless society for the restored Jerusalem.

II

In an age of revolutions Hess thus announced his own, the Jewish Revolution. His messianic programme had some affinity with that of his fellow communists. In the messianic era of which both he and they dreamed, the acquisitive instincts of man would be curbed, the oppression and exploitation of labour would come to an end, the wolf would lie down with the lamb. Moreover this would be achieved through the process of a Hegelian historical dialectic. Pressures set up in history itself would cause the unjust society to collapse, whilst the tyranny of the state would be overthrown by a wave of indignation sweeping through the minds of men. Enlightenment, reason and moral passion would prevail. All this sounds like orthodox communism, but there were basic differences even here between Hess's position and that of his fellow radicals.[15] Hess believed that historical necessity would not of itself produce the messianic change in the structure of society of which they all dreamed. Moral principles, such as those which he found in the Hebrew Bible, would have to be applied; men would have to become good; they would have to overthrow the evil in themselves before they could cure the ills of society. It would not be enough simply to destroy the economic structure of capitalism if the destroyers turned out to be as avaricious and as unscrupulous in their methods as the exploiting class that they were striving to overcome. This was a vital distinction. Marx scorned Hess not only for his reactionary nationalism but for his sentimental idealism also, his utopian faith in man, his call for a spiritual change.

Clearly the path of modern communism has followed the course set for it not by Hess and his friend, Ferdinand Lassalle, but by Marx and Engels. The dialectical process itself has been held sufficient as history has proceeded by an iron necessity towards its fulfilment, but the fulfilment itself seems to have eluded their grasp. Hess, if he were to look around today in search of a reformed society after his own heart, would not, I think, feel particularly consoled by what orthodox communism had achieved in the Soviet Union, but he might take comfort from some aspects of Israeli life, the social services, the *kibbutzim*, the compassion and love shown in the Ingathering of the Exiles. What has prevailed there, on the whole, has not been the Marxist dialectic of inevitable class war and revolution, but the Jewish ideal of humanity and social justice, the quest for the good life which starts in the heart and moves outwards into the relations between man and man. 'Righteousness, righteousness shalt thou pursue, that thou mayst live and inherit the land which the Lord thy God has given thee' (*Deuteronomy* 16:20). Marx scorned such outworn religious slogans as the hypocrisy of priests and the self-deceptions of the multitude. But for Hess such words represented the essence of the revolutionary idea, and if that sentence from *Deuteronomy* combines the notion of social obligation ('righteousness, righteousness shalt thou pursue') with that of national and territorial rights ('that thou mayst live and inherit the land'), it is because classical Judaism does, in fact, combine the two.

In the West the left- and right-wing revolutions have been fundamentally opposed to one another. A good internationalist who believes in humanity and progress cannot easily be, at the same time, a fighter for his own nation and land. To be progressive has often come to mean to despise 'tribal' loyalties – especially if they happen to be Jewish loyalties. Many of the younger generation of today seem to regard love of country (as well as love of family) as a kind of original sin of the bourgeoisie. Hess might claim, in answer to this charge, that his left-wing credentials were sound enough; after all, he had helped Marx and Engels to wage the first battles against capitalism and class privilege. But he might also claim that he was part of a revolution which did not, in the last analysis, attach much importance to the terms left and right. In the good life which the prophets of Israel foretold there would be social justice and reform, but there would also be much marriage and giving in marriage; and there would be nations, each cultivating its own traditions, Israel amongst them, rejoined to its ancient land.

Hess thus provided the revolutionary idea with a specifically Jewish character. He found no incompatibility between the dream of national rebirth and the dream of social reform, for he saw them both as rooted in moral obligation. And he found no contradiction between reverence for the past and a reformatory zeal for the future, because both are included in the dynamic pattern of Judaism. In such a system there is work for priests and prophets, for conservatives and radicals alike. New frontiers have to be crossed, but at the same time ancestral pieties have to be guarded. Thus if the Jew is, like Disraeli, often fanatical in his attachment to the past, he is also, like Hess, everlastingly discontented with the present. In fact the 'good Jew' is both these persons at the same time: that is the ultimate paradox of the Covenant.

III

Hess's special Jewish contribution to the messianic thinking of his generation is contained in his use of the phrase 'the Sabbath of History'. Just as Nature has its sabbath, the seventh, culminating day of Creation in which the work of Creation is sanctified (*Genesis* 2:1–3), so history, too, has its sabbath, its final stage of fulfilment:

We Jews have always, from the beginning of our history, cherished the faith in a future Messianic epoch. This belief is symbolically expressed, in our historical religion, by the Sabbath festival. The celebration of the Sabbath is the embodiment of the great idea which has always animated us, namely, that the future will bring about the realization of the historical Sabbath, just as the past gave us the natural Sabbath. In other words, that History, like Nature, will finally have her epoch of harmonious perfection. . . .[16]

The social world, he says, will celebrate *its* sabbath, the completion of its historical labour, by introducing the messianic epoch. Hess is clearly working with Hegelian categories here, but he is giving them a specifically Jewish orientation.[17] The dialectical process of history will correspond to the six days of labour, and the fulfilment of that labour will be the messianic age, the 'Sabbath of History', when history will achieve its consummation.

The biblical language used here to describe this quasi-Hegelian movement towards a perfected harmony is, for Hess, indispensable. He is thinking not merely of an equilibrium of social and economic forces, but of a flowering of the spirit of man; he is thinking of a sabbath peace in which the good life is consecrated. Although Hess is committed to the realm of the historical, time is nevertheless shot through with sanctity. Above all the use of biblical terminology underlines what for Hess is essential, the mediatory role of Israel in bringing about the paradisal state for which men yearn and towards which the whole creation moves. This provides a new perspective for the nineteenth-century dream of progress. The goal at which we aim is the 'far-off divine event' which the Hebrew prophets have foretold. Thus we are not speaking of a mechanistic development imposed by inevitable laws, but of a willed progress of redemption in which man and Nature joyfully participate. This is the mystery intimated in Hess's use of the term 'Sabbath of History', the final aim of which is justice and obedience, and a world reconciled to its Maker. But the path to this is through the political process: the seventh day of history is being prepared for by the liberal revolutions of Hess's time, by the rise of the new nations, by the spread of socialist doctrine. All these are dialectically related to one another and are part of one development. But the central thread in the whole pattern – that which will give meaning to the rest – is the regeneration of Israel in its land. Through Israel's rediscovery of its true vocation, history will ultimately be redeemed and the aims of all the other revolutions achieved.

The Jewish Revolution was thus, for Hess, a radically modern phenomenon. Judaism, with its life-affirming emphasis on Nature and history, belonged with the forces of progress rather than with the spiritual, other-worldly civilization of the Middle Ages. It was not so much the precursor of Christianity as, paradoxically, its successor. The great phase of Judaism, he claimed, was still to come. It was destined to establish the divine commonwealth from which light would radiate to the nations. Religious though Hess's emphasis was, he was, in fact, not so far from the mainstream of modern European thought as might appear at first sight. For behind the secular messianism of Rousseau and Tom Paine in the eighteenth century there lurked the Protestant dream of a religious commonwealth dedicated to the fulfilment of a divine promise derived from the Scriptures. The revolutionary theme had already been sounded in the year 1644 by the English poet, John Milton, when he declared: 'For now the time seems come, wherein *Moses* the great Prophet may sit in heav'n rejoicing to see that memorable and glorious wish fulfill'd when, not only our sev'nty Elders, but all the Lords people are become Prophets.'[18] Truth and prosperous virtue would, he said, now prevail, transforming the political and social life of Europe in the era of revolutionary Protestantism now beginning.

We may smile today to think what has come of the messianic ambitions for world reform entertained by Cromwell, Milton, the Diggers, the Levellers and all the millenarian and democratic sects of the seventeenth century in England, Scotland and America; and yet it is impossible to think of the American Declaration of Independence except against this earlier background of prophetic enthusiasm, based on the fulfilment of the biblical prophecies of Isaiah and Micah. Behind all such revolutionary processes lurks the tradition of Western Protestant energy with its zeal for reform. It may be claimed that in this sense the original religious ferment of the Reformation produced much that is good. Essentially a middle-class phenomenon, it helped to generate the current of modern liberalism prevailing in the West. And yet it also produced much evil. As R. H. Tawney and others have shown, the element of Christian other-worldliness in this revolution implied, very often, an indifference to social-ethical questions and thus helped to create the conditions for the development of modern *laissez-faire* capitalism. It gave rise not only to the American dream of freedom, but also to the American nightmare of unrestrained free enterprise and self-seeking.

And here is where we may locate the peculiar historical significance of Hess. He reincorporated the vague, secular messianism of his day into its original biblical frame, giving to the revolutionary idea a Jewish content and purpose and thus saving it from moral distortions. For, as we have said, Jewish messianism, as understood by Hess, remains unequivocally ethical. It proclaims the reign of righteousness between men and nations. The great Jewish Revolution which he formulated was in fact a revolution of unique scope: it combined national, social and spiritual elements in a dynamic synthesis. And if we take Hess to be the first modern Zionist, then it is this revolution and nothing less which is to be understood by the term 'Zionism'.

Rome and Jerusalem is thus a religious document.[19] It announces a plan of redemption in which the particular religious genius of the people of Israel will find expression. The Jewish spirit elevates the material life of men to the realm of holiness. It is, he says, opposed equally to the gross sensuality of the ancient Baal worship, the worldly spirit of modern technology and the unworldliness of evangelical Christianity, which removes the emphasis from Nature and society by placing man's destiny in the world to come. Judaism bridges the gap and urges man forward through the challenges of history towards salvation and goodness, to be achieved within the temporal, this-worldly order. After the six days of trial, error and revolution will come the 'Sabbath of History', the seventh day of universal blessing. But even that will be achieved within the world we know and its blessings will be those that mortal men desire.

The essential condition for this revolution, however, was the return of the Jewish people to its homeland. Hess was clear about the physical, territorial aspect of his programme. He quoted the very practical reflections of a non-Jewish French contemporary, Ernest Laharanne, who had not only paid tribute to the mysterious providence which had kept the eternal people alive through its age-long martyrdom, but had also examined the political situation of the Near East in the light of the new balance of power.[20] His conclusion was that the time was propitious for the restoration of the Jewish state in Palestine. No European power would oppose it and the Turks could easily be bought off. Laharanne saw the main difficulty as stemming from the cowardice and weakness of some of the Jews themselves. He had particularly hard words for the assimilated Jews of Germany, whose claim was that they had only one Fatherland, namely, the land in which they had been born! Hess was directly influenced by another practical writer of a different stamp, the cabbalistically inclined Rabbi Zewi Hirsch Kalischer of Thorn, whose work on the restoration of Israel was concerned to a great extent with the restoration of sacrifices in the rebuilt Temple in Jerusalem.[21] But Kalischer had also gone into the questions of providing agricultural instruction for the farmers in the new Jewish settlements which he envisaged, of establishing a police force and, above all, of attracting capital for the new enterprise. Hess, too, as his published correspondence shows, was much exercised by problems of practical implementation.[22] The Jewish people needed a physical base, and that base could only be the Holy Land to which it was bound by age-long love and loyalty.

He was in this sense a realist, an enchanted realist. There was no substitute for the land of Israel. And yet it was not land as such that he craved, but a land from which salvation would spring. Nahum Sokolow said of Hess:

> He claimed a centre, not in a shallow technical sense for transporting a number of individuals from one place to another in order to improve their condition; he claimed it for active, living and self-conscious Judaism, which he explored and made his own by learning, and for which he wanted a revival.[23]

Zionism was thus like Jacob's ladder: its foot was set on the earth and its top reached the heavens. This was a mighty truth of the spiritual imagination and one, moreover, which history would corroborate.

IV

Images, literary metaphors play a part here. 'Jacob's ladder' has just been mentioned. Hess himself gave great weight to the 'Sabbath of History'. Such figures of speech, alien to the positivist language of such contemporaries as John Stuart Mill or Auguste Comte, are an essential ingredient of Hess's political doctrine. The Zionism that we are concerned with in this study cannot in fact be understood without its poetic element, often derived from the poetry of the Bible. It may be defined as the transfer to the realm of practical affairs of a whole system of potent metaphors preserved alive in the consciousness of a people. Probably other revolutionary movements can be explained in this same way. Marxism harbours within it the archetypal vision of a paradisal state, the Eden of the classless society. As is well-known, the modern phenomenon of space-travel began as poetic image in the Romantic Age: it has now simply clothed itself in technological form. Zionism, we may say, is the space-programme of the Jewish people, except that it sticks to this planet even whilst it soars in vision to a new society to be founded around the 'holy hill' of Zion.

The images used by the more visionary Zionist thinkers should therefore be taken seriously. Let us consider in detail one of Hess's typical images. Throughout *Rome and Jerusalem* he uses the imagery of *growth* or *organism*: 'Humanity,' he declares, 'is a living organism of which races and peoples are the members.' (George Eliot echoed this notion some years later in her 'Zionist' novel, *Daniel Deronda*.) The Jewish people is part of the larger organic unity of mankind, but it is also an organism in its own right, with its own principle of growth and vitality. In fact if we view Israel in these terms, Israel's spiritual endowment, remarkable though it is, seems to be part of its natural condition, part, almost, of its biological character. Thus, he says, Judaism is a seed preserved alive through the centuries like the grains of corn found in the Egyptian tombs. Immortality is a blossom, he says, the roots of which are to be found in the Jewish love of family. The Jewish social-historical religion is 'the germ out of which future social creations will spring forth'.[24] The dominant notions here are those of generation and regeneration. False developments (dogmatic Marxism, modern technology) are mechanical; true developments (national cultures) are organic.

This will help to explain the rather sentimental tale with which he virtually concludes the exposition of his Zionist philosophy. He tells of a knight who makes a pilgrimage to the Holy Land. On his return he visits his friend, a learned rabbi, to whom he presents a dried rose which he had plucked from a wayside spring in Jericho and which he had carried with him throughout his long return journey to Europe.

The Rabbi took the rose from his friend and watered it with his tears. And behold a miracle! It bloomed afresh and brought forth a sweet fragrance. Said the Rabbi: 'Marvel not my friend. For Israel is that dry and withered flower, and she too will again blossom like the rose when she is restored to the garden of her youth.'[25]

Hess could claim today, with a measure of justification, that history has proved him right. His fable has become fact. Not only has the Jew brought fertility to an arid land, making the desert bloom, as all agree, but the land has also brought new life to the Jew, a fact less often noted but even more impressive. A new Jew has been born, displaying new powers and burdened with new problems. The entombed grains of wheat have proved to be capable still of vital growth.

There is, of course, nothing original about Hess's use of this type of imagery. Starting with Goethe, it was current in the work of many nineteenth-century thinkers in England and Germany. Coleridge thought primarily in terms of organism and Carlyle viewed all history as branches of the tree Igdrasil! Hess himself traced the organicist view of life and society to Spinoza and to the Hebrew Bible. As far as the latter source is concerned, he was probably thinking of such a verse as: 'In days to come, Jacob shall take root, Israel shall blossom and bud, and fill the face of the world with fruit' (*Isaiah* 27:6) – a verse which might stand as a text for Hess's book in its entirety. Hess seized eagerly upon such evidence of Judaism as a religion addressing itself to natural man, man in his material condition, needing family, territory, nationality, social organization, just as a plant needs earth and air, and only flourishing when supplied with these natural necessities. And he was surely right in sensing that the Hebrew Bible, through its characteristic imagery, supports such a view of the human condition. Man is as earthbound as the plants and trees, and Israel is to this extent part of mankind.

But here we should remark that this kind of imagery in the Old Testament has another significance. In the chapter immediately following the above quotation from Isaiah the prophet inveighs against 'the drunkards of Ephraim', the 'fading flower' of whose 'glorious beauty, which is at the head of the rich valley, shall be as the first ripe fig before the summer; which when one sees, while it is yet in his hand he swallows it up' (*Isaiah* 28:4). It is quite clear that the flower imagery can define both the strengths of man and his weaknesses. Jacob, when restored to his inheritance, blossoms and fills the face of the world with fruit; but, by the same token, the wicked are no more than a fading flower or an early fruit hastily consumed.

There is an element here which Hess, dialectical though his inclination was, had failed to grasp. Man is organism, but he is also much more than organism. 'The tree of the field is, as it were, a man', declares the author of *Deuteronomy* (20:19), and therefore fruit-trees are not to be wantonly felled during a siege. But the same words can bear the opposite sense: Is the tree of the field a man, that you should lay siege to it? In the Jewish exegetical tradition the verse has been interpreted both ways. Man participates in the vital growth of Nature and is subject to the same laws as trees; but man is also summoned to inhabit a different reality.

It is the wicked who sink into the mere life of Nature, who 'spring like the grass', whilst on the other hand 'The righteous shall flourish like the palm tree; he shall grow like a cedar in Lebanon' (*Psalm* 92:7,12). The psalmist, lacking an abstract vocabulary, presents his dialectical notions concretely. The wicked who 'spring like the grass' and the righteous who 'flourish like the palm tree' both clearly share the life of Nature. But the grass fades away rapidly in the fierce summer heat of Samaria, leaving only dry stubble behind, whilst the palm tree, when properly tended, brings forth fruit in its old age (verse 14), and the cedar may attain permanence by being 'planted' in the house of the Lord (verse 13). The Psalmist is evidently thinking of the cedar beams from which the Temple was constructed. Organism has here ceased to be mere organism. It has become integrated in the life of service. Man is summoned to transcend the natural by becoming a servant of his Creator and thus 'flourishing in the courts of our God'. The natural is caught up in the realm of that which is beyond Nature, as the life of man becomes part of the artifice of eternity.

This is the ultimate implication of the biblical Covenant. Man is a creature, a fading flower, but, through his capacity to enter into a direct and unmediated relation with his Creator, he may in his human condition nevertheless 'see God'; he may transcend the merely natural and organic. Here is a mystery which Hess did not fully comprehend, but it is surely fundamental to an understanding of Judaism. And since (as Hess would be the first to admit) the Return to Zion is the contemporary expression of a living Judaism, then this mystery, too, must in the end be included in a full account of the meaning of that Return.

5

Myth and Metaphor

I

THE METAPHOR OF ORGANISM which we noted as pervasive in Moses Hess also pervades the writings of many other Zionist thinkers down to the time of the creation of the Jewish state. It is, in fact, a fundamental metaphor. Israel is a tree to be replanted in its soil; this will assure its material rebirth. The spiritual and moral effects of that rebirth are the blossoms on the tree. The image suggests vitality and also liberation: the Jewish people, long artificially uprooted from its natural environment, will now resume the life granted to all natural, healthy organisms. It also implies a reaction to a bourgeois, urban culture and an implicit affirmation of the value of living by what Wordsworth called 'natural sympathy': the life of the field and farm is held up in preference to that of the market-place and the house of study. This metaphor reminds us that Zionism in its modern form belongs to the age of Thoreau, Whitman and Tolstoy and was, in fact, profoundly influenced by the mysticism of the earth which is part of the Romantic love of Nature, formulated in the nineteenth century.

An anthology of Zionist writings could be assembled around the metaphor of growth and organism. A prominent name in such a collection would be that of Aaron David Gordon (1856–1922) who, at the beginning of this century, taught the sanctity of labour as an absolute value. William Morris had formulated a similar doctrine thirty years earlier, and Thomas Carlyle about twenty years before that, but the Zionist application was original, as was the messianic drift of Gordon's conception. Salvation would come when the new Jew laboured in the earth, the earth of the Home-

land, achieving primary contact with it through physical toil.
Support for this notion is provided by the imagery of vegetation:

> A normal people is like a living organism which performs its various
> functions naturally, and labor is one of its basic organic functions. . . .
> We come to our Homeland in order to be planted in our natural soil
> from which we have been uprooted, to strike our roots deep into its
> life-giving substances, and to stretch out our branches in the sustaining
> and creating air and sunlight of the Homeland. . . .
> The center of our national work, the heart of our people, is here in
> Palestine, even though we are but a small community in this country,
> for here is the mainspring of our life. Here, in this central spot, is
> hidden the vital force of our cause and its potential for growth. Here
> something is beginning to flower which has greater human significance
> and far wider ramifications than our history-makers envisage, but it is
> growing in every dimension deep within, like a tree growing out of its
> own seed, and what is happening is therefore not immediately obvious.
> Here, in Palestine, is the force attracting all the scattered cells of the
> people to unite into one living national organism. . . .[1]

What is important here is not only the repeated image of growth
and vitality but also the accompanying tone of revelation. Gordon
is preaching a gospel of salvation and is strongly aware that what
he is calling for is a total revolution, a reappraisal of values, a
turning to a new source of inspiration. After all other peoples have
known manual labour all through their history, whilst Jews have
rediscovered it after a break – a rift of two thousand years. Zionism,
as understood by Gordon, comes to repair that rift: 'We who have
been torn away from nature, who have lost the savor of natural
living – if we desire life, we must establish a new relationship with
nature.'[2] The new connection with Nature which Gordon desires,
and which he experiences as a pioneer in the first *kibbutzim* in the
Jordan Valley, becomes a kind of new religion to replace the old
religion of Judaism. In returning to the soil of Palestine the Jewish
people is doing two things; it is restoring itself to its own ethnic
roots and it is also achieving an expansion of soul, a cosmic life
which links it with the whole life of man and Nature. There is,
Gordon says, a cosmic element in the return to the soil of the
Homeland.

What Gordon records is undoubtedly a religious experience, but
we may add that it involves a religion of a certain kind, one distinct

from that of the Law and the prophets. From the biblical point of view we may say that we have here a resurgence of something like the worship of the *Bealim*, the gods of the earth, who lend vitality to man and animals and to whom we owe the cyclical course of Nature. Many Israelites of old worshipped these *Bealim* whom they had taken over from the Canaanites, but the prophets (we remember Elijah confronting the Baal priests on Mount Carmel) were unequivocally opposed to this form of worship which they regarded as morally reprobate and as a deviation from Israel's true religious vocation. For them salvation and blessing are offered to us by a transcendent, 'calling' God, who is independent of the life of Nature. Gordon's doctrine suggests the reaffirmation of a non-covenantal mode of religious experience, one which has as its base the communion of man with Nature itself. He points to the cthonic realm, to the absorption of the self into the dark life of the earth. This does not mean that Gordon does not have a strong ethical drive; in fact his emphasis on love and justice and his sense of the higher life to which we must aspire marks him out as the idealist of his generation of pioneers. But the higher life is the life of Nature itself. It is, so to speak, within us. Primary experience, which is intuitive, is superior to consciousness, which is cognitive. Gordon rejects the radical Nietzscheanism of his contemporary Micah Joseph Berdichevsky, who, in his avowal of life and Nature, tended to see biblical Judaism as an aberration. Gordon stops short of this; nevertheless for Gordon, too, the Bible has undergone a basic revaluation. The Garden of Eden in Gordon's exegesis represents the life of spontaneous innocence in communion with Nature, rather than, as in the normative tradition, a communion with a God who has created the natural world and stands apart from it in a posture of command. For Gordon it is hardly possible to speak of a commanding God, for divine inspiration flows into us when we become part of the cosmic life of Nature:

Unfathomed depths stir within you. At times you imagine that you, too, are taking root in the soil which you are digging; like all that is growing around, you are nurtured by the light of the sun's rays with food from heaven; that you, too, live a life in common with the tiniest blade of grass, with each flower, each tree; that you live deeply in the heart of Nature, rising from it all and growing straight up into the expanses of the vast world.[3]

Z.R.—3

This mode of inspiration is, as we have said, very much part of the post-Romantic world of Europe in the nineteenth century. It belongs to what has been termed the 'Orphic vision' (Orpheus being the poet who visited the underworld and was able, through his music, to charm rocks and trees).[4] What is involved is a spiritual descent into the region of the unconscious where the organic life of man and Nature join together. It suggests a religion of immanence rather than transcendence, the spiritual life being a function of growth, vitality and organism rather than a meeting with some 'otherness'. Nietzsche had distinguished between the Apollonian and the Dionysian spirit. Both, he said, represented powerful spiritual forces, but the Dionysian is related to the gods of the earth, whilst the Apollonian is related to the sun and that which is beyond the earth.[5] The Dionysian mode of inspiration, we may add, is related to the matriarchal principle, the worship of the earth mother. As against a father-god we have the mother-goddess, Maia, or Hera or Isis, who invites us into her bosom. Nature is the womb to which we desire to return. For Gordon, too, the land is a loving mother who cherishes us, claiming us, at the same time, body and soul.[6] In the natural state we are like infants, he says, suckling at the breast of the mother.[7]

The sexual overtones of this kind of Nature mysticism are strongly marked in the work of those who had gone further than Gordon along the 'Orphic' path. The settlers of the Bittania commune in the Kinneret region, we are told, were wont to think of the relation between the pioneer and the soil in frankly sexual terms. They were 'its bridegroom who abandons himself in his bride's bosom . . . yes, thus we abandon ourselves to the motherly womb of sanctifying earth'.[8] This is similar to the primitivism that we find at this period in the writings of D. H. Lawrence and the biblical prototype, as we have said, is in the religion of Baal.

In the early pioneering days such a 'return to Nature' made a powerful pseudo-religious appeal to the new settlers. It was part of the spiritual revolution which Zionism had set in motion and it gave meaning to their life and work. They were not disturbed by the strongly untraditional quality of the spiritually involved. On the contrary, whatever was different from the Judaism of the ghetto was *ipso facto* good, for these pioneers were for the most part in active rebellion against the faith and practice of their parents. But there was also a positive advantage to the new spirituality, for it seemed to them to link them with the labouring classes all over the world in a mystic union of labour. This was, in a way, the ultimate achievement of the Emancipation – each nation had its own identity, its own seed of growth (shades here of Moses Hess), but in expressing this identity, in realizing its potential for growth, it joined itself to all other nations which, apparently, had likewise rooted themselves in Nature and were currently redeeming themselves through the toil of their hands. Neither A. D. Gordon nor his followers were to know that the sanctity of labour was not exactly the religion of the European proletariat at this time, nor could they know where the Dionysian principle was to lead Europe during the first half of the twentieth century, or what disastrous consequences were to follow from that 'return to Nature' which, as children of the nineteenth century, they had greeted with such innocent joy. In the aftermath of Auschwitz we have learned that work as such does not necessarily make us free, and that mankind, in descending into its own primitive depths, does not discover the path of salvation.

II

To place A. D. Gordon side by side with Rabbi Abraham Isaac HaKohen Kook (1865–1935)[9] is to exhibit in its fullest extreme the paradoxical nature of the Zionist Revolution. They have at first sight much in common, both in personality and in world view. Both are, in a manner, mystics, who yet affirm the positive value of this-worldly striving. For both men physical toil in the land of Israel has a messianic value; for both the Return to Zion is seen as holding within it the key to a process of spiritual regeneration which will eventually involve mankind as a whole. Both men owe much to the cabbalistic tradition; they owe to it their strong sense of a cosmic harmony of which we are part, an occult unity which underlies phenomena and endows our striving with significance.[10]

And yet, in spite of these and other similarities, no more vivid contrast can be imagined than that between the naturalism of Gordon and the supernaturalism of his younger contemporary, Rabbi Kook. This can best be illustrated by returning once again to the question of metaphor. Rabbi Kook frequently uses the metaphor of organism so pervasive in Gordon. For him, too, Israel is a fertile field irrigated by sacred influence and yielding a growth of enlightened souls.[11] In Rabbi Kook's case the image is probably derived from the eleventh-century philosopher, Judah Halevi, who had spoken in the *Kuzari* of the nations as branches of one tree whose fruit would be the Messiah.[12] But the dominant image in the writings of the Rav Kook is light, a supernal light streaming down from above. His emphasis is upon transcendence. He is fond of quoting the Talmudic saying: 'From the day that the Temple was destroyed the clear light of heaven has not been seen.'[13] That clear blue light will now become visible again, suffusing all things: 'The light of the sanctuary, of the prophecy and the Kingdom is already sent forth and strikes our eyelids. We are summoned to prepare ourselves to meet the great light.'[14] In every page of Rabbi Kook's writings, in the title of almost every book, the image of light occurs. It is seen in contrast to the darkness of the Exile, that of the nations who labour in blindness and ignorance. The light of the Torah shines out amid the darkness of the world's evil: it is the supreme and central reality. We may term this imagery Apollonian, in contrast to Gordon's Dionysiac imagery, though the immediate sources for Kook are Hebraic, biblical. His sense of the great light about to dawn, by which all the shadows will be dispersed, is nourished, as one would expect by the oracles of Isaiah, the most eschatological of the prophecies.

Arise, shine for thy light is come, and the glory of the Lord is risen upon thee. For behold, the darkness shall cover the earth, and gross darkness the peoples: but the Lord shall arise upon thee, and his glory shall be seen upon thee. And nations shall walk at thy light, and kings at the brightness of thy rising. (*Isaiah* 60:1-3)

These verses acquire in Rabbi Kook's presentation an extraordinary immediacy and power; they become a veritable key to the events of his own time. In the First World War darkness covered the earth, but now a new light is arising in Zion as the dawn breaks for erring humanity. It is 'the light of the Messiah', and as it comes to shine ever brighter the nations will abandon their impurity and join together to 'nourish themselves upon the dewdrops of sacred light', thus partaking of the blessings of Abraham as offered to all humanity.[15] Israel, when joined to its land, thus becomes the

source of a transcendent spiritual glory, a glory which will trans-
form the world, raising the everyday and the profane, including
art and literature and the life of man in society, to the order of
holiness.[16]

We may note here an important new principle, that of *holiness*.
In sharp contrast to the earthbound spirituality of A. D. Gordon,
we have an emphasis on a spiritual quality which unites man with
God and at the same time separates him from the world. In this
Kook clearly stands on the ground of classical Judaism: 'Be you
holy for I the Lord your God am holy' (*Leviticus* 19:2). The people
of Israel, even when they labour on the soil – and Kook was almost
as positive about this as Gordon himself – are performing a priestly
task. They have to elevate the merely earthly, sanctifying it
through the observance of the commandments, restoring it, as it
were, to its divine ground. Jerusalem and the rebuilt Temple
signify the ultimate sanctification of the earthly. We have come
beyond the cthonic realm of Gordon's teachings. For Kook, a
priest himself, it is clear that man and Nature can fulfil their
messianic role only when both are sanctified by the light that
comes from beyond them, from 'the holy One of Israel'. Thus the
poet of Israel will never be able to rest content with a mere celebration of the surface beauty of Nature; he must see it with the eyes
of the soul, unveiling the heavenly beauty by which the material
world is ultimately transfigured,[17] for this is the true ground of all
reality. The truth is that there is no sphere which cannot be thus
sanctified. This applies to the phenomenal world and the sphere
of human action alike. And above all it applies to the processes of
history. There is, in fact, no secular history, for the Providence of
God is manifest in all the affairs of men, their wars, their triumphs
and their defeats. The *enlightened* man is he who perceives the
providential pattern and bears active witness to it.

In joining himself to the political enterprise of Zionism Kook
did not see himself as compromising the sacred character of
Judaism by an alliance with secularists and apostates (the view
taken of him by some of his opponents), but he felt, on the contrary, that he was helping to perform the most profoundly religious
task of all, that of rescuing the fallen 'husks' of divinity and thus
helping to bring about the harmonious unity of all things. In the
Exile Judaism had shrunken within itself; holiness had been

confined to a limited sphere. The priesthood of Israel had expressed itself only within the family, within the Diaspora community and its daily pieties, but the covenant of priesthood required for its full exercise the entire realm of human relationships, political and international, and the entire arena of man's relationships with the natural world. Only through the Return to Zion would it be possible to achieve this fullness, to restore the light of holiness to its full glory. The Return would, in fact, be the harbinger of a spiritual awakening, in which Israel would discover its true vocation as 'a Kingdom of priests and a holy nation' preparing the ground for that cosmic movement of return for which the whole world waited.

Rabbi Kook did not deceive himself about the sinful character of his generation. He was painfully aware that a majority of those who had settled in the Jewish National Home by 1920 or thereabouts, in order to take part in the Return, were no longer faithful to the Law and the Commandments, the true and only vehicle of holiness. Materialism and apostasy were more in evidence in their lives than holiness. In dealing with this issue Rabbi Kook makes use of two major arguments. One is dialectical: he maintains that depravity, on the scale which we witness around us, is itself an indication that the Messiah is near. Rebellion, contumacy (*hutzpah*) are themselves eschatological signs, making the coming of the divine light of salvation not only necessary but inevitable. This notion, originating in the Talmud, is a commonplace of cabbalistic thought. Second, he argues that though individual Jews, even very large numbers of them, might transgress the Law or repudiate its authority, the nation as such, the mystical body of Israel (*Knesset Yisrael*), can never abandon its religious vocation as witness and source of divine inspiration.[18] This is the central nerve of Kook's teaching. The mystical body of Israel is more real than its constituent members; its religious vocation and integrity guaranteed to all eternity: 'A covenant is entered into with the whole Knesset Yisrael that she will never become altogether unclean.'[19]

Here, too, is the source of his confidence in the messianic character of the movement now under way. The individual can become alienated, but the mystical body of Israel, never. The collectivity of the Jewish people is true to its religious destiny, held to it by laws which are as irrefragable as the laws of Nature. Kook owes something to the teaching of the famous sixteenth-century rabbi, Judah Loew of Prague (the so-called *Maharal*), who had developed a theory of nationality according to which each nation has its land and its national rights and is subject to the laws of its own destiny. The destiny of Israel is indivisibly bound up with the land of Israel and the vocation of both is to be the eternal partner of God in his plan for world salvation. The election of Israel is for all time: it can never be annulled, even if individual members of Israel prove faithless. For Israel has a unique role, one which will inevitably unfold itself on the stage of history, which can never be forfeited even in the darkn essand humiliation of the exile, far less in the exalted epoch of national restoration.[20]

Rabbi Kook's extraordinary messianic optimism constituted both the strength and weakness of his position. Although he foresaw that the national rebirth would be marked by darkness and storm, these would be merely the 'birthpangs of the Messiah'.[21] If there was still evil in the world, it was only because 'the grapes are unripe'. The evil of the latter days would be swept aside by the light streaming down upon the world from above, or in another metaphor, 'the lees will sink inevitably to the bottom of the barrel'.[22] He obviously could not take the storm and darkness of the twentieth century as seriously as he took the light. He was aware of the world's troubles and had witnessed the Arab hatred of the Jewish National Home – evinced in particular by the murder of Jews in Hebron and Safed in 1929 – but his reading of Zionism and of the Jewish destiny in the modern era does not provide us with any means of comprehending the nature of the Nazi Holocaust which took place so soon after his death, nor does it really enable us to account for the full fury of Arab hatred as we have experienced it in five wars, the unwillingness of Israel's neighbours to tolerate the existence of the Jewish state and the indifference (if not worse) of a majority of the nations to this hatred. The world, in fact, shows little readiness to welcome the word of the Lord from Jerusalem. Whilst Rabbi Kook placed all emphasis on the words 'Arise and shine, for thy light is come', history has actually borne stronger witness to the continuation of that verse: 'For behold darkness shall cover the earth, and gross darkness the peoples.' Isaiah, though holding firmly to the ultimate positives of his messianic

faith, had, it seems, a far keener perception than Rabbi Kook of the
dialectical elements involved in his prophecy. His last words
(*Isaiah* 66:24) do not speak of joy and fulfilment but of eschatological disaster, of a world decimated by divine anger, by the
undying worm and the unquenchable fire.

Rabbi Kook had undoubtedly seized upon the essence of the
messianic idea. In his apprehension of a sacred bond linking God,
people and land together from the beginning to the end of days he
is in the authentic biblical tradition. To this extent his followers,
both in his day and since, have been right in hailing his doctrines
as an authoritative formulation of spiritual Zionism. Nevertheless
we are justified in asking why he went so wrong in his reading of
modern history. Is there something missing in his presentation of
the Zionist idea? Or has some alien factor intervened?

I would suggest that the first serious deficiency to be noted is
the metaphor of light itself. It betrays, no less than Gordon's
metaphor of organism, an element of over-simplification. As in
Platonism – and Kook is clearly in the Platonic tradition – spirit
becomes the only reality. This was probably also true of the
illuminist Quakers in the seventeenth century whose attitude
('God is Light') was mild and optimistic, in contrast to the grimmer
theology of the Calvinists of that time, with their harsh doctrine
of human depravity. One has the impression sometimes with
Kook that evil need not be actively resisted because it has no true
reality; it is simply shadow. Hugo Bergman remarked that for
Rabbi Kook 'there is no such thing as evil'.[23] To put it another
way, just as man has little or no share in creating the light by which
the world is redeemed, so he cannot really shut out that light. The
light will stream down almost inevitably; it is, so to speak, *given*.
It does not challenge us to active response, nor it is likely to be
permanently obscured or diverted by any failure on our part.*

This will help to explain Rabbi Kook's remarkably pacific
attitude towards the deep divisions within Zionism in his time, in

* But Kook's position is not always as simple as this. In his *Arfile Tohar*
('Mists of Purity'), consisting of a series of rather personal meditations, he
shows himself often powerfully aware of the evil which besets us in the
world, and also of the psychic darkness which threatens the saint from
within. He seems to have believed, along with the cabbalistic masters, in a
kind of cosmic Fall. But this can be repaired by action of a mystical kind,
without prejudice to the fundamental harmony of the Creation.

particular between the religious and the militantly secular elements. He naturally condemned the latter and called upon them to acknowledge the true Torah vision as that which gives meaning to Zionism,[24] but he was unwilling to acknowledge the radical nature of the threat posed by secular Zionism. It is true that his conciliatory attitude helped to moderate the positions of many individuals such as Berl Katznelson and Chaim Greenberg, both leading publicists of the Labour Movement; but it is also true to say that during his tenure of office as Chief Rabbi of the Jewish *Yishuv*, and during the most creative period of his literary work, the secular and religious polarization within Zionism hardened into a kind of institutional *apartheid*, giving to Israeli society the character which it has retained to this day. Neither his personality nor his writings served to arrest this development in any fundamental way.

The second and more basic limitation in the Rav Kook's life and work is bound up with the fact that he wrote almost exclusively from within the Jewish rabbinical tradition; he had not inwardly encountered the full impact of modern European thought.[25] He was first and foremost a man of the sixth Jewish millennium, and to a much lesser extent a man of the nineteenth and twentieth centuries. If the European Emancipation represented what Emil Fackenheim would call an 'epoch-making event', that is, an event which totally transforms the Jew's sense of himself and the world, then it was one which Kook had not genuinely and fully experienced. He had not interiorized the revolutionary challenge of the Enlightenment – that challenge which had so deeply affected the minds of men as different as Moses Hess, Theodor Herzl and even, in his way, A. D. Gordon. Naturally this gave to his world view a marvellous serenity, coherence and strength; he was spared the kind of agonizing choices which so many other leading Jewish figures of the nineteenth century had to face, but at the same time he was not equipped to conceive of the nature of the break which had occurred in the modern world for both Jew and non-Jew. He presented a thesis, and a convincing one at that, which is still relevant for men in our generation, but without fully understanding the nature of its antithesis. He had not comprehended the full power of the secular revolution which had begun in Europe at the time of the Renaissance and which had hit the Jewish people at the end of the eighteenth century. He still tended to see the secularists as simple transgressors against the Law who might be corrected by chastisement and instruction, instead of which they were, like himself, men of faith.[26] Their faith lay in the power of man over Nature (that faith proclaimed by Bacon, the architect of the modern mind),[27] or in the power of man to shape his own condition and to control the forces of society and economics (the faith proclaimed by Karl Marx) or in the power of man to master the soul itself and dispel its mystery (the faith proclaimed by Freud and others). All this may add up to a diabolical faith. It was, if you like, an abyss. Many had fallen; others had drawn near and gazed over the edge of that abyss. Kook had done neither. He was thus able to treat the problem of good and evil, of faith and apostasy, in terms which had little relevance to the situation of men like J. Klatzkin or Y. H. Brenner, the great apostates of his time. He sensed the enormous gap between himself and them, but he still believed that they inhabited the same world of discourse. If they were evil-doers and evil-thinkers, then evil itself was no more than an absence of light. What he did not reckon with was that in the modern world man had made his own light which would challenge in its destructive brilliance the light of the sun itself! Kook was happily innocent of such awareness. He did not even feel constrained to throw his inkstand at the devil.

III

With Martin Buber (1878–1965), the most brilliant writer and thinker to date to concern himself with the meaning of Zionism, we are clearly in the mainstream of modern thought. If he draws upon the biblical and post-biblical Jewish tradition in his formulation of Zionism, it is because he is convinced that those terms can still be made meaningful for men who have endured the full force of the intellectual and political revolutions of the past three hundred years. His messianic reading of Zionism is, therefore, of extraordinary interest in itself and also as a counterweight to the presentations we have already noted.

Buber's central image immediately alerts us to the radical difference between his formula and that of Kook or Gordon. Instead of light or organism he speaks of dialogue. The Return to

Zion is not part of some pre-determined natural law, nor is it part
of a stream of tendency designed to bring the natural and the
divine worlds into harmony with one another; it is something
much more dramatic than either of these – a meeting, an encounter
through which the loneliness of modern man is cancelled. The
whole history of Israel, as he reads it, is a meeting between the
human and divine partners to the Covenant. It is a challenge
thrown out, a response given or withheld. In this meeting there
are dramatic tensions, possibilities of failure and success. What is
involved is the creation of a sacred community charged with
mediating salvation on behalf of itself and the world. But this
community has to be created in the here-and-now; it has a concrete human and social dimension; it is enacted in physical space
on the stage of history. The contemporary relevance of this reading
of Zionism is obvious. Buber is addressing himself not so much to
the immediate political condition of the Jew in the post-Emancipa-
tion era as to his spiritual condition, to what we have earlier
described as his alienation. The sacred community comes as an
answer to the loneliness of spirit from which the Jew – and by
wider implication, modern man at large – is suffering. In the
existential void created by the de-personalization of modern
existence, love and dialogue provide us with a remedy. The Jew
is, above all, that man who is called upon to mediate salvation for
mankind by means of the creation of a 'sacred community' bound
together by bonds of mutual love and obligation, a community in
which individual human striving will be of significance. The Bible
is the record of repeated attempts – never wholly successful – to
create this sacred community out of the materials of everyday life,
to fashion the political and religious institutions necessary for its
implementation. This is the demand placed upon Israel. It is a
demand of extraordinary difficulty but also of extraordinary
importance, for it involves nothing less than the creation of the
Kingdom of God, the fundamental theme of the Covenant: 'In the
historical hour in which its tribes grew together to form a people,
it became the carrier of a revelation. The covenant which the
tribes made with one another and through which they became
'Israel' takes the form of a common covenant with the God of
Israel.'[28]

The Covenant, as we have already noted, has three partners:

God, people and land: 'In Israel the earth is not merely, as in all other primitive peoples, or people that preserve their primal energy, a living being, but it is also the partner in a moral, God-willed, and God-guaranteed association.'[29] Buber quotes the *Zohar*, according to which 'the world can be redeemed only by the redemption of Israel and Israel can be redeemed only by reunion with its Land'.[30] The land to which the people of Israel is bound is not mere earth, supplying the materials for organic growth, as in Hess and Gordon, nor does it dissolve and lose its concrete character in the incandescent glow of a spiritual emanation from beyond, as in the philosophy of Rabbi Kook. The land for Buber is an actor in a drama. By yielding or withholding its blessings it tests our faith: 'The very nature of the land of Canaan bears witness to the unremitting providence of God. And it is its nature that qualifies it to be the pledge of the covenant ... In Canaan Israel realizes that rain is a gift and it recognizes the giver.'[31] The encounter with the land is thus an existential encounter. It is not (as with A. D. Gordon) simply a matter of replanting the organism in its natural soil and allowing it to grow. The relationship with the land is a covenant relationship, and it is consequently burdened with risk, tension, responsibility: 'In other respects, the people of Israel may be regarded as one of the many peoples on earth, and the land of Israel as one land among other lands; but in their mutual relationship and in their common task, they are unique and incomparable.'[32] The bond between Israel and Zion is a mystery, but it is a mystery which lies at the base of Israel's existence. Not only does the history of the Jewish people bear witness to its continuing force, but the fact is that the Jew cannot find stability within, or security without, except in the full acknowledgement of this union. It is part of the moral task which Israel is unable to relinquish, for it is the very ground of his reality: 'If Israel renounces the mystery it renounces the heart of reality itself.'[33] Israel has to create the sacred community. The Return to Zion in the twentieth century signifies a renewed attempt to fulfil the mission for which Israel is elected; a society has to be created, institutions have to be forged which will express the meaning of the Covenant. 'Hebrew Humanism', as Buber calls it must be formulated anew in a relationship of love between man and man and between man and God. For above all the sacred community is formed from the materials of the world we know and has relevance to its concrete social and political problems.

And yet there is a paradox here, for whilst Buber's teaching would seem to point to a practical involvement (comparable with, say, that of Sartre) in the day-to-day life of his generation, the fact is that after his immigration to Palestine in 1938 Buber remained largely aloof. He took no interest in the institutionalized religion which he found in Palestine (in which Rabbi Kook had, for instance, been so much involved) feeling, evidently, that it was irrelevant to the fulfilment of Israel's religious mission. He also remained aloof from the hyper-fervid political and social activity of his surroundings in the years immediately preceding the rise of the Jewish state, and to the extent that he was involved (as an associate of Dr Judah L. Magnes in the so-called 'Peace League'), it was in a quixotic attempt to reverse the tide of history and prevent the Jewish state from being born. What Buber was aiming at was a bi-national federation of Jew and Arab, for which there was little support among the Jews and less among the Arabs. Buber had some influence during these years on the social and cultural world of the *kibbutzim*, but by and large it may be affirmed that he failed to influence the wider community. The effect of his personality and teaching was felt almost exclusively among intellectuals, especially those who lived in the charmed circle of the academy where he taught.

We may well ask why this should have been so. Why should he have proved less effective a force than, say, A. D. Gordon or Rabbi Kook in the life of that community whose prophet he implicitly claimed to be? A partial answer lies in the fact that Buber's original conversion to Zionism was brought about largely through the example and influence of Ahad Ha'am (Asher Ginzberg) (1856–1927), a man of less originality than himself, and intellectually his inferior. Ahad Ha'am had argued for Zion as a 'spiritual centre' without giving a really satisfactory definition of what this meant. The Judaism that he professed was really a Judaism without God, though he retained his faith in the 'prophets' and in the special character of Israel as the 'chosen people' – chosen, presumably, by itself.[34] Ahad Ha'am, writing at the turn of the century, provided an undogmatic version of Judaism suited to the children of the Enlightenment, who had abandoned the authority of the rabbis but felt themselves still inwardly constrained by their origins and their Jewish traditions. He was the Matthew Arnold of the Zionist Movement, teaching 'sweetness and light' and a community founded on culture rather than power. Ahad Ha'am was also a skilled rhetorician, who tended to simplify complex situations and flatten them into a form which could be easily managed for polemical purposes.

Buber was able to see later on that Ahad Ha'am's religious sense was inadequate, that the dimension of eternity was lacking and that there was no otherness to which Israel might turn in faith as the ground of its election and as the covenanting partner in establishing its bond with the land.[35] Nevertheless he accepted to the end Ahad Ha'am's rather facile antithesis between the Zionism of the Spirit and the Zionism of Power. Ahad Ha'am argued that what was needed was a solution of the problem not of the Jews but of Judaism.[36] Thus, in opposition to the political Zionism of Herzl and Nordau, he had appealed for a modest programme of small-scale colonization, sufficient to provide a territorial base for an élite community, which would symbolize the centrality of Zion in Jewish life and thought. Buber never wholly subscribed to the notion of a Jewish state which might be unique in its character but no less a nation-state than other nation-states. For most of Ahad Ha'am's idealistic followers his teachings ceased to be relevant with the radicalization of the Jewish situation following the First World War and, later on, the rise of Nazism. The issue was then not a 'spiritual centre' but free immigration. And when this proved impossible under the conditions imposed by the British Mandate, the cry went up for an independent Jewish state. Buber remained committed to the end to the 'spiritual centre'.

But Buber's reluctance to come to terms with Zionism as a political movement exercising power on behalf of national aims was bound up with the limitations of his existential thinking. Buber, in effect, denied the validity of objective structures of authority whether in state, society or religion. Valid forms of life were for him dialogic, personal. All institutions, codes of law, courts and parliaments belonged to the world of the I/It; they remained necessarily outside the sphere of the I/Thou in which salvation is truly sought and accomplished. This limitation was particularly evident in Buber's negative attitude towards the

Halakhah, the codified system of law, biblical and rabbinic, which has traditionally regulated the daily life of the Jew. The *Halakhah* stems, of course, from an original revelation (i.e. an I/Thou encounter) but it has been crystallized, objectified and converted into a system. As such there was no place for it in Buber's scheme. 'Centralization and codification,' he declared, 'undertaken in the interests of religion, are a danger to the core of religion.'[37] To many Jews – even those who do not regulate their lives strictly by the *Halakhah* – this inevitably appeared to be a renunciation of the essential practical substance of historic Judaism. G. Scholem accused him of 'religious anarchism'.[38] But it was not only a question of religion; in politics and society, too, every structure of authority, every mode of regulation outside the dialogic sphere tends to be suspect. As in the earlier novels of E. M. Forster, personal relations were all-important, but then Forster did not claim to be formulating a social or political gospel.

This is, perhaps, the weakness of all manner of existential thinking. No doctrines or systems, except such as might be discovered in the immediacy of experience, have any real place; they belong to the realm of fantasy, illusion or absurdity. Political attitudes have to submit to this same existential criterion. The result is a fastidious distaste for politics, a kind of stoic apathy, which inhibits any genuine identification with the organs of state power.

Even this, however, does not quite fit Buber's case, for the fact is that in his writings on biblical subjects, notably in his important work, *The Kingship of God* (1932), he by no means separates Jewish spirituality from the realm of political action and state power. On the contrary, he portrays the history of Israel in Bible times as originating in a vivid experience of the divine kingship under which the people fight the wars of their God and create a society directly ruled by him. Power is thus paramount. The Sinaitic Covenant is one which creates a national community founded upon faith but dedicated also to a dynamic programme of conquest and liberation. 'This active covenant and the leading, divine, covenant-Lord'[39] remain the constants of Israelite political life down to the end of the period of the Judges and the founding of the united kingdom under David, when 'naive theocratic enthusiasm'[40] is replaced by a settled order in which a human king rules by 'hereditary charisma'. And however much the original polity, based on the total acceptance of divine rule over a united people, may have been weakened as a result of later political developments, the prophets of Israel never abandon this vision. They continue to visualize the divine kingship under which power is wedded to faith as the model for a more universal, revived theocracy in the messianic era: 'The all-embracing rulership of God is the Proton and Eschaton of Israel.'[41]

In view of these and similar sayings one might have expected that Buber's theo-political understanding of the biblical record would have led him to support an active political Zionism in his time. And yet Buber had no sympathy for such a leader as David Ben-Gurion, who rather consciously evoked the model of Joshua and the Judges. Quite the contrary, he violently condemned the 'will to power' which he found among the Zionist leadership of his day as so much 'patriotic bombast' and 'national egoism'.[42] For him the appropriation of the biblical prophecies for the justification of an active policy of national self-determination in our time was a matter of false messianism. The kingship of God was apparently not to be achieved by such crude means as those proposed by Herzl and later employed by the leadership of the Jewish state. There was, it would seem, a kind of historical fall from grace which, temporarily at least, inhibited the realization of the eschaton. He claimed that the political Zionists were offering 'power without faithfulness'.[43] This may have been true; but then they might have retorted with equal justice that he was proposing faithfulness without power. And this is surely – on Buber's own terms – equally unsatisfactory.

The fact is that Buber's attitude to the biblical Covenant was highly ambivalent. Like the Protestant theologians by whom he was undoubtedly influenced and whom he also influenced in his turn, Buber was sometimes guilty of a certain spiritualization of the Old Testament vision. Whilst the Bible celebrates historical events, conquests, wars and the like, the final vision of the prophets implies, he says, 'the messianic overcoming of history'.[44] Biblical leaders such as Joshua, Deborah and David bear witness to the divine kingdom, but each attempt to establish that kingdom fails; these leaders turn out to be no more than 'foreshadowings of the dialogic man'[45] in whom history is to be fulfilled and at the same time transcended. Existence will ultimately be transformed into an unbroken dialogue of man with man, and man with God. This language is remarkably like the typologies used by Christian theologians, who see in Moses and Joshua foreshadowings of Jesus, the truly spiritual Messiah who renounces all earthly ambitions in favour of a divine kingdom which is 'not of this world'. Such Christian ways of thinking are, in fact, not altogether foreign to Buber, though they are balanced by his existential stress on the achievement of the sacred community in a this-worldly context.

But the ultimate explanation for Buber's relative detachment from the historical crisis which led to the foundation of the Jewish state is nearer at hand. For him the model of the sacred community is found in Hasidism, in particular the later Hasidism which he portrays in his legends of Rabbi Nahman of Bratzlav: 'The Hasidic teaching is the consummation of Judaism'.[46] Here were, he believes, 'little communities bound together by brotherly love',[47] groups of men living the life of dialogue in conditions of idyllic simplicity and faith. From this point of view, as Will Herberg has pointed out, 'his [Buber's] Zionism is essentially a call to take up the task which Hasidism attempted and at which it failed'.[48] The Hasidic groups in eastern Europe at the end of the eighteenth century constitute, for him, the true prototype of the halutzic or pioneering societies being set up in Palestine in his time. He also suggests that in their feeling for the land of Israel (Rabbi Nahman lived for some time in Tiberias) the Hasidim were the true precursors of modern Zionism in its authentic spiritual character.

His presentation of Hasidism is, in this respect, highly selective. He gives little or no weight to the observance by the Hasidim of the Law and the Commandments, to their interest in the occult world of the *Kabbalah* or to their veneration for the leader or *Zaddik*. What impresses him most is evidently the political – or rather apolitical – character of the Hasidic movement. He stresses its detachment from violent revolutions designed to change the course of history. The messianism of the founder of Hasidism, the Baal Shem Tov, and of his followers and disciples is a messianism of the inward life – 'daring incarnation fantasies are displaced by the quiet experience of intercourse with the divine in daily life.'[49] Buber discerns, correctly, that Hasidic spirituality represented among other things a reaction against the political convulsions of the era of Shabbetai Zwi, the false messiah who, in the latter half of the seventeenth century, tried to 'force the end' and led a large part of the Jewish people in a vain attempt to re-establish the Jewish kingdom. The result was a crisis of bitter frustration which left its mark on Jewish life for a hundred years. In this respect the Hasidic model is normative for Buber. Not only are we bidden to create in Palestine a community of faith such as that known to us from the world of Hasidism, but we are to do so without incurring the perils of false messianism.[50]

IV

We are now in a position, I think, to summarize the main strengths and weaknesses of Buber's Zionist doctrine. There is no doubt that in his theology of dialogue and meeting he laid hold of the strong central core of Judaism. Here is to be found the inner meaning of that call to go up to the mountain of God with which the Hebrew Bible begins and ends. The story of the Jewish people opens with a life-transforming encounter in which God addresses Abraham, saying: 'Get thee out of thy country and from thy kindred, and from thy father's house, to the Land that I will show thee' (*Genesis* 12:1). There is a challenge and a response. A man is walking along the road and he is suddenly confronted, chosen, addressed. The I encounters the Thou, the Other who speaks to us in the countenance of our fellow man as well as in the word of revelation. In addressing him, our lives take on significance; we discover the ground of our own being. Here is a metaphor more fundamental than that of either light or growth. In the Covenant God addresses us and we address him. It establishes henceforward the parameters of our existence, giving to life a purpose and a direction. Moses, wandering with his sheep in the desert, 'meets' God and receives the task which he will never be able to relinquish. The Covenant is re-enacted when the tribes later meet that same God at that same place. It is the moment in which a true community is created, a people founded in freedom but also in obligation. A bond, too, is established with the land, a land not yet seen which will also participate in the extraordinary adventure of the Covenant. Here, again, is challenge and response.

Buber did not go wrong because he placed undue stress on

dialogue. He went wrong, I will suggest, because he did not take the principle far enough. There is, for instance, his remarkable insensitivity to the *Halakhah*, the code of righteousness which regulates the lives of Jews who adhere to the Law. The *Halakhah* – literally a 'walking with God' – also represents a mode of dialogue, one carried into the minutiae of daily life. The devout Jew lives from the moment he rises in the morning to the moment he lays himself down to sleep at night in the life of dialogue. 'Know him in all thy ways,' says the wise king (*Proverbs* 3:6), and in pursuit of this principle the *Halakhah* sets about sanctifying the small world of the individual, his dress, his speech, his home, his food, his joys and sorrows. Sanctity invades the most intimate details of family life as well as the public celebration of fast and feast. This may be termed the *micro-dialogue* of the Covenant, a realm of existential awareness which brings the Covenant home to men's businesses and bosoms.

But Buber was insensitive not only to micro-dialogue; he was also insensitive to the realm of what may be termed *macro-dialogue*, the element of challenge and response which constitutes the course of Jewish history. For God, we are assured, addresses us in the great events which mark our wandering: he goes before the camp in a pillar of cloud by day and a column of fire by night. He bids us halt or go forward. Thus Rabbi Jokhanan ben Zakkai correctly read the meaning of the great and tragic events of his day. When the Temple was destroyed he set up his academy in Yabneh. And he was not deceived. In responding thus he laid the foundations of the home – the home of the Torah – in which the Jewish people would live through the long night of the Exile. Here was a prophetic understanding of history. The modern history of Zionism has similarly been a following of the pillar of cloud and the column of fire. Herzl and Pinsker, too, responded to the pressures of their times: the intolerable discrimination suffered by the Jews on the one hand, and on the other, the new opportunities offered by the liberal revolutions of the nineteenth century and the growing respect for the rights of nations. In his day Chaim Weizmann saw the clear sign inscribed in the Balfour Declaration and drew the necessary conclusions. The Zionist movement has been, in this sense, profoundly pragmatic and also – and blindly – dialogic.

Sometimes it is the entire people which hears the sound of the trumpet. Emil Fackenheim has said that out of the darkness of Auschwitz the God of Israel addressed a command to his people: it was, in effect, a command to live and thus deny to Hitler a posthumous victory.[51] In the light of this imperative obligation the demand for Jewish independence became more importunate, and out of the courage and despair of those years the Jewish state was born. History is, in this sense, the realm of dialogue; a dialogue in which we are addressed and we respond, or in which we cry out from the depths and are answered. Here is a covenant dimension as meaningful as the dimension of personal relations which governs the life of the community from within. Buber was less receptive to this dimension than one might have expected. He lacked a sense of historical crisis. Though himself a refugee from Nazi Germany, the Holocaust found no real expression in his work; it did not cause him to revise his notion of dialogue, of a relation of love existing between all men.* Nor did it cause him to revise his Zionist philosophy in any fundamental way; he went on employing the categories of Ahad Ha'am. By contrast a leading politician and publicist such as Berl Katznelson, though spiritually less gifted than Buber, proved himself much more acutely aware of the demands made on us by history. In 1931 Katznelson was speaking, rather in the fashion of Buber, of an accommodation with the Arabs, and of shared sovereignty under benevolent international auspices. By 1943, however, he was voicing an urgent

* On the other hand, it is fair to point out that in 1940 he wrote his longer Hasidic fiction (Gog u-Magog) on the theme of the Napoleonic wars. He describes the atmosphere as one of 'telluric crisis' (see English translation by Ludwig Lewisohn under the title of For the Sake of Heaven, New York 1958, p. xi). The terrible events of the time of writing are indirectly reflected in this work. Mr Roy Oliver, in his valuable study of Buber (The Wanderer and the Way, London 1968, pp. 10–13, 76, 92, etc.), gives weight to Buber's response to the Nazi regime in his famous letter to Gandhi of 1939 in which he spoke of the martyrdom of the Jews, and later in his speech on receipt of the Peace Prize in Frankfurt-am-Main in 1953. There he expressed 'reverence and love for those Germans who opposed Hitler and suffered martyrdom', at the same time declaring that he could not feel hatred for the Nazis themselves, since they had 'radically removed themselves from the human sphere'. However it is difficult to find in these statements or others like them evidence that the Holocaust had totally and radically affected his view of man and the world.

demand for the full assertion of Jewish rights in an independent Jewish state. The issue was now free immigration and to this the Arabs were implacably opposed; this left no option except full Jewish independence in however limited a part of the country. The change in Katznelson's attitude had been brought about both by the violence of Arab hostility and by the apocalyptic events in Europe, the full scope of which was even then not apparent. The column of fire was on the move and Israel was bidden to go forward.

Nor is it only in darkness and disaster that the God of Israel speaks, demanding an answer. He speaks also through great acts of deliverance. Such an act, the mass of the Jewish people felt, occurred with the triumph of the Six Day War, by which they were not only delivered from mortal peril but also restored to Jerusalem and to the cities of Judah. Everyone felt the triumph and the joy. It was a moment full of significance and obligation. Put at its simplest, there was an obligation to renew one's Zionist faith, to re-dedicate oneself to the larger vision. Not everyone was prepared to formulate this in prophetic biblical terms, but for all it was self-evident that there was no way back from 1967. As one teacher, addressing his class in the University in Jerusalem on the morrow of the war put it, 'We are not the same people as we were before this War'. He referred to the inner change, the inward liberation. But there was also to be an outer change. All vowed that there would be no return to the condition of territorial vulnerability which had given occasion to that war. Yitzhak Tabenkin, a veteran leader of the *kibbutz* movement (*Hakibbutz Hameuhad*), whose vocabulary lacked all theological reference, drew the conclusions with absolute clarity. The territorial outcome of the war simply could not be reversed: 'The sense of *there being no alternative* was and is the basis of our struggle. It is that which moulds our power and which has transformed our enterprise in this Land into a State.'[52] He maintained that there was a continuity between Hitler's war and Nasser's war in 1967. We were coerced by history, left with no option. From scattered colonies to a National Home; from a National Home to a state in a fraction of the land; and from that to the liberation of the land of Israel as a whole on behalf of the Jewish people: here was a process which we did not initiate; at each stage we had no option but to respond to a demand made on us; we are manifestly coerced by the logic of tragedy and redemption.

Shall all this be dismissed as false messianism? Shall we conclude that the whole of modern Jewish history from the First Zionist Congress in 1897 to the Yom Kippur War of 1973 has been a record of delusion and error? Is it not truer to say that it is a record of agonizing choices taken in circumstances which have left us, as Tabenkin recognized, no alternative? Surely a distinction is called for here between the messianism of fantasy, such as that of Shabbetai Zwi, and a messianism born of great and manifest historical events to which we are required to respond. The former is monologue: it has no firm outer reality to support it. The latter is dialogue: it goes hand-in-hand with history. We are actors in a drama which we do not write for ourselves, but we have to act our part and come in on our cue. And this – although Buber does not seem to have allowed for it – is truly a condition of the Covenant.

6

The Double Calendar

I

MARTIN BUBER declared, with characteristic insight, that the division between the 'Zionists of Zion' and those who supported the Uganda plan in 1903 was really the fundamental and continuing division within Zionism to this day.[1] On one side were the political schemers who thought in terms of a territorial base for normalizing the Jewish condition; on the other side were those for whom 'Zion' bore its full semantic weight of myth and yearning and for whom the Return carried with it a hope which went far beyond mere national self-determination. For one group it is almost true to say that the national solution of the Jewish problem was to be the means, once and for all, of ridding the world of the scandal of Jewishness, and the Jewish people of its mystery. For the 'Zionists of Zion', on the other hand, it was to be the fulfilment of Judaism in acknowledgement of the mystery; it was to be a return to transcendent tasks and origins. In 1905 the Uganda offer (if it was ever a true offer) was rejected by the majority of the Zionist Congress, but the attitudes that had encouraged an earlier majority to support it (including large numbers of religious Zionists) did not evaporate. It was so much easier to leave the Book where it belonged – in the synagogue. Zion then became the place where Jews would go to end their abnormal condition in the world (for according to the common formula Jewish abnormality was due to the fact that Jews were a minority in all lands and a majority in none). It was as simple as that. Therefore to round off the syllogism (and at the same time solve the Jewish problem) all one had to do was to convert the Jews into a majority in one land. And if Zion could be that land, so much the better.

There are those who, in consequence, see Israel as a state like any other state – for, if not, the whole enterprise has failed; and there are those for whom Zion remains Zion, its meaning only to be comprehended in terms of age-old covenant responsibilities and promises: 'For out of Zion shall Torah go forth, and the word of the Lord from Jerusalem' (*Isaiah* 2:3). Of course this is not so much a conflict between groups (for there are few groups which subscribe totally to either proposition) as an ambiguity within the movement as a whole, one which cuts through parties and groups and, indeed, through the souls of the individuals composing those groups; so much so that it is almost possible to say that what unites the Zionist movement as a whole is precisely an unwritten consent to harbour this ambiguity!

Such consent, as a matter of fact, is not altogether unwritten, for it is explicit in the one particular document which regulates the nature of the state of Israel to this day. I refer to the Declaration of Independence, drawn up by the founders of the state thirty years ago. And since it is all that Israel has in the way of a written constitution, it deserves close scrutiny. I begin with the end: 'Placing our trust in the Rock of Israel, we set our hand and testimony to this Declaration, here on the soil of the Homeland, in the city of Tel-Aviv, on this day, the eve of the Sabbath, 5th Iyar, 5708, 14th May 1948.'

Now this, as well as being a most moving and solemn sentence, is also a very ambigous one. In the absence of initial capitals in the Hebrew text, there is no way of knowing whether 'the Rock of Israel' refers to the divine Father and King to whom the devout Jew is wont to address himself both in joy and in sorrow, or to the rocky collectivity of Israel, that composite national will which, according to Rousseau (and later Ahad Ha'am), directs the destinies of nations, a sort of Greek chorus personifying past, present and future. Obviously the phrase means all things to all men *and this was the intention*. The former president of the state, Zalman Shazar, was sometimes heard using the more emphatically theological formula, 'the Rock of Israel and his Redeemer'. This is a concession, however, which the original witnesses to the Declaration of Independence did not permit themselves.

'The soil of the Homeland' is a phrase no less hedged about with ambiguity. Nowhere in the Declaration are the borders of the 'Homeland' defined; there is no way of knowing where it begins and ends (except that the city of Tel-Aviv is part of it), and yet, on the other hand, there is nowhere in the document any acknowledgement of the partitioning of the Homeland by the resolution of the United Nations in November of the previous year. Even though a majority of the signatories to the Declaration had agreed to the partitioning of Palestine, such agreement was never, in fact, read into the constitution and is therefore no part of the basic law of the land. We are again in the region of profound and calculated ambiguity.

But the most ambiguous of all the components of this sentence is the last. The 'eve of the Sabbath' in Hebrew could mean simply 'It is now Friday noon', but it could also mean 'We are standing at the threshold of the sabbath, the holiest of holies of the Jewish year, that sign of the unbroken Covenant ratified week by week between God and Israel.' Some signatories intended it in one sense, some in the other. Some kept both meanings fused in their minds, in a kind of solution, a form of mental equivocation. But at the end of the sentence equivocation ends and gives way to two clear, parallel and separate measurements of time: '5th Iyar 5708' and '14th May 1948'.

Arthur Koestler, in one of his journalistic reports on the new Jewish state, made a quip about the Jewish habit of counting from the Creation (*anno mundi*) and thus ignoring all that science has taught us about the age of the universe.[2] Like so much else that he discovered about the Jewish state, this represented to him an absurd gesture towards tradition. On the other hand we may well ask: what is so logical and scientific about counting one's days from the birth of the Christian saviour? The truth is that, by establishing 14 May 1948 as the date of the foundation of the state, the authors were saying nothing about Christian salvation (it is fairly certain that none of the signatories to the Declaration had that in mind); what they were saying was that the state was founded in the twentieth century, and that the Jews who had come back home in the year 5708 *anno mundi* would have to learn to live in the twentieth century and adapt themselves to its ways, its sciences and its pressures. It is the eve of the sabbath, but it is also the middle of the twentieth century, and though these represent two very different measurements of time, it is impossible, as things are, to live in one dimension and ignore the other. So the Jewish state abides uneasily in both. That seems to be what they were saying. There are some dates which belong purely and simply to one calendar: the outbreak of the Six Day War is recorded as 5 June 1967, but the Liberation of Jerusalem occurred on 28 Iyar 5727. There is good reason for this: wars are, we may say, part of the grim reality of the twentieth century and we pray for a time when they will be no more. In the meantime we must struggle to secure a place for ourselves in the twentieth-century jungle, surrounded by hatred and bitter suspicion. The twenty-eighth day of Iyar, on the other hand, is a date which is felt somehow to belong to that permanent calendar dating from the Creation and pointing forward to the final era of redemption. For our connection with Jerusalem does not begin and end with the twentieth century. To bring these two notions of time together and to endure their contradiction is a work of paradox and pain; and this is what the signatories to the Declaration of Independence took upon themselves to suffer.

There are some who deceive themselves that they can get along with one calendar only. Among them are the 'Canaanites', so-called because they have decided to reject all that is Jewish in Israeli nationality and to return to some purer, non-Judaic identity based on land and language.[3] They represent the Nietzschean revision of Jewish history and the Jewish value-system carried to its extreme. They believe they can live in the twentieth century without coming to terms with the fifty-eighth century *anno mundi*. For them there is neither sabbath nor sabbath-eve. Their complaint against the Jewish state is that as well as being founded on 14 May, it was also founded on 5 Iyar. This is for them a scandal and an absurdity. For the 'Canaanites' there is neither history nor promise, but only the affirmation of contemporary existence. Or if there is history, it is pre-Judaic, the history of Terah, the father of Abraham. What then happens to 28 Iyar? How are they to explain those deeper vibrations of the Jewish soul, the sudden joy of a people returning to its sanctuary, to the Eternal City? What for them is the meaning of the 'Rock of Israel', with or without capital letters? And why is Tel-Aviv the soil of the Homeland?

Whose Homeland? Presumably that not of the Jewish people, which has ceased to exist, but of the long-dead Canaanites. If so, whence comes the passion to restore those 'Canaanites' to their Homeland from the far-flung corners of the world? What is the bond between them, if not their Jewish identity, their Jewish hopes and memories? To pursue the 'Canaanite' philosophy to its absurd extremity (which some of its proponents do) is to deny the ongoing existence of the Jewish people and even to question the validity of the Ingathering of the Exiles, i.e. the process on which the whole dynamics of the Return is based.

So much for the 'Canaanites'. There are other minority groups of the opposite persuasion. In the Mea Shearim quarter of Jerusalem there is a group of extremely pious Jews, the so-called *Neture-Karta* (Guardians of the City), who refuse to come to terms with the twentieth century. Their problem is that the Jewish state was founded on not only on 5 Iyar but also on 14 May. Because the Jewish state has taken upon itself the trials and burdens and perils of twentieth-century man and strives to accommodate itself to them, these Jews have decided to opt out of the state. The *Neture-Karta* are, as a matter of fact, the remnant of a much larger and more important section of Jewry which not only opposed the idea of a Jewish state but, until the period of the Nazi Holocaust, opposed the Zionist Movement as a whole. The main organization through which this group articulated its views was the *Agudat Yisrael*, founded in Katowicz in 1912 by some of the leading rabbis and communal leaders of the time. But this organization was merely a symptom of the profound distrust which the Zionist idea aroused at the beginning of the century in the minds of the great majority of spiritual leaders of east and central European Jewry. The signal to return to Zion was not given. Instead of this the great Talmudic luminaries of the generations before the First War and between the wars fought Zionism and did their best to discourage their followers from emigrating to Palestine to take part in the Zionist enterprise. They included the great Rabbi Chaim Soloveichik of Brest-Litovsk, the Hassidic rabbis of the dynasties of Satmar and Munkacz and many others. Their combined authority outweighed that of such eminent leaders as Rabbi Isaac J. Reiness, Rabbi Meir Berlin and even Rabbi Kook, who at that time were trying to mobilize the support of the reli-

gious masses for Zionism. Here was a tragic division – tragic
because as a result of it hundreds of thousands of Jews from
eastern Europe who might have possibly come to settle in the
Jewish National Home following the Balfour Declaration were
discouraged from that course; instead they emigrated westwards,
or remained where they were, to be swallowed up later in the
Holocaust.

What were the motives behind the religious opposition to
Zionism? It would be too simple to conclude, as some observers
have done, that these men were 'waiting for the Messiah' and were
unwilling to act unless a clear sign was given them from heaven.
The fact is that Rabbi Chaim Soloveichik and others were practical-
minded leaders who knew very well that God acts through human
agency. The Talmud, after all, teaches that in a dispute on a point
of law between an angelic voice and a constituted human authority,
the human authority wins.[4] Had they been convinced that Zionism
was an authentic Jewish phenomenon and that its programme
would have furthered the spiritual as well as the physical well-
being of Jewry, they would not have hesitated to give it their
support. But they sensed – correctly – that Zionism was the offspring of the Emancipation, and the Emancipation represented for
them the intrusion of an alien life-style and an alien calendar into
the life of Jewry.[5] Zionism had to be resisted for the same reason
that the whole assimilatory trend of the nineteenth century had to
be resisted. If individual Jews had to be prevented from surrendering their Jewish identity, then the collectivity of Israel had
to be prevented no less from following a path designed to turn it
into a nation like the other nations, its way of life determined by the
norms of twentieth-century civilization.

What the men of the *Agudat Yisrael* refused to recognize, and
here the leaders of the *Mizrachi* such as Rabbi Meir Berlin and
Rabbi Isaac J. Reiness revealed a more profound insight, was the
powerful impulse for Jewish self-authentication which also operated
within Zionism. Whilst the Zionist movement was indeed the
offspring of the Emancipation, it was also, paradoxically, the
offspring of Jewish prophetic history, and this paradox had to be
endured until the time came to bring the two calendars together
and somehow redress the disjunction between them. Some (like
Rabbi Kook) thought the time was near when 'all the Lord's

people would become prophets'; others thought the work of redemption and regeneration would take longer, but this hope, or something like it, was what sustained those religious leaders who had taken the daring step of allying themselves with the secular Zionism of Herzl, Pinsker and Nordau. They knew that ultimately Zionism could no more deny its connection with the Jewish calendar than its connection with Zion. If it did so, it would betray its inner theme and motive.

The religious opponents of Zionism and of the Jewish state were, therefore, mistaken. They failed to discern that 14 May 1948 was also 5 Iyar 5708. The signatories to the Declaration of Independence had realized – all of them – that without that Jewish dimension there would have been neither a Jewish people nor a land of Israel. And this they had inscribed very clearly at the beginning of that Declaration in the following words:

In the Land of Israel the Jewish People took its rise: here its spiritual, religious, and political character was formed: here it lived in sovereignty; here it shaped its national and universal cultural treasures, and from here it has given the world the Book of Books.

14 May was thus not the only date that mattered to the 'Zionists'. 5 Iyar was no less real, even if for some it was a kind of *dybbuk* – a haunting presence – from which they would much rather have been released.

There can be no doubt that in our time the great mass of orthodox Jewry, ranging from the *Agudat Yisrael* to the Hassidic followers of the Lubavitcher Rabbi and the entire body of oriental Jewry which has never known anything of the compromises of nineteenth-century Reform Judaism, are committed to Zionism. The *Neture-Karta* are, in this respect, no more than an insignificant relic of some earlier day. The change for the parent organization itself, the *Agudat Yisrael*, came with the foundation of the state – or more precisely with the recognition of the full enormity of the Holocaust at the time of the Second World War. Here the historic sense of responsibility of rabbinic Judaism reasserted itself. It was not possible to ignore the commandment written in blood upon the soil of Europe. A whole civilization, that of east European Jewry, lay in ashes. Not only had the bodies of six million Jews been incinerated, but the great Torah centres of

Volozhin, Ponivezh, Satmar, Munkacz, Mir and Slabodke had ceased to exist. There was no way back to eastern Europe, to its values, to its social norms, to its religious solidarity, to its simple Jewish calendric system. There was, in fact, only one way forward, and that was towards a Jewish Palestine, with all the perils for the soul of Jewry that that implied. For these men too, as for Berl Katznelson and Ben-Gurion, the fundamental logic of *en brerah* ('There is no alternative') was at work. The Jewish state was accepted as an inexorable necessity. When the *Agudat Yisrael* representatives joined the Provisional Government of Israel in 1948, they showed that they, too, understood that Jewish history is the arena of dialogue, of existential challenges and responses which test our religious faith. Nor is it always possible to find the responses written out for us in a book. For history is a book which we help to write ourselves, a covenant drama in which we act freely and are yet 'constrained by the Word', never knowing quite how the drama will unfold from scene to scene.

But if the great mass of the faithful threw in their lot with the Jewish state at its foundation and have remained more or less committed to it ever since, a subtler logic was at work also. It may be suggested that in the religious heart of the Jewish people a new truth had been revealed. That truth was, to put it very simply, that the Emancipation no longer held the key to the future. The Torah sages of the nineteenth century had not been taken in by the promise of the Emancipation. By and large they had warned that it was an empty dream, and that in exchange for our acceptance of their paganisms the nations would offer us only shame and suffering. But they could not have known how horribly their prognosis would be confirmed by events. If the Jewish life of Europe lay shattered by the Holocaust, then the dream of the Emancipation – that dream of Moses Hess and so many of his contemporaries – lay shattered also. The great liberal hope first proclaimed at the time of the French Revolution had come to an end. Europe had seemed, for a century and more, to be holding out a promise of liberty, fraternity and equality, a secular messianism in which the differences between men, black and white, Jew and Gentile, would melt away. The Holocaust had changed all this. The remnant of European Jewry was sickened not only by its bereavement but also by the new glimpse it had had of the hidden face of Western culture, its Heart of Darkness. No one knew quite what the future held, but it was clear that it would not be the future of progress and universal goodwill by which the children of the Emancipation had been beguiled. Thus in the cataclysm of the war years the hope of the Emancipation, that which gave it its spiritual content, had largely burned away. It may be that Israel was not ready for the Jewish Messiah, but there would be no non-Jewish Messiah either. The sting had, so to speak, been taken out of the non-Jewish calendar.

The second great moment of truth came with the Six Day War. Here, you may say perhaps, the opposite process occurred – the revelation not of the spiritual poverty of the West, of the emptiness, the ultimate meaninglessness of the calendar which marks out the centuries of progress for Western man, but the revelation, suddenly that summer, of the full meaning of the Jewish calendar which binds us to a past echoing with ancestral obligations and a future of promise and redemption. The amazing triumph of those six days, coming as it did so quickly after three weeks of dark menace, created what Buber called 'an abiding astonishment'.[6] He used the term to describe the Israelites' experience of the great deliverance at the Red Sea. It was a truly religious moment, the experience of miracle, of sudden illumination. And what was illuminated was the significance of Jewish existence. We were suddenly living in the fullness of our own covenant history. It is here that we should locate the special metaphysical character of the Six Day War. The outcome of the war did not only call in question the armistice lines set up in 1949 between the divided halves of Palestine; it also challenged the lines which divided the Israeli people from within, the lines which divided their Jewish past from their contemporary existence in the twentieth century.

The Six Day War revealed a new dynamic in the Jewish calendar. It was as though archaeology had come alive, or rather as though the past had become a key to the future. Those who jumped off the weapon-carriers at the Lions' Gate on 7 June 1967 were not in search of archaeological relics. Indeed it is doubtful whether anyone could be persuaded to storm a walled city in a half-track out of a mere academic interest in the past. And yet when they reached the Western Wall what they found there, and what they found in themselves, was the Jewish past. A few were too shocked

444

444

4444

4

at the immediate sense of personal bereavement to respond in this way, but the overwhelming sentiment was that of fulfilment and joy. Israelis who had never known they were Jews suddenly awoke to their inheritance, and it was clear to all that this discovery would have momentous consequences for the future. The books do not tell us where we go from here, but without the books there is no way of explaining how we got here in the first place.

II

In a collection of taped conversations between soldiers from the *kibbutzim*, taken down and printed shortly after the Six Day War, two things emerged: with an almost monotonous insistence, as though afraid of making too perilous a leap, the heroes of the secular tradition insisted that they were not religious, but they also insisted that they had suddenly realized that they were Jews:—

So *even though I'm not religious, the Wall meant an awful lot to me.* And again it was because I felt that the Wall wasn't just a wall, that it wasn't just a collection of stones, but expressed something. It's enough for me to know that it's served as an address for all Jews, whenever something hurt, whenever something oppressed them. It symbolizes everything.

The first experience was Jerusalem. In my unit we heard the news on a transistor radio. When we heard of the conquest of Jerusalem there wasn't a single one who didn't weep, including me. Then for the first time, *I felt not the 'Israelness' but the Jewishness of the nation.*

It didn't have a religious connotation – at least so it seems to me. Today, when I try to explain it to myself, I can't find an exact answer – but it seems to me that *for us the Old City was a symbol of something unfinished* ... it's difficult for me to know exactly why. But it's clear that at that moment it didn't have a religious significance.

Personally I say that whenever you hear 'Jerusalem', you feel another feeling ... I have no religious sentiment. *No-one can accuse me of that.* But this is something that touches us all. It gave us more than anything.[7] (Author's italics throughout.)

One has to understand that the very word for religious, *dati*, inevitably connotes in modern Hebrew a rootedness in the past, a

refusal to address oneself to the future. That is why the secular
youngsters are so afraid of the label. And yet the newly felt wonder,
the newly acquired identity, threaten the careful semantic barriers
which the secular have erected against the religion of their ancestors, just as they threaten the ideological barriers implicit in the
Declaration of Independence. But those barriers are coming
down.[8]

The dialogues were resumed a year after the war in the circle of
a *kibbutz* of the *Hashomer Hatzair* (*Mapam*), and there the participants were even more outspoken, linking the new-found
religious consciousness with the bankruptcy of their traditional
communist faith revealed after the Twentieth Party Congress:

The fact is that there is to-day a slow but uninterrupted return to
tradition. . . .

You can call it reactionary, you can say it's no good, that it's medieval
– but in my opinion it's a fact. . . .

We are now in a period of return to the tradition, towards the Jewish
people and our connection with it. . . .

Another speaker was just as emphatic about the breakdown of her
socialist faith but less optimistic about the possibility of a return
to Judaism:

But we had one blow from the 20th Congress. It began then and now
it's complete. That was really a powerful blow which left us without a
faith. And I don't believe that we can get back to a religious faith. We
had the sort of rationalist education which makes it impossible for us
to go back.[9]

From the above extracts two striking and perhaps contradictory
conclusions emerge: one is that the Jewish dimension of existence,
that symbolized by the Jewish calendar, had suddenly acquired
enormous significance for the heirs of the secular tradition, and
the other is that in spite of this, and in spite of the moral shock
occasioned by the sudden realization of the emptiness of that
secular faith which had hitherto sustained them, there was no
simple way back to Judaism ('It is impossible for us to go back').
The history of 1967 was what the poet Wordsworth called one

Z.R.—4

of the 'spots of time', a moment of illumination which seemingly gives life new meaning. It left those who lived through it changed but also confused. Hitherto guarded beliefs and standards were called in question. Barriers were down, but who was to step over them? And what were we to find on the other side? Perhaps it would be better not to step over them, but just to leave them where they had fallen and imagine that they still existed. This was true of the physical map of the Holy Land and it was true of the soul of the Jew. It was still possible to hope that we would be allowed to return to a 'normal' condition. General Yitzhak Rabin, the victor of 1967, assured the armoured brigade in Sinai shortly after the fighting that no miracle had occurred ('It is all your doing');[10] there was no reason to think in terms of the extraordinary. (It is only fair to note, however, that Mr Rabin spoke in a different strain when receiving an honorary doctorate at the newly restored campus of the Hebrew University on Mount Scopus. On that very stirring occasion he described how the soldiers had experienced the victory of June 1967:

But the strain of battle, the anxiety which preceded it, and the sense of salvation and of direct confrontation with Jewish history itself cracked the shell of hardness and shyness and released well-springs of emotion and stirrings of the spirit. The paratroopers who conquered the Wailing Wall leaned on its stones and wept – in its symbolism an act so rare as to be almost unparalleled in human history. Rhetorical phrases and clichés are not common in our Army, but this scene on the Temple Mount, powerful enough to break through their habits of reticence, revealed as though by a flash of lightning truths that were deeply hidden.[11]

Mr Rabin here very accurately catches the emotions as well as the spiritual reverberations of the victory. He tells us that 'truths' were then revealed, but he cannot tell us what those truths were. They remain 'deeply hidden', evidently, from the heirs of the secular tradition.)

As though to reassure a shaken public that there was nothing the least bit 'apocalyptic' in the events of 1967, some of the military people a few years later were saying that Israel had not even been under the threat of annihilation. It was a case of a military operation undertaken as the most reasonable of several options, and it had worked out well. No need to think of the Lord of Hosts riding

upon his chariot with an outstretched arm as in the exodus from
Egypt. These generals were, of course, in flight from Jewish
covenant realities. They were proposing an alternative myth, that
of Israeli normality, by which they hoped to persuade us that we
were a people like any other, without any special *dybbuk* from the
past to disturb our lives in the present, without any special
messianic responsibilities or apocalyptic terrors to mark us out
from others. Our calendar was basically the same as that of other
peoples; if we needed to use the old-fashioned Jewish calendar, we
should keep it for tombstones only. It did not need to interfere with
our normal lives, our international relations, our posture as reasonable men seeking an accommodation with our neighbours in what
was, after all, a normal dispute about borders between sovereign
states.

It is against this background that the third moment of truth
occurred, that signalized by the Yom Kippur War. It is no good
talking about the October War; every Jew, every Israeli knows in
his bones that this was the War of the Day of Atonement. It was
the war that 'made one': it made us not only one people, but a
people subject to a special destiny, to special stresses, to special
existential perils, a people with one calendar which stretches back
from Creation through the agonies and storms of the present,
through a wilderness where only the pillar of fire and the column
of smoke mark the path to the future. No one dared to doubt this
time that we were under threat of annihilation. This was no normal
international dispute, no quarrel about borders. It required no
special gift for making historical analogies to see that in the joint
onslaught on Israel made by the Arab armies and their helpers
from a dozen lands there was a genocidal intent, a continuation of
Hitler's war against the Jewish people. The issue was not this or
that piece of land; the issue was Israel's right to national existence,
the Jewish people's right to physical space.[12] But there was a
metaphysical dimension also. The war was launched on Yom
Kippur, because it was thought that on that day the front-line
soldiers would be less on the alert than on other days of the year –
this was an important tactical consideration. But there was also
what may be called the spiritual strategy. For the modern secularized imagination of the West and of many Zionists it is difficult
to grasp fully the concept of a 'holy war', a *Jihad*, as a twentieth-

century reality. But for the Arab world the crusade against Israel has never been other than a holy war. It is not a war on behalf of the Palestinians; quite the contrary, the logic of the holy war can even dictate (and does, in fact, dictate) the sacrifice of the Palestinian Arab people to its imperative demands. It is a religious war. The Zionists who came to settle in Zion long refused to recognize this, seeking to assure themselves and the international community that this was a 'normal' international dispute. But for the Arabs the purpose of this war is the liquidation of the Jewish entity in Palestine in the name of the integrity of Islam. The enemy is Judaism, for the claims on which a 'Jewish state' is based are manifestly religious in origin, just as the aims on which such a state is founded cannot be understood except with reference to Jewish messianic beliefs. This was a major theme of the Fourth Conference of the Academy of Islamic Research held at the Al Azhar University in Cairo in September 1968. In his address to that Conference Dr Kamel el Baker, President of Om Dorman Islamic University, referring to the Declaration of Israel Independence, maintained that what is spoken of is, specifically, a '*Jewish* state' and that the full implications of that term could not be ignored:

> Thus the usurping state of Israel declares that it is a religious state based on asserting the existence of the Jewish people *vis-à-vis* other peoples in the area. This is an evident fact, for it is obvious that describing Zionism as a 'political' movement is associated with the means it adopts to achieve its ends. Because Zionist means are really political that is why it was described as a political movement. Its end is the same end as that of Judaism, for Judaism, like Zionism, calls for the return to the Promised Land (of Zion), with a difference in the methods employed. Judaism associates the return with a purely religious aspect – the appearance of the expected Christ [sic] – when the Jews would restore their power, while Zionism resorts to political action.
>
> Difference in the methods employed has no relation whatsoever with the essence. Judaism is a 'religion' in which the believers follow certain creed. Zionism is the same as Judaism, but it seeks to achieve the end sought by Judaism but through political action. The document declaring the establishment of the state of Israel asserts this fact, for it does not hide that the state of Israel is but a name for a Jewish state. Zionism, therefore, is the means employed by the Jewish religion for self-realization, and the Jews' method of establishing their unity *vis-à-vis* others in

the area. Who, then, is the other party concerned in the conflict? Resorting to the law of the majority as the closest criterion to natural justice emphasizes beyond doubt that the establishment of a Jewish state in Palestine means a confrontation of Islam and Moslems, for the cultural and demographic superiority in the usurped land is for Islam and Moslems.

And he went on to say, 'This, then, is the essence of the Palestinian problem – a religious Jewish state founded by Zionists. . . .'[13] Dr el Baker understood that the Declaration of Independence speaks of the 'Rock of Israel', of the 'Book of Books' and of 5 Iyar 5708. And if Israel represented the revival of Judaism as a twentieth-century political phenomenon, then his horrifying conclusion was that it must be destroyed entirely.[14] There was no room for political compromise.

Those were the terms on which the Yom Kippur battle was joined five years after the Al Azhar Conference had defined its ideological basis. The irony is that whilst one side was clear about the ideological issue, the other, the Israeli side, was confused; it was still attempting to deceive itself that this was a conflict susceptible of solution by the ordinary means of international mediation. And this confusion, which conferred on Israel a certain charming innocence as a surviving representative of Western liberalism and rationalism, did nothing to strengthen its political position. Quite the contrary, the refusal of the Arabs on ideological grounds to negotiate with Israel face to face gave force to their demands, whilst Israel's proclamations of peaceful intent and willingness to compromise merely encouraged the view that her claims were infinitely weaker than those of the opposing party. And, needless to say, it was a confusion which was, above all things, damaging to morale. The *Jihad*, pernicious and barbaric as its conclusions were, gave the Arabs a motive beyond mere self-preservation. Israel, having failed to define its covenant faith and responsibilities in political terms, was at a disadvantage, just as the West, with its emasculated liberal faith, is at a disadvantage in the face of an aggressive, self-confident and doctrinaire communist enemy.

But the Yom Kippur War and the world-wide offensive against Zionism which has followed it have had the effect of driving Israel towards a more profound spiritual reassessment. Much more evidently than Nasser's war in 1967 the Yom Kippur War was directed, as we have noted, at Israel's spiritual essence, at the 'Rock of Israel', at the 'Book of Books'. Launched on Yom Kippur, at the most sacred hour of the Jewish year, it was a challenge to the Jewish calendar and all that it stood for, namely, the whole historical pilgrimage of the Jewish people, its covenant destiny. A metaphysical shudder, as it were, passed through the body of Israel. Corresponding with the moment of exaltation, the triumph, the sudden joy of the reunion with Jerusalem on 28 Iyar 5727, and in dialectical association with that moment, was this moment of metaphysical horror on Yom Kippur 5734. It was not so much an act of aggression as a blasphemy. It challenged the Jewish people at the root of its existence. Like the Assyrian invader in the time of the prophet Isaiah (chapter 37), the enemy had 'reviled and blasphemed the Holy One of Israel'. The Jewish dimension of the struggle could no longer be ignored, and for the common soldier the occasion was one for the deepest heart-searchings. The searching was even more emphatic than that recorded in the taped conversations of 1967 quoted earlier. In the weeks following the outbreak of the Yom Kippur War, amid the shelling and the subsequent battles of attrition in Sinai and on the Golan, there was not an army unit in which the issue of Jewish identity, of the Jewish meaning of the struggle, was not in the forefront of discussion. It was not merely a blind reaching out for some religious hope in the midst of calamity (though there was that also); it was a search for a faith more sustaining, more vitally informed with a sense of the Jewish past and the Jewish future than that which secular Zionism had so far offered. And the search went on.

It went on through the crisis of November 1975, with the United Nations (UN) Assembly's vote against Zionism. That, too, was a kind of metaphysical outrage, a blow directed against the intimate core of the faith of Israel, of faith in the Jewish future. No longer was it possible to affirm with any confidence that we were engaged in a normal conflict with a normal enemy. The problem became one of defining the specific character of the struggle. The child suddenly exposed to the manifest uniqueness of Israel's situation will ask, 'Why is this nation different from other nations?' It will no longer do to tell him that when we become a majority in our land all will be well. We are already a majority and all is not well. It is no good saying to him that other nations also have to struggle for their existence. He sees only too clearly that other nations, which came into existence in circumstances far uglier than those surrounding Israel's struggle for independence have long been accepted by their neighbours, their natural borders long recognized by the international community. Israel has to endure a double standard. The 600,000 Jewish refugees who fled from Arab lands in 1948 do not count; they are not remembered. Only the 600,000 Arab refugees from Israel are to be considered;[15] their rights are to be the subject of repeated UN resolutions, each one more hostile than the last. These facts constitute the special environment in which Israelis, individually and collectively, find themselves. It leaves them with no alternative to the Jewish myth from which the Zionist enterprise has risen. It means the acceptance of a covenant destiny, with all the constraint and freedom, all the exaltation and agony, that that implies. There is literally only one calendar left: the Jewish calendar. Israel's enemies have seen to that.

Giving urgency to this quest for meaning is the universal nature of the crisis at the centre of which one is seemingly placed. Israel and the Jews are exposed to world-wide attention of an extraordinarily disturbing kind. There is no escaping the awful spotlight. If only the nation could be inconspicuous, like Albania or Nicaragua! But it seems that this is not to be. Its destiny is to defend its right on a high platform, before the gaze of all. The question of who we are and what we are doing here is directed at us from all quarters of the globe. The Jewish need for survival has to be balanced against the world-wide fear of a renewed Arab oil boycott, or even a new world war. Inexplicably it is the Jews who have remained in Jerusalem, the Jews who hold on for dear life to the plateau of the Golan and the mountains of Judea who threaten world peace, not the hydrogen bombs which China and Russia point at one another day and night. Inexplicably it is the plight of the Palestinian refugees left over from 1948, whom the Arab states with all their wealth and their vast spaces refuse to absorb, which most exercises the nations, not the starving millions in India or Nigeria. There is pressure upon Israel to rediscover the sources of its own spiritual strength, to reformulate its destiny in terms which can match the importunity of the demands made upon it, to discover a validity in ourselves to match the seeming validity of the questions addressed to us. It is a strangely apocalyptic moment.

High up on one of the great Herodian blocks of the Western Wall of the Temple the hand of a scribe many centuries ago engraved the following words from the prophet Isaiah: 'And when you see this, your heart shall rejoice, and your bones shall flourish like the grass' (*Isaiah* 66:14). Perhaps he meant the words for us, knowing that we should one day return to that Wall and that mountain. However in the sequel to the verse, which tells of war and flames and of the punishment of evil-doers, there is little obvious cause for rejoicing. We have to look a little further on to see what the prophet meant, and then we shall find two infallible grounds for hope. One is the knowledge he has of the deathlessness of the Jewish people: 'For as the new heavens and the new earth, which I will make, shall remain before me, says the Lord, so shall your seed and your name remain' (verse 22). And the other source of rejoicing is his intuition of the day when the nations will marvellously acknowledge the truth which it is Israel's task to bring to the world, that message of justice and peace of which the holy mountain is the visible symbol: 'The time shall come that I will gather all the nations and tongues; and they shall come and see my glory. And I shall set a sign among them' (verses 18, 19). To speak of the abolition of the double calendar is really to speak of a hope almost too daring to be breathed. It is, as the prayer book for Yom Kippur expresses it, that 'all the nations will unite to do thy will with a perfect heart'; that all will one day learn to live with the biblical calendar, counting from Creation to salvation; that all will acknowledge the one Lord of history under whose providence we live our lives. When that day comes we shall know for whom the Jew has suffered through the long centuries, in whose name he has been reviled, whose priest he is and whom he is called on to serve in Zion, the City of the Great King.

7

Who are the Jews?

I

IN A BOOK, the English version of which was overtaken by the June War of 1967 almost as it came off the press, Georges Friedmann, the French sociologist, wrote:

> There is no Jewish nation. There is an Israeli nation. The state that came into existence as a result of Herzl's prophecies is not a 'Jewish state'. The Israeli state is creating an imperious national community that is conscious of itself but does not include in that consciousness belonging to a 'Jewish people'. There seems to be a widening gap (among the extremist zealots it is an impassable abyss) between that part of the population that sees itself as essentially Israeli and that other part, consisting of the orthodox, that regards itself as essentially Jewish.[1]

The statement was not true even when it was written. It overlooked the problematical character of Israeli nationhood and the love-hate relationship between the religious and non-religious sections. The deep friendship between David Ben-Gurion and Rabbi J. L. Maimon at the time of the establishment of the state was not without significance for the forging of bonds (the so-called religious *status quo*) on which the co-existence of religion and the state has since been based. This was not just a marriage of political convenience, a truce, but an expression of a collective Jewish identity. Of course there are tensions, but these express the force of the connection between the two groups. If religion is dead you don't have to drive your vehicle into the Orthodox sections of Jerusalem on the sabbath, as people sometimes do, to demonstrate the fact;

and if the violators are not themselves Jews, the Orthodox don't
have to throw stones at them to express their outrage. After all
there is nothing outrageous about a non-Jew, a mere 'Canaanite',
driving his car on the sabbath! If such scenes occur, it is because
the sabbath is still a central issue for the consecrators and dese-
crators alike. Both sides are Jews.[2]

The national community of Israel is unable to exclude from
itself what Friedmann called 'the consciousness of belonging to the
Jewish People', because that consciousness is not the possession
of a minority group of 'zealots', as Friedmann supposed: it
belongs to the people as a whole. Over the years the secular
majority had tended to behave as though they were liberated from
the discomforts and embarrassments of Jewishness and as though
these could be somehow projected upon the Jews of the Diaspora
or the old-fashioned religious section of the Israeli community as
their special responsibility. But this psychological manoeuvre no
longer seemed to work after the Six Day War. There was, as we
said earlier, a new situation. The barriers were down as the average
Israeli discovered that he was more Jewish than he had supposed.
It was a shock which everyone experienced, secularists and religious alike. What everyone felt was that this was a Jewish and not
an Israeli war.[3] And it was an experience which millions of Jews in
London, New York, Paris and Moscow shared with their brothers
and sisters in Israel. Georges Friedmann had maintained, 'there is
no Jewish nation'. Now in 1967 the Israelis discovered precisely
the opposite, that 'the People of Israel lives – *am yisrael hay!*'

II

The crisis of *Yom Kippur* which came six years later was parallel
and yet different. Then, too, an electric shock passed through the
whole Jewish people and then, too, the Jews of the Diaspora were
involved. But on that occasion there was a shock of a different
kind; it left behind not relief and thanksgiving, but rather anxiety
of a profoundly unremitting nature. But perhaps this was no less a
sign of a deepening Jewish consciousness! Georges Friedmann
concluded his book, *The End of the Jewish People*, with a witty
epilogue in which he warned that the new Israelis might be losing
one of the most important constituents of Jewishness – *anxiety*, the

source of so much Jewish creativity and striving. It was 'the eighth virtue which conditions the rest'.[4] From this point of view it seemed to Friedmann, writing in 1965, that Israel was moving in a new, non-Jewish direction! There was still a lot to worry about in the new Israeli society, including the Arab threat, the economic difficulties and a certain unappeased *malaise* of the spirit, but nevertheless there was much complacency, abundance, happiness, and a desire for a 'normal' life which seemed to be within reach of large sections of the population. In these circumstances, could it be that the restlessness, the traditional *Angst* which had characterized the Jewish soul in the Diaspora was about to disappear? 'There are still cases of living anxiety in Israel,' he concluded, 'but how much longer will they last?'[5] Yom Kippur gave us the answer to that.

If the Yom Kippur War has proved one thing, it is that Jewish anxiety has not come to an end, nor is it likely to come to an end in the foreseeable future, in spite of the extraordinary peace initiative of President Sadat and Prime Minister Begin in November 1977. Politically speaking, the use of the oil weapon means that Israel is now subject to pressure by the West in their attempted conciliation of the Arabs – this is probably the most important factor in the current situation – and yet in the long term it is clear that the pressure will be directed not against Israel but against the oil-producing states themselves, whose economic stranglehold must eventually prove intolerable. But the anxiety remains. In fact it is the anxiety itself, not the external causes of it, which constitutes the basic difference between the condition of Israel in 1972 and 1978. If the outcome of the Six Day War was renewed Jewish hope, the outcome of the Yom Kippur War was renewed Jewish anxiety. What both of these states of mind add up to is that the 'Jewish people' is still remarkably Jewish. But is the Diaspora Jewish to the same extent? In this connection we may note a certain reversal of roles. The Israeli social psychologist Simon N. Herman shows how young American Jews arriving in Israel in the early sixties were often disappointed at finding Israeli *sabras* (native-born Israelis) less Jewish than they wanted and expected them to be.[6] The young Israelis projected an alien 'un-Jewish' image and were seemingly indifferent to the Jewish traditional practices which still meant so much to their American counterparts. If we define 'Jewish consciousness' in terms of observance

and synagogue attendance, this may still be partially true, but if by
'Jewish consciousness' we mean the sense of belonging to a people
subject to a special Jewish fate which differentiates it from other
peoples, then it is clear that Israeli youth in 1978 are more acutely
Jewish than their counterparts in the Diaspora. They have felt
'the badge of shame, the branding tool, and the bloody whip' in a
way that their fellow Jews in the Diaspora have not. Following the
UN Assembly vote against Zionism and Jewish 'racism' in 1975,
the Jews of Israel live in the vivid awareness that they are the
object of a world-wide anti-semitic reaction. Many Israelis try to
repress this awareness – as Jews did, no doubt, in czarist Russia a
hundred years ago – but it is there nevertheless, now manifestly a
part of Israeli existence. Not so for the emancipated Jews of the
West! Even their synagogue attendance and other forms of
'ethnicity' do not serve to isolate them from the society to which
they belong. In America these Jews are part of the pluralist pattern
of American middle-class culture, and in other Western countries
the Jewish youth have merged with considerable success, though
perhaps with less show of 'ethnicity', into the general culture of
their surroundings. The well-known signs of a special Jewish
condition – that which was traditionally defined by anti-semitism –
have passed over to Israel!

A Marxist writer, Karl Kautsky, declared in the early part of the
century that Jewish consciousness, Jewish culture, Jewish nationality and, indeed, the Jewish religion itself are no more than functions of anti-semitism. Anti-semitism is thus the very ground of
the existence of the Jewish people, a point reaffirmed thirty years
later by Jean-Paul Sartre. When anti-semitism ceases (as according
to the Marxist myth it will with the achievement of the classless
society), then the Jewish people will come to an end also: 'When
the Jews shall have ceased to be persecuted and outlawed, the
Jews themselves will cease to exist,'[7] Kautsky declared. We have
seen in an earlier chapter that this account of the nature of Judaism
and the Jewish people fails to do justice to the positives of the
Jewish myth.[8] Ultimately the Jewish people is not defined by anti-
semitism but by its inward sense of mission and responsibility.
Jewish anxiety is, at bottom, the anxiety born of a covenant task
needing to be discharged. Nevertheless no account of the Covenant
can be adequate which does not give weight to the negative factors

on which the Marxist writers lay their emphasis, namely, the
radical isolation of the Jew and the pressure of a hostile environment as that which conditions Jewish existence. If the hatred of
the Jews stems from Sinai, as the rabbis declared, rather than from
the dialectics of the class struggle, it is hatred nevertheless. And if
we define anti-semitism as a theological sign of election, the badge
of the suffering servant of Isaiah, rather than as a sign of the
unsolved problems of a bourgeois society, that does not make it
any the less anti-semitism; it merely makes it easier for the faithful
Jew to live with it. It becomes elective suffering, the dark side of
the Covenant. If the Six Day War enables one to glimpse the bright
promise of the Covenant, the joy and salvation it offers, then the
Yom Kippur War gave one a glimpse of the menace and radical
isolation which are the price of that salvation. And in that shadow
we now live.

III

We may now summarize the bearing of these two covenant
moments on the interrelation between Israel and the Diaspora. In
May and June 1967 what was felt overwhelmingly was unity – the
recovered unity of the Jewish people throughout the world. But
the Yom Kippur War was in some way different. True, there was
the sense of shared outrage; but the outcome, as we have said, was
a recovered sense of isolation and anxiety. And this was an experience which divided rather than united. It served to divide those
who identified themselves fervently with the Jewish lot from those
who did not. This aspect of Yom Kippur has been brilliantly
defined by Emil Fackenheim. He remarks that, 'The Six-Day War,
if but for a moment, united the whole Jewish People, including
some of the most marginal. The Yom Kippur War, if but for a
moment, divided the most committed.'[9] There are many Jews for
whom living in the new, perilous world created by Yom Kippur
is too agonizing a trial. For Israelis – those at least who choose
to remain in Israel – there is seemingly no alternative to accepting
the burden of isolation. But for the Diaspora Jew it is possible to
opt out, or so it seems to him. Whilst many, no doubt, have been
brought nearer to their brethren in the land of Israel through the
fierce pressure of these 'terrible days', others have chosen, often

unconsciously, to disassociate themselves. There has been a polarization of Jewish identity.

If we are honest we will realize that this is not something quite new. The polarization we are speaking of was already implicit in the creation of the state of Israel itself in 1948. In the cold light of Yom Kippur one was simply able to see the true contours of an already existing situation. And what we saw was a Jewish people bound together, indeed, in kinship and memory but separate in their existential condition. There is, in the last analysis, no way of ignoring the separate identities of the Jews of Israel and the Diaspora. It is the former who carry on their back the burden of the Covenant; for the latter it is now a matter of voluntary self-identification. And no amount of rhetoric can gloss over the sharp contrast between these two situations.

A brief chapter of British parliamentary history will, I think, make clear what actually happened with the creation of the state of Israel. During the years from 1945 to 1948 Jewish aspirations in Palestine were being opposed by the British government, which assumed an unashamedly pro-Arab posture. The Foreign Secretary of the day, Mr Ernest Bevin, took his stand from the British White Paper of 1939 which had the effect of severely limiting Jewish immigration. This meant that the doors of Palestine were virtually closed to hundreds of thousands of survivors of the Holocaust still languishing in Displaced Persons' centres throughout Europe. When the Government was finally forced to accede to pressure (from America as well as from such sharp critics at home as Winston Churchill) and to agree to hand back the mandate for Palestine to the United Nations, in order that a Jewish state might be established, it did so with obvious bad grace and, in the process of handing over to the warring communities in Palestine, clearly tilted in favour of the Arabs. The Arab Legion of King Abdullah of Trans-Jordan, which invaded western Palestine to prevent the implementation of the United Nations decision, was openly supported by the British and was, in fact, commanded by a British colonel. During this period of 'strained relations' between the Jewish people and the British Government there was no stronger critic of the Government than Mr Barnett Janner, the Member of Parliament (MP) for Leicester and a member of Mr Bevin's own party. Mr Janner lost no opportunity to voice his solidarity with the *Yishuv* in Palestine and his abhorrence of Mr Bevin's policies. It is clear that at this time the sense of responsibility for the Jewish fate and the Jewish future rested squarely on the shoulders of Diaspora Jews, especially the leaders of the Jewish community such as Mr Janner. The question of dual loyalties scarcely arose, for the issue was too clear and the sense of Jewish duty too imperative.

If we move ten years forward to 1956 we see a dramatic change. By then a Conservative government was in office, headed by Sir Anthony Eden, and Janner, along with sixteen other Jewish MPs, was a member of the Labour Opposition. When the Suez crisis exploded in November of that year the Government came under fierce attack from the Opposition for its aggression in Suez in collaboration with the French. The British-French action had been timed to coincide with that of Israel which had launched an offensive across the Egyptian lines into Sinai in October. From the Israeli point of view, Israel was fighting for its life, reacting, in fact to intolerable Egyptian provocation in the form of attacks by *fedayeen* (armed infiltrators) made almost daily from the Gaza strip into Israeli territory; this was also the position taken by Sir Winston Churchill. But for the Labour Opposition headed by Mr Hugh Gaitskell, Britain was an aggressor and Israel no better than a 'burglar' breaking into the home of a peaceful householder, as he expressed it. During the first week of November the parliamentary debates reached an unprecedented peak of bitterness, almost hysteria, reflecting the high state of tension throughout the country. Sir Barnett Janner, by then president of the Zionist Federation of Great Britain and Ireland, as well as president of the Board of Deputies of British Jews, at first refrained from voting with his party in order to do nothing that might serve, however indirectly, to weaken Israel in its struggle. But in the final, critical division on a vote of censure (the division which was eventually to bring about Eden's resignation) Janner, along with *all* the other Jewish Labour MPs, many of them declared Zionists, entered the division lobby in support of their party.[10] This betrayal of Israel's interests – as it seemed to many – led to acrimonious personal attacks on Sir Barnett and his colleagues in many sections of Anglo-Jewry. But the truth is that this was not a personal matter, a display of cowardice on the part of Sir Barnett, but rather a symptom of a profound historical change. A change had occurred in the existential condition of Diaspora Jewry as a result of the emergence of the state of Israel. To be a Zionist after that date meant no more than to be a friend and supporter of Israel; it did not mean actually to bear responsibility for the Jewish fate. That responsibility had passed to Israel itself and to its constituted government.

To use the theological vocabulary which is surely appropriate here, we should say that the whole burden and charge of the Covenant had now passed to the people and state of Israel. What had occurred was a kind of changing of the guard. The Jews of the Diaspora would participate by proxy in the joys and trials of the Covenant, but the covenantal centre of gravity itself had passed to Israel. There was no conscious abandonment of responsibility, but the burden had shifted nevertheless. Jewish history was to move into a new channel; those who wished to participate in it would have to become part of the new enterprise in the land of Israel. If they did so they would experience an extraordinary sense of renewal, of power; but they would also have to endure the scandal and embarrassment of otherness. In short, they would become 'the Jewish People'. For the Jewish people is defined not only by those common ancestral memories which Israel shares with the Diaspora communities, but also by a unique fate, and this burden of uniqueness now rests exclusively, it seems, upon the new nation that has arisen in the land of Israel. The Jews of the Diaspora are in the position of having carried the burden to this point; and it is with an unconscious sigh of relief that they have discharged it and placed it on younger shoulders.[11]

IV

The conclusion we have reached may seem, on the face of it, not essentially different from that of two distinguished and sharp-sighted observers, Arthur Koestler and David Ben-Gurion. Both saw the coming of the Jewish state as an event which called in question the very meaning and purpose of Jewish corporate existence outside Israel. For Koestler Jews in the Diaspora were now faced with the choice between becoming part of the new Hebrew nation or renouncing any conscious or implicit claim to separate nationhood. A few would take the first course, but the majority, himself included, would choose the second. Judaism, as he rightly discerned, is more than a religious confession; it involves national and historical purposes, and these latter had been finally transferred to where they belong, the national community in Israel. The Jews of the Diaspora had thus discharged their task:

Now that the State of Israel is firmly established, they are at last free to do what they could not do before: to wish it good luck and go their own way, with an occasional friendly glance back and a helpful gesture. But nevertheless to go their own way, with the nation whose life and culture they share, without reservations or split loyalties.[12]

He concluded his book, *Promise and Fulfilment*, with a word of farewell to the Jewish people of the past: 'Now that the mission of the Wandering Jew is completed, he must discard the knapsack and cease to be an accomplice in his own destruction.'[13] This closing sentence of Koestler's actually echoed the words of Karl Kautsky thirty years earlier. Kautsky had ended his book, *Are the Jews a Race?* (1914), by announcing the imminent disappearance of the Jewish people: 'Ahasuerus, the Wandering Jew, will at last have found a haven of rest.'[14] Koestler had obviously read Kautsky's book and here was either consciously or unconsciously reproducing his notion of the approaching term of the Jewish people's historical pilgrimage. This, on the face of it, was odd, since Koestler was a professed Zionist and was powerfully impressed by the vitality of the new nation-state of Israel, whilst Kautsky was an anti-Zionist and saw no more significance in Jewish aspirations in Palestine at the time that he wrote his book than he did in Jewish separate existence in the Diaspora.

The truth is, however, that both Koestler and Kautsky were agreed on one thing, and that was that the 'Jewish people' had no further purpose to fulfil. Koestler did not see the new nation-state of Israel as taking over where Diaspora Jewry left off: like the new *sabras* of the 'Canaanite' persuasion, and like Georges Friedmann in the passages quoted earlier, he saw Israel as a new departure. 'One thing seems fairly certain,' he remarked in 1949, 'within a generation or two Israel will have become an entirely un-Jewish country.'[15] He was as it were, apologizing to secularists and universalists like Kautsky for the reappearance of Israel on the stage of history. True, Israel had transformed itself into a nation-state, but there was no need to fear a revival of the Jewish myth, for the career of the Jewish people, *as such*, was over and Israel was fast becoming a nation like any other nation. This was the implication of his words about the Wandering Jew putting down his knapsack. Koestler could hardly sustain this thesis in 1978. Even if he were to deny the signs of a resurgence of the Jewish myth within the consciousness of the Israeli people, he could hardly deny the resurgence in the minds of others of those irrational hopes, phobias and hatreds which have conditioned the existence of the Jewish people in the past and which condition the life of Israel at this time.

Koestler's arguments will not, therefore, serve as a support for the view set out here, namely, that Israel has somehow inherited the mystery, becoming the bearer of the peculiar burden which has been with the Jewish people since the beginning of its history. David Ben-Gurion would seem to be more our man. Like Koestler he made a sharp distinction between the roles of Israel and Diaspora Jewry; and like Koestler he, at bottom, denied the validity of any continued purpose for the Diaspora. A true Jew and Zionist was one who chose to identify himself, body and soul, with the Hebrew nation as reconstituted in the land of Israel. But Ben-Gurion differed from Koestler in claiming that the new nation of Israel would not be like other nations. It would be exemplary, chosen, a 'light to the gentiles'. Ben-Gurion visualized Israeli nationalism and leadership in biblical terms. His models were Joshua, King David and the prophet Amos, and there can be no doubt of the strength and sincerity of his attachment to the ideals represented by those heroes. It is really what made him unique among the modern liberators who have helped to create the new nations of Africa and Asia. It gave him a messianic sense of purpose, resembling in some way that of the early American settlers in New England. For them, too, the biblical inspiration was a source of dynamic energy; it legitimated an unflinching use of political power for exalted ends. But unlike most of the American Puritans, Ben-Gurion's biblicism included certain very strong ethical restraints which, whilst they were not applied with complete consistency, were nevertheless very remarkable. He laid down a stringent code for the rank and file of the army, which included long terms of imprisonment for looting. The kind of excesses which were common in the history of the conquest of the North American continent, for instance, were almost unknown during Israel's wars against the Arabs; and much of the credit for this belongs to Ben-Gurion. Nor did he derive his moral fastidiousness from the tradition of Western liberalism as did his pacifist opponents. For him it was biblical, and could be combined with an equally biblical vigour in conquering the Promised Land for the Chosen People.

And yet there is something very vital missing in Ben-Gurion's use of the Hebrew Bible. His inspiration is messianic, prophetic, and yet in some subtle way it is also non-prophetic. Like so many of the earlier Zionist philosophers and guides he, too, had carried out a radical revision of the Hebrew myth. Ben-Gurion, in one of the last television interviews that he gave at the end of his life, declared his belief in God as that without which he could not conceive of reality. But for him it is clear that God is a non-personal force, a stream of tendency. Ben-Gurion's God resembles the Bergsonian *élan vital*, with a dash of Buddhism and more than a dash of Spinozism. The world of Nature and history testifies to a divine movement, but there is no real dialogue between God and man. Ben-Gurion did not meet God in prayer; there was no dialogue such as that which Martin Buber saw at the centre of the experience of biblical man. There was thus no sense of personal dependence, no fear and trembling, no existential anxiety, no true biblical humility. This may, perhaps, seem an advantage for a political leader charged with the task of raising up a new nation; for such a task pride and courage may seem more to the point than fear and trembling. However Israel's peculiar circumstances, as we have come to understand them since Ben-Gurion's death, and especially since 1973, make the qualities of humility and anxiety directly relevant to its political situation. For this Ben-Gurion, unhappily, did not prepare his people.

V

The spiritual failure of David Ben-Gurion and his generation can be grasped most clearly if we consider what may be termed his Nietzschean revision of the Holocaust. The Holocaust of European Jewry between the years 1941 and 1945 lies, of course, at the very heart of Israel's modern history as a nation. It gave to Israel's demand for nationhood political and moral force, as well as endowing the defenders of the new state with the extra ounce of desperate energy that was needed to fight off the invaders of 1947 and 1948. Nevertheless the Holocaust phenomenon also contradicts the basis on which the state of Israel is seemingly founded. For to understand the psychology of the victims there is no alternative to employing the categories of humility, of fear and trembling. The biblical metaphors which fit their case are those associated with the 'suffering servant' of Isaiah: they gave their backs to the smiters; they were led like lambs to the slaughter. These images, however, would not do at all for the Israel which Ben-Gurion wished to establish. They did not conform with the basic myth of the Second *Aliyah*. The 'worm of Jacob' had to be buried and replaced by 'Israel who does valiantly'. Ben-Gurion had forgotten that the Jewish people combines both characteristics. Jacob, the meek tent-dweller, struggles, indeed, through the long night of terror and wins the name of 'Israel', signifying triumph over unbelievable odds (see *Genesis* 32:25–30). But he does not lose his earlier personality; he carries it with him through his historical pilgrimage as wound and as inspiration.[16]

Ben-Gurion and his generation altered the balance of the Holocaust, turning its memory into a celebration of physical heroism. The day devoted to the commemoration of the Nazi slaughter became not simply 'Holocaust Day' but 'The Day of Holocaust and Heroism'. An enormous emphasis was placed on the record of the few examples of organized resistance, in particular the Warsaw Ghetto rising of April and May 1943. It was made to seem as though the last amazing bid for freedom by the starving remnants of the Jewish community of Warsaw was somehow characteristic of the whole period during which the Nazis pursued their policy of systematic extermination of European Jewry. Little attention was paid to the fact that for every Jew who resisted, a thousand others were paralysed by terror, helplessly ground down by the machinery of destruction. The truth was, of course, that in the situation in which they found themselves physical resistance was about as relevant for most of them as it would be for the victims of an aerial bombardment. But what the Israeli youth gathered about the Holocaust from the teaching they were given (and perhaps even more from the silences of their teachers) was that a portion of the Jewish people had resisted – these were the true heroes, the prototype of the new Israeli generation – whereas the others showed the cravenness characteristic of Diaspora Jews, the lack of dignity and courage associated with the beaten Jews of the European ghetto.[17] The suggestion was that never again would Jews, now that they had achieved independence in their own land, bend their backs to the smiters in the pusillanimous fashion of their ancestors. This was not usually expressed in so many words, but it was the clear implication of the manner in which the Holocaust was presented in schools and in the media. In keeping with this, little emphasis was placed on the many examples of heroism of a non-violent kind with which the history of the Holocaust abounds; that, for instance, of Rabbi Mendel Alter of Kalisch, who bid his many followers continue their study of the Torah in the death camps themselves; that of the many children who risked their lives to bring a piece of bread to their starving parents; that of the mothers who refused to be separated from their children even to save their own lives; that of the millions, in short, who preserved the human image in conditions of unbelievable degradation; that of the thousands who, as Elie Wiesel has reminded us, continued to rejoice at the Festival of the Law in the very jaws of death.[18] There would be respectful mention of such matters, but the young Israel was never bidden to *interiorize* such models of heroism as relevant to himself, for the day of Jacob was over and the day of Israel had begun. The fact that Jacob has his own special dignity, his own moral superiority to evil, was ignored.

The capture and trial of Adolf Eichmann in 1960 is rightly regarded as one of Ben-Gurion's greatest achievements. This was an act of historic justice but, more important, it was a means of bringing the past and its traumas into proper focus. The trial served to catalyse the attitudes to the Holocaust of Ben-Gurion and his generation. From this point of view its most significant aspect was not the hollow man in the dock, or the just sentence meted out to him – though that had its symbolic value – but rather the depositions of the many witnesses. In their collective testimony we have a fully documented and dramatic reconstruction of the physical and psychological horror of the Holocaust. The witnesses were not limited to any one aspect of their experience, and the result was that the story they had to tell was both frank and comprehensive. But there was a certain intention behind the trial, nevertheless, and it was revealed in the questioning. Time and again survivors of the camps and ghettoes would be asked, 'Why did you not fight back?', and the question was echoed by the public in numerous forums. Many of the witnesses had difficulty in comprehending the question at all, since it seemed so irrelevant, for the most part, to the situation of the Jews in Treblinka or Auschwitz.[19] The truth is that it was, in the exact sense of the term, a rhetorical question. No answer was expected from the witnesses: the answer was provided, rather, by the staging of the trial itself, its scenery and backdrop. The implication was that through the capture and trial of Eichmann Israel was somehow making good the failure of those who had died without resisting. The demonstration of state power that made the trial possible was a source of great and justifiable pride to the Israelis, including the hundreds of thousands of Holocaust survivors. But the trial was also intended to be the means of purging the Jewish people of the shame of the past. The secret agents, the police, the whole setting for the capture and the state trial were symbolic compensations for the shortcomings of a weak-kneed generation which had allowed itself to be led like lambs to the slaughter. This was the unconscious assumption behind the very agonizing trial – more agonizing, it often seemed, for the witnesses and the public than for the defendant.

Such was the assumption, but it did not work out exactly as planned. The seemingly endless record of suffering gradually penetrated the consciousness of the Israeli public, especially that of the young for whom this was the first full-scale confrontation with the Holocaust, and what it produced was a sense of identification between the victims and those to whom the tale was being related.[20] It was not so much the question 'Why did you not resist?' that stayed with the audience, but another kind of question, an inner interrogation: Am I not that man? Am I not that woman? Are these not my people? In the state's handling of the prosecution much was made, both implicitly and explicitly, of the analogy between the Nazi plan to exterminate the Jewish people and the pan-Arab design to liquidate the state of Israel. This comparison was intended, naturally, as a warning, as though to indicate that

Jews would never again be led helplessly to the slaughter but would rise up, if necessary, and overthrow their enemies. And the force of the warning was attested in 1967 when Israel, spurred on once again by memories of the Holocaust, took up Nasser's challenge and fought back. This was the external meaning of the analogy. But, as we have noted, the identification between the Jews of Europe and those of Israel was also evident within Israel itself. Each and every Israeli, during those harrowing weeks of the trial of Eichmann, learned to identify himself imaginatively with the victims – not only those who resisted but also that vast majority which did not and could not resist. It was a symbolic participation in the tragic destiny of the Jewish people of the Diaspora, and in this sense was for many, especially the young, a new and shocking kind of history lesson. Its importance would be grasped years later in the three weeks preceding the Six Day War, in the Yom Kippur War and in the years that followed. We were then to learn that the role of the suffering servant was not quite played out.

As a matter of fact that ghost of the Holocaust walked a year before the Yom Kippur War, in Munich (of all places) in September 1972. Then the world watched while eleven Israeli sportsmen attending the Olympic Games were marched, bound and helpless, to be murdered by their Arab captors. Pride and self-sufficiency were not always to guarantee a sharp distinction between the fate of the Israelis at the hand of those who sought to destroy them and the fate of the Jews of Europe in 1942. Israel tasted at that moment the bitterness of the Jewish fate. The analogy was ironically illuminated by the fact that a few days before the massacre the Israeli sportsmen had declined a suggestion made from Jerusalem that they attend a memorial meeting for the victims of the Holocaust at the site of the nearby concentration camp in Dachau. Evidently they thought themselves sufficiently free of the ghosts of the past to make it unnecessary for them to attend. Dachau, in the end, came to them. The shock was felt in every Israeli home. There was anger, but there was also frustration. No matter how hard one tried to be like everyone else, the special Jewish condition, the special Jewish fate, would not let us be. A few weeks later, predictably, the murderers were released by the German authorities.

The state of Israel was to have been the antithesis of the Diaspora with its sorrows, its hopeless trust in gentile justice, a justice that always seemed to be denied to the Jew. Instead Israel seems to have inherited that very same condition.

VI

The historical role of Jewish peoplehood has thus been transferred for good or ill to the new nation of Israel. And it must be sadly noted, in addition, that some of the sicknesses regarded formerly as characteristic of Diaspora existence have also passed on, by inheritance, to the state and citizens of Israel. One of these is an economic sickness. The Zionist pioneers at the beginning of the century despised the Jews of the 'old *Yishuv*' in Jerusalem, Hebron, Tiberias and Safed, who lived on the *haluka*, i.e. on a dole provided by their brethren in the Diaspora who regarded it as a pious duty to maintain those who were prepared to live and die on the sacred soil of Palestine. The Zionists rejected this system. In the village of En-Gannim (where Ben-Gurion, Y. H. Brenner and A. D. Gordon all lived at one time) the first of the workers' small-holdings had been acquired around the year 1908 with the help of a loan from the Jews of Odessa. But within a few years the loan had been repaid and the new settlers were able to stand on their own feet. It was a proud achievement. The new Hebrews were to be self-supporting above all, no longer meek and dependent on others. Indeed self-help was a basic element in the philosophy of the Second *Aliyah*. If, in fact, the 'new' *Yishuv*, and later on the independent state of Israel, were assisted throughout their history by large subventions from Diaspora Jews, channelled through the Jewish National Fund and other agencies, then this was no dole but rather – so Israelis always assured themselves – a temporary expedient to enable the state to establish itself. It seems that after thirty years of statehood this assumption no longer holds. Far from becoming less dependent, Israel has become, with the passage of the years, more so! Nor is this just a matter of a growing defence budget or a heavy burden of expenditure for immigrant absorption. The fact is that the total structure of the economy is clearly based on a kind of *haluka*. Israelis do not receive a personal dole like the members of the old *Yishuv*, but the enterprises they manage and the organizations for which they work are more often than not artificially supported by state subsidies, and these in turn are made possible by constant subventions from abroad. The motives of the Jews who provide this help are not essentially different from those of an earlier generation of Montefiores and Rothschilds. Charles Liebman has pointed out that, 'as far as most of the Diaspora is concerned, Israel represents Judaism.'[21] Now as in the past, Jews from abroad who still identify themselves as Jews send their donations to Israel in acknowledgement of the pious duty to maintain those who are prepared to live and die on its sacred soil.

Ironically Israel tends more and more, therefore, to project an image not essentially different from that of the old-world Jews whom the new Zionists ostensibly came to replace. It is an inauspicious state of affairs, especially as it is not merely a matter of dependence on other Jews. It goes deeper than that. In the early fifties vast, unearned sums of so-called 'restitution funds' from Germany were injected into the Israeli economy. This blood-money, the acceptance of which was bitterly attacked in Israel at the time, introduced a certain flaccidity into the economy and habits of luxury from which Israel has not really recovered. Much of that money found its way into the hands of entrepreneurs, managers and middle-men who have grown into an unproductive middle class enjoying an artificially high standard of living based on hand-outs. And since the sixties there has been the growing economic dependence on annual grants and loans made by the United States Government. And this is much more serious, for it is clear that economic subjugation carried to such extremes leads to political impotence. The old brave spirit of 1948 will become more and more difficult to sustain as Israel's very economic viability comes to depend on the annual goodwill of Congress and the United States administration. How long, one wonders, can that goodwill be relied on? And what happens when the United States Government uses Israel's economic dependence on it to force Israel to adopt policies at variance with its own vital interests? At that point survival itself may well be conditional on Israel's discovering within itself the spiritual resources necessary for economic recovery. Only a motive as powerful as the original pioneering spirit of fifty years ago can generate the kind of programme of economic self-denial and sacrifice that Israeli society so sorely needs.

Thus what appears on the surface to be an economic problem proves to be, at bottom, a problem of political stability and spiritual health. In its stance, especially before the change of government in May 1977, Israel tended to show less tenacity than when the state was poorer both economically and militarily. And this weakening of fibre suggested a spiritual condition not so different from that which the fathers of Zionism detected in the so-called *Galut* Jew of western and eastern Europe. For Leo Pinsker in 1881 the typical Diaspora Jew of the Age of Emancipation was sick, a tragi-comic figure ultimately unable to control his destiny; for Ahad Ha'am the Jews of the *Galut*, vainly seeking freedom and equality, were, in fact, enslaved, subject to every whim and pressure of their environment.[22] It was hard not to be reminded of these typical judgements when one viewed Israel's uncertain political posturings during the three years or so following the Yom Kippur War. In an ironical reversal of roles Henry Kissinger, the assimilated *Galut* Jew, the *Hofjude* of tradition, applied the pressure on Israel, whilst the liberated Israelis, sons of the founders who cast off the weakness of the *Galut* in order to achieve independence of body and mind, weakly submitted! When Israel goes, cap in hand, to beg favours of such a Jew as Bruno Kreisky, the Chancellor of Austria – the classic example of the Jew in flight from his Jewish identity – one is bound to recognize that the Nietzschean revolution did not work out exactly as planned.

It will be retorted that Israel's isolation and relative helplessness at that time were due to circumstances over which Israel had no control, that it was a matter of great-power politics, brutally exercised in an attempted pacification of the Arab oil moguls. True, but this in itself suggests a role for Israel not so different from the traditional role of the Jew in history. Israel has become, like the Jew of medieval society, the barometer for registering the moral state of the nations. When the world is menaced (as by the Black Death, for instance) the Jew is made to pay.

But there can be no doubt, also, that Israel has been at least partially responsible for the position of extreme political vulnerability into which she has been manoeuvred. As we have seen, over the years Israel has allowed itself to become dangerously dependent on others in the economic sphere. It also tended to lose the sense of moral aim which should give meaning to statehood and independence. Statehood is not enough and Zionism, unsupported by the full content of the Jewish myth, has not been able to provide any other *raison d'être* for statehood than statehood itself. There are still great resources of strength within the country, there are courage and creativity in abundance waiting to be summoned into life but these assets are not always exploited.

What all this adds up to is very simple. The early Zionists diagnosed the Diaspora sickness correctly and they were also right in urging that to cure his parasitic condition the Jew needed to live as a free man in his own land. But they were wrong in thinking that true freedom meant the abandonment of Jewish values and Jewish beliefs and their replacement by a socialist ideology. The effect of this has been twofold: in losing his Judaism the new Jew has lost the deeper source of his strength and self-respect, that which made *Galut* existence bearable, and the socialism that the settlers of 1908 brought with them has provided a poor substitute. As the prophet declared: 'For my people have committed two evils. They have forsaken me the fountain of living waters; and they have hewn them out cisterns, broken cisterns that can hold no water' (*Jeremiah* 2:13). The very children of the socialist pioneers, and often the pioneers themselves, created a society more grossly parasitic than that of the inhabitants of the 'old *Yishuv*', who asked for little more from their benefactors than bread and olives on weekdays and a little extra for the sabbath. In a play by the *kibbutz* writer Nathan Shacham, *Call Me Siomka*, which appeared as early as 1950,[23] the dramatist sharply exposed the graft and corruption to be found even within the ruling left-wing establishment. Siomka is an innocent idealist, an unspoiled survivor of the generation of founders, who is suddenly confronted by the moral degeneration of the society he has helped to create. It is a moment of tragic disillusionment.

Shacham can suggest no remedy, but in the twenty-eight years since his bitter satire was written much has happened. Among other things the moral inadequacies of the original socialist-Zionist ideology have become more glaring. The problem has become radicalized: it is no longer a matter simply of social and economic ills, but of Israel's very ability to maintain an independent existence, an ability which is itself contingent on her capacity for moral recovery. It was the deeply felt need for such a recovery that helped explain the results of the May 1977 election in Israel. There was a general feeling that something had to change, not only in Israel's posture *vis-à-vis* the outside world, but also in the internal balance of Israeli society. The negative aspects of that desire for change were most in evidence: the new proletariat of the development towns clearly withdrew their support from the traditional socialist-Zionist parties, rejecting the Marxist option and also, perhaps, the link with Western policies which had characterized the ruling class up to that time. But what of a new vision, a new spiritual motive?

Following the Six Day War and subsequently the Yom Kippur War, the mantle of Jewish destiny has clearly fallen on the state of Israel. In these circumstances it would be surprising, indeed, if Israel were not to rediscover those inward sources of life and hope which have all along constituted for the Jewish people the very ground of its existence. The positive search for a regenerate society and a fresh national theme is less articulate than the manifest rejection of former policies and attitudes, but it is evident nonetheless. Israel is looking for its way and the feeling that this must be a *Jewish* way is deep and widespread.

8

Who are the Christians?

I

WE HAVE SPOKEN of the events of 1948, 1967 and 1973 as moments of crisis for the Jewish people, involving a restructuring of relationships between metropolitan Israel and the Jewish Diaspora. We are now bound to add that these were also testing times for the Christian Church, when a re-appraisal was demanded of the relationship between Christians and Jews. If for the Jew there was a crisis of identity, then it is hardly an exaggeration to state that there was a crisis of identity, too, for the professing Christian. He was constrained to re-evaluate his relationship not only with Jews and Judaism, but ultimately with himself and with his Church as the putative heir of the Old Testament covenants.

We have noted a polarization among the Jews of the Diaspora in their attitude to Israel: there was a drawing near for some, a moving away for others. A similar polarization was to be remarked within the Christian establishment, at least among those who took their religious profession seriously. Some Christians were disturbed by the thought that the 'Old Israel' of the flesh whom the Church came to replace was not merely alive but flourishing and even victorious as well.[1] And for others there was the exaltation of knowing that the God of Israel – who is also, of course, the God of the Christians – was still mighty to save. Not a few Christians have been stirred to their depths by the sign of Grace extended by the God of Abraham to his suffering but still unrejected people. They find themselves echoing the words of the apostle Paul: 'Hath God cast away his people? God forbid, for I also am an Israelite of the seed of Abraham, of the tribe of Benjamin. God hath not cast away his people which he foreknew. . . .' (*Romans* 11:1). And if God has not cast away his people, then there is hope for the world also, hope for the branches of the wild olive tree grafted, as in Paul's parable, on the uncorrupted native stock of Israel.

Many Jews and Christians alike have complained that in 1967 and 1973, when Israel faced mortal peril, few official Christian bodies spoke out in support of Israel.[2] There was an ominous similarity with the silence of the Churches when the Jewish people was being systematically murdered at the time of the Nazi Holocaust. The Rev. A. Roy Eckardt, a leading American Methodist scholar and theologian, rebukes his Church for its silence during the crisis of June 1967: 'No influential Church group,' he says, 'declared the right of Israel to defend herself.'[3] And yet, even if this were true, we might declare: '*Ecce homo!*' Mr Eckardt himself proves through these very words that the Church is not silent. And when he goes on to say, speaking as a Christian, that 'the Covenant with Abraham and his people is an abiding Covenant',[4] he is speaking with just as much authority as Dr Millar Burrows, or Father Daniel Berrigan, or the late Archbishop Garbett of York. He bears witness to a Christian principle as authentic as those invoked by his adversaries. And Eckardt is not alone. We recall the position taken by Reinhold Niebuhr, surely no mean spokesman of twentieth-century reformed Christianity,[5] on behalf of Israel's absolute right of existence and self-defence. We recall the unwavering friendship of James Parkes, whose passionate avowal of Israel's rights stems from a long tradition of humane and undogmatic Anglican piety. Parkes might well claim that his is the central tradition of his Church. And on the Catholic side one thinks of so distinguished a leader and philosopher as Jacques Maritain, who is on record as declaring that the return of the Jewish people to its land is a sign of divine favour:

I have no doubt that this event, mysterious as it is for Jews and Christians alike, bears the sign of God's faithful love for the people which always is His. It therefore seems to me that, once the Jewish People has set foot again on the Land which God has given it, nobody can take that Land away from it.[6]

Of course neither Maritain nor Pope John XXIII a little earlier represent the Church as a whole, but their pro-Jewish position is as orthodox and commands as much support in the rank and file as do the more anti-semitic doctrines of other Catholic clergymen. One group are the spiritual heirs of those many priests and laymen who hid and protected Jewish families at the risk of their own lives during the Holocaust; the other group are the heirs of those officials of the Vatican who aided the escape of so many Nazi war-criminals to South America in 1945.[7] To understand the crisis of twentieth-century Christianity we need to attend to the witness of both groups. It is as though Peter's Church was founded not on one rock but on two.

The situation is thus essentially dialectical. Perhaps the common assumption about the silence of the Church owes its currency to the fact that pro-Zionist Christianity is often voiced not by official spokesmen of the Church but by those who strive to act out their Christian faith in a practical fashion, without invoking theological precepts. The late General Jan Smuts was a Christian Zionist of this kind and so was President Harry Truman, who congratulated himself on having acted the part of Cyrus in encouraging the return of the Jews to their land and in recognizing the new state when it was declared. In fact one cannot think of the rise of modern Israel without reference to these men and others like them, just as we cannot think of their contribution without reference to the powerful and still active biblical impulses at work within them. Nor is this biblical response to Israel's restoration at an end thirty years after the establishment of the state. To get a balanced impression we must consider the witness of individual Christians of all denominations who visit the state of Israel in their thousands year by year. Which of them is not stirred by the visible signs of Israel's rebirth? Which of them does not recall half-forgotten biblical prophecies when he sees the Jewish people rising once again, a great host, from the valley of dry bones, the young and old together 'singing in the height of Zion' (*Jeremiah* 31:11)? The word 'Zion' still retains its mystery for the vast majority of Christian believers, and few of them remain indifferent when confronted directly with the reality of Israel's restoration to the Holy Land – power, so to speak, returning to Judah.

The problem, of course, is power. The idea that the 'God of Israel gives strength and power to his people' (*Psalm* 68:35) is attractive to some, repellent to others. It was repellent to General de Gaulle, a good Christian and a good Catholic. For de Gaulle Israel's victory in 1967 evoked the image of 'an élite people, self-assured and domineering'.[8] A self-assertive Israel erupting on the stage of history and exercising, like other nations, the privileges of power was irreconcilable with de Gaulle's concept of Israel's true place in the spiritual economy of mankind. Professor David Flusser reports meeting with a Dutch Church television team in Jerusalem shortly after the war of 1967.[9] They said openly how much more beautiful for them were the eyes of the Jews saved from Auschwitz than the proud looks of the soldiers whom they witnessed thanking God at the Wailing Wall. They saw the latter as a deplorable example of Jewish militarism. The Rev. Millar Burrows argues on doctrinal grounds that the Jewish combination of religion and militarism revealed in the state of Israel is ana-thema.[10] To the Jews as adherents of a religion (or as a dispersed ethnicity), everything: to the Jews as a nation dwelling on its own land, nothing.

Which, then, is the dominant strand in modern Christianity – those for whom Israel, degraded and humbled, bears witness to Christian truth, or those whose Christian faith can even be fortified by the thought of Israel's salvation and victory? It must be empha-sized that we are not here concerned with the numbers of believers in either camp. It may be that a numerical majority of professing as well as nominal Christians in Europe during the years 1942–5 actually connived at the massacre of Europe's Jewish population, but this does not render less significant the witness of those few who chose the path of martyrdom rather than aid the devil in his work. Jews are surely the last to dismiss the importance of the 'righteous remnant', since we are taught that the survival of Judaism itself depends on no more than just such a handful of the faithful. However here it is a case not so much of a righteous remnant as of two opposing righteous remnants! Christianity as a whole is in retreat before the overwhelming tide of secularism, and what the current situation reveals are two kinds of residual Christianity, one pointing towards Israel as the actor in a divine drama of salvation and the other pointing towards Israel as a kind of anti-christ. Both of these attitudes, contradictory though they are, evidently have their place in the classical Christian tradition. Could it be, then, that there is some kind of contradiction within the substance of Christianity itself? That the debate between Father Flannery and Father Berrigan is not really about the character of the state of Israel, but about the character of Christianity?

The issue seems to be whether Christianity acknowledges the religious significance of events within human history, or whether the God of the Christians is emphatically and unequivocally one whose 'kingdom is not of this world'. If the former position is adopted, then there is room for Father Edward H. Flannery's claim that not only may Zionism be tolerated by Christians, but the marvellous rise of the state of Israel may be regarded as a sign of the religious vocation of that state.[11] But if the latter position is taken, then the Zionist state will be seen as a blasphemous attempt to give a spiritual, divine value to the doings of fallen man in this world of principalities and power. And against such attempts the true warrior of Christ is bidden by the apostle Paul to put on the whole armour of God – which is precisely what Father Berrigan and the Rev. Burrows are doing. In leading the battle against Israel they are taking action against the world, the flesh and the devil.

Naturally the Church over the centuries has urged counsels of moderation. Compromises have been found to enable Christians to pursue their other-worldly vocation in the manner of the address of Jesus to Nicodemus (*John* 3) and at the same time to live and work in this earthly city of fallen mankind. The most evangelical of Christians have learned to accommodate themselves to an earthly city which makes no messianic claims, seeing in it an arena for the exercise of their zeal and energy. The problems arise when we are confronted with an earthly state whose very warrant for existence depends on biblical evidence. Here no compromise is possible, for the implicit claim of such a state is that it bears witness to an enduring history of salvation. It is part of *Heilsgeschichte*, a divine historical programme. And on this the Christian is bound to take a stand, not for or against Israel as such, but for or against *Heilsgeschichte*. Are human history, politics and wars to be viewed as part of a divine drama, the last act of which will include salvation for man and the world, or is that salvation already achieved on a non-historical, non-material plane, without reference to what seems to be happening to the world? Does faith seek a confirmation in the world of politics, or is it content with its inward evidence, the spirit bearing witness for the spirit?

Faced now with the gross materiality of Israel, the Christian is obliged to define his own faith. He cannot remain neutral. The leaders of Israel may strenuously renounce any theological claims; they may proclaim thrice daily that Israel is a state like any other state, but for the Christian the name 'Israel' cannot be freed of its special semantic load. The problem for such Christians is not whether the Jews recognize the Christian Messiah, nor whether the Jews respect the Christian holy places: these are secondary issues. Nor does it really make any difference whether the Jews are faithful to their religion or have become freethinkers. It is not a question of what Jews believe or do not believe; the very intrusion of the Jewish people into world history is what disturbs. This constitutes the existential challenge, the fundamental dilemma. Does the new Covenant, which is altogether spiritual, supersede the old earthly Covenant of Israel (for this is what the Rev. Millar Burrows maintains)?[12] Or may Israel still successfully claim a place under the sun by virtue of 'the faithful covenant loves of David' (*Isaiah* 55:3)? This is the position of the Rev. Franklin H. Littell. 'The restitution of Israel,' he declares, 'is the event which challenges Christianity to take events, history, and the world seriously again.'[13] The attitude towards Israel is thus crucial to the Christian's attitude to himself and to his own Covenant. It involves a very basic question, Christianity's relationship with the world as a possible arena of divine action.

There has always been tension for the Christian believer between the more 'Judaic' gospels of Matthew, Mark and Luke (the so-called 'synoptic gospels'), with their emphasis on the physical and temporal setting of the Christian story, and the more metaphysical fourth gospel, that of John, with its stress on regeneration and the inner light. But from now on the exigencies of that tension are inescapable. Those who, like Rudolf Bultmann and his followers, have turned their backs on the historical side of Christianity itself will have no difficulty in ignoring the contemporary challenge posed by Israel's irruption into history. If Christianity itself can be 'demythologized', its essential message stripped of the circumstances of time and place, then the physicality and historicity of contemporary Israel can be safely ignored also.

For historical evidence can then neither aid faith nor subvert it. Faith (in the manner of so much German Protestant theology of the nineteenth century) has been firmly consigned to the inner realm of the psyche; it belongs to the soul, and the world of struggling men and women may be left to its barbarian devices.

But there are other Christians who are unwilling to abandon history and politics to the devil: they have always sought to bring the Christian message into association with the life of the world. For some of these Christians the Holocaust and the subsequent rise of the state of Israel have a radical meaning. Many of them now feel that they must choose between a sterile righteousness of faith and an active righteousness of works. After the Christian moral failure at the time of the Holocaust, compromise on this issue is no longer possible. 'The Jewish People carried history,' writes Dr Littell, 'while the Christians fled headlong from their professed vocation.' There must now be a revaluation. Dr Littell speaks for a 'righteous remnant' for whom the fundamental *kerygma* (saving message) is today a crucified and resurrected Israel, the reference being to the European Holocaust and the rise of the state of Israel which followed close upon it.[14] Here is the hope for mankind, the 'good news', we may say, for modern man. 'The hope of Israel,' says Dr Roy Eckardt, 'is the hope of mankind';[15] and, after 1973, he adds: 'The one divine opportunity for our period is Jewish sovereignty.'[16] Few Christian Zionists (or Jewish Zionists either, for that matter) express their sense of the meaning of current events as strongly as this: nevertheless Eckardt and Littell are not alone in affirming the revolutionary nature of the drama now being enacted by Israel on the stage of history, and its implication for Christianity now and in the future. There are many silent fellow witnesses among Christians of high and low degree. They have heard the Word issuing from Zion and have made their response out of the depths of their Christian conscience and memory.

Roy Eckardt speaks of 'the hope of Israel'. A little more than three centuries before him the Dutch rabbi and philosopher, Manasseh ben Israel, had addressed a tract to his Christian friends in England and elsewhere under the title of *Spes Israelis* ('The Hope of Israel') (1650). Its burden had been the necessity of providing a refuge for the Jewish people as a prelude to its

ingathering and final redemption, an event on which the Christian
hope of salvation likewise depended.[17] The official Church bodies
seem to have ignored his appeal, but many Christians heard it, and
that response had momentous consequences. The Jews were, in
fact, re-admitted to England, and for a while the destiny of the
Jewish people and the history of England flowed in the same
channel. It was as a result of that confluence that in 1917 there
finally came from England the word of hope and encouragement
which was to set in motion the return of Israel to its land.

II

Now, as in the days of Manasseh ben Israel, there are Christians
who see the Children of Israel as 'under the curse', and there are
others who look with longing and hope to their deliverance. But
there has been a radically new development. With the rise of the
state of Israel, the burden of Christian ambivalence concerning the
Jewish Covenant has passed from the Jews of the Dispersion to the
new Jews of the land of Israel. It is they who are now seen as either
under the curse or under the blessing. By contrast the Jews of the
Diaspora are, so to speak, 'off the hook'. Perhaps this is the
strongest evidence for the argument advanced in the previous
chapter, namely, that the covenantal centre of gravity has shifted
to Israel and its people. *The proof that Israel has now inherited the
burdens of Jewish history is that for the Church the Jews of the
Diaspora no longer constitute a problem.* For the poet Coleridge at
the beginning of the nineteenth century the shuffling Jewish pedlar
in the East End of London was the problem. He demanded to be
related to the prophet Isaiah and yet he was a figure of profound
ambiguity: he was both saint and beggar; prophet and worm. How
was one to deal with him? It is this paradox which fuelled Christian
anti-semitism and which also explained the frustrations and
agonies of the Jewish search for acceptance as normal members of
nineteenth-century society. Dr Millar Burrows is clearly, with
regard to the Jews, in the hoary tradition of Luther and William
Prynne, and yet we detect in him none of the animus towards the
Jews of the Exile that we find among earlier Christian anti-semites.
His best friends are, truly, Jews; his enemies are the Israelis. And
the same applies to spokesmen of other denominations. In fact one

can scarcely think of any significant expression of Christian anti-semitism at this time which does not have specific reference to Israel. Typical of this trend was the sermon delivered in Washington Cathedral by the Dean, the Rev. Francis B. Sayre, Jr, on Palm Sunday 1972, in which he re-echoed the most medieval of anti-semitic slanders, including the charge of deicide ('Even as they [the Jews] praise their God for the smile of fortune, they begin almost simultaneously to put Him to death'). Applied to the Jewish middle classes of the great American cities, this would have seemed, even to the more bigoted at this time, a grotesque anachronism, but the words were applied instead to the new Jews of Israel, 'the oppressors of Jerusalem', as Mr Sayre termed them.[18] And for some this gave his words a seeming connection with reality. Even when the Jews of the Diaspora are concerned in bitter debate or the defence of Jewish interests, the issue of Israel, its legitimacy and the crisis in the Middle East are rarely far away. This is the new development.

The relative lack of theological tension affecting Jewish existence in the Diaspora has created a certain euphoria in some Jewish circles. Many Diaspora leaders, for instance, have been impressed by the new ecumenical spirit of the Vatican. In 1965 the second Vatican Council, in a conciliar declaration entitled *Nostra Aetate* ('In Our Time'), absolved the Jews of the charge of deicide! At a stroke of the pen the bitterness of two millennia of anti-semitism was ostensibly wiped away. Jews are no longer, it seems, to be regarded as under the curse. This gesture was followed, in January 1974, by the new 'Guidelines' outlining the Church's relation to the Jewish people. In spite of certain reservations necessitated by theological consistency, these 'Guidelines' make remarkable reading. They speak of 'the spiritual bonds and historical links binding the Church to Judaism'; they speak of the need for dialogue and mutual respect; they condemn 'all forms of anti-semitism'; they affirm the need for Christians to understand the religious tradition of the Jews as Jews themselves experience it, and they even encourage 'a common meeting in the presence of God'. It would seem that centuries of strife and prejudice have, indeed, been swept away. The Jewish representatives who went to Rome at the time of the publication of these 'Guidelines', in order to confer with the Catholic officials concerned, were deeply im-

pressed by the cordiality of their reception. There was no prosely-
tizing, no mark of disdain or superiority. The visitors were served
with kosher food, of which both Catholic and Jewish participants
partook, and the room where the sessions were held was cleared of
all Christian symbols.[19] Many of those present were struck, no
doubt, by the contrast between the atmosphere on this occasion
and that evoked, say, by Browning's description of the Jews
attending a compulsory sermon at Rome on 'Holy Cross Day'
some centuries earlier.

All this may seem remarkable, but what is much more remarkable is the omission from the 'Guidelines' of any mention of
Israel, Zionism or the Jewish feeling for Jerusalem! The Church
speaks of the necessity of understanding how 'Jews define themselves', and yet fails to point out that they have always defined
themselves as a nation with a connection with a certain land,
namely, the land of Israel – a fact more obvious today than ever
before. By avoiding mention of this fact the authors of the Vatican
document showed clearly where the shoe pinches. The ecumenical
spirit of *Nostra Aetate* is gratifying, but to see it in perspective one
has to set beside it the fact that to this day the Vatican has not seen
fit to accord even formal recognition to the state of Israel.

The truth is that the Vatican has sensed more clearly than have
the Jews of the Diaspora themselves the fateful and irreversible
change which has taken place in the Jewish condition with the
Return to Zion. The Church has no further argument with the
Jews who are not part of the Zionist venture. The real problem
for the Church has never been the 'beliefs', as such, of the Jews,
or even their refusal to accept Christian beliefs. The problem has
been the existential relation of the Church to the 'old' Israel. The
tension has always been in a sense 'political', occasioned by the
separate historical existence of the Jewish people as the proclaimed
bearers of a unique destiny.[20] This uniqueness, which the Jewish
people has never renounced – and, indeed, the terms of their
contract make it impossible for them to renounce it – has now
transmitted itself to the people of Israel in the land of Israel. They
are the bearers of the blessing and the curse, as a glance at the
headlines of almost any daily paper will tell us. The Jews of the
Diaspora, therefore, who have, in effect, abdicated the burden of
historical responsibility, no longer constitute a theological problem.

Quite the contrary, if they can be effectively detached from those who now bear the charge of the Covenant, that will make it easier to deal with the question of Israel where the real theological strain is felt.

A parallel phenomenon may be noted in the Soviet Union. Although the state is atheist and clearly finds Jewish 'beliefs' and practices repugnant, that aspect of Jewish existence has never been the real underlying ground of tension between the Russian regime and its Jews. The problem is Jewish peoplehood, with its overtones of transcendence and idealism, and the revolutionary implications for the Russian state and system itself of such peoplehood. For, ultimately, communism too claims to be the vessel of *Heilsgeschichte*; it claims to be the religion of the future. Jewish peoplehood, expressed in the form of active dissidence and even martyrdom, implies a hardness of heart which challenges the very ideological foundations of communism. The cry 'Let my people go!' makes it clear that for a significant minority (a minority which, it should be remembered, had a central role in the original ferment which brought about the communist revolution) true liberty is no longer to be sought within the communist world. The object of policy, therefore, will be to isolate and neutralize this obdurate minority. The many Jews who do not count themselves among the activists and are prepared to make their peace with the regime while at the same time abjuring the international Zionist conspiracy, may well be allowed, from now on, to pursue their peculiar religious practices within the Soviet system.[21] These Jews will be allowed to feel that they are preserving their Jewish 'identity'. There are signs that such an 'ecumenical' move is on the way. If so, it implies a degree of subtlety on the part of the Russian leadership, as well as an understanding of the real dialectic governing the history of the Jewish people at the present time.

But let us turn to the far more intimate and complex question of the Church and its relations with the Jewish state. Here no simple formula is possible, for no matter how hard some leaders of the Church may try to ignore the new reality of the state of Israel, even to the point of denying it political recognition, the fact is that the fate of the Jewish people and the fate of the Holy Land are ultimately of the most profound concern to Christianity. The Church is linked with the Jews for good or ill, both in its origins and in its hope for the future, and above all it is linked with the Jews by a common concern with the Holy Land. We have spoken of *Heilsgeschichte* as though that was the fundamental common ground as well as the fundamental ground of contention between the Church and the Jewish people. But there is also what might be termed *Heilsgeographie*.[22] The Church can never wholly resign its interest in the Holy Land. It may etherealize it; it may strive to 'demythologize' Christianity so completely that geographical space is no longer relevant to the saving message, the *kerygma*. But the Holy City is a presence not to be put by. When theology has banished it, it will return to the Christian in his dreams.

III

The Christian attitude to the Holy Land has changed over the centuries but the dream element remains. Helena, the mother of Constantine, we are told, was shown the site of the Holy Sepulchre in a dream. She became, in a way, the first Christian pilgrim, and her son the Emperor, inspired by her, undertook a vast programme of building in and around Jerusalem to emphasize the bond linking Christians with the Holy Land.[23] These were the centuries of what might be termed 'total Christianity'. The spiritual, political and territorial aspects of the Christian faith were still undifferentiated, and that being so, the Holy Land played a central part both in Christian memory and in the Christian hope of salvation. It is the land where the Saviour lived and ministered, and so it was natural to suppose that it would also provide the physical setting for the *parousia*, his longed-for Return. The Crusades of the later Middle Ages can only be understood against the background of such messianic dreams. Meanness, greed and the desire to loot and murder were forceful motives, but we are still left with the power of a dream as the mainspring of the Crusaders' whole amazing enterprise. Gibbon relates that after the forces of Godfrey of Bouillon had conquered the city of Jerusalem in 1099 and had indulged themselves in every excess, including the murder of all the Jews and Moslems they could find, they made their way to the hill of Calvary and 'bedewed with tears of joy and penitence the monument of their redemption'.

We may ask what has become since of this passion and this

dream of redemption? Of course the failure of the Crusades brought with it, as time went on, a weakening of the 'territorial' claims of Christianity. The Church concerned itself more with the New Jerusalem in heaven and less with the earthly city which beckoned from the East. Nevertheless it would be wrong to suppose that with the sublimation of Christian belief and the weakening of the political power of the Church, the dream of Zion ceased to haunt the Christian imagination. The need for a holy place as the meeting-ground between heaven and earth is too imperious a need of the imagination of man to be thus abolished. The numinous, the sense of the presence of the holy, is, we are told, a fundamental category of human experience;[24] and it may be suggested that this sense of divine presence attaches itself above all to 'the holy hill of Zion'. This does not mean that Christians any longer desire or need to conquer the soil of the Holy Land, but it is there that the spiritual imagination seeks its satisfaction. It remains the land where God dwells. Behind every Utopia, every vision of human progress, there is at least a hint of a renewed Jerusalem.

Thomas Fuller, a leading writer and divine, devoted a lengthy and detailed treatise in 1650 to an account of Palestine, its length and breadth. In spite of many apologies to his fellow Christians who might find an element of superstition in his book, he makes clear the intensity of his interest in the places made sacred by biblical history. As he approaches the subject of the Temple of Solomon he 'falls flat in veneration of the God thereof'.[25] Nothing of Palestine and its environs is alien to him.

We have here what may be termed a displaced Christian myth. The interest in the land of promise itself as an object of Christian hope or effort has moved from the centre of theology to the periphery, but it still expresses itself there in various quasi-religious forms. The long history of pilgrimage, exploration and even colonization on the part of Christian groups and individuals continues to the present day. The myth is even transferred to other locations, which come to partake of the sacred character of the land of Israel and on which the hopes for redemption become focused with something of the original biblical charge and intensity. The poet William Blake dreams of Jerusalem rebuilt 'in England's green and pleasant Land'. The Mormon Church of the

Latter-Day Saints has a similar feeling about various locations in the United States. Indeed for many settlers and pioneers, North America became, in effect, the Promised Land and gathered to itself the messianic hopes and metaphors which had hitherto belonged to the Holy Land of Israel. Thus George Washington promised the Jews of Newport in 1790 that in the new land 'everyone shall sit in safety under his own vine and fig tree and there shall be none to make him afraid.'

But these notions will not ultimately satisfy. Only Zion, it seems, remains inalienably sacred. It does not allow itself to be permanently displaced. The Zionist idea, the dream of a renewed *Jewish* commonwealth in the land of Israel, is to a very great extent – more than is usually realized – the dream of Christians who need the land of Israel as the physical setting for the drama of salvation. They cannot themselves take part in this drama; their own theology has, so to speak, removed itself from the earthly sphere; but someone must bear witness to the continuing function of the land. That will be the task of the 'Israel of the flesh'. Thomas Fuller, interestingly, appends to his treatise, *A Pisgah-sight of Palestine*, a discussion of the possibility of the return of the Jewish people to the Holy Land 'after the fullness of the gentiles shall come in'. And though he ends up by dismissing the notion as a Jewish dream induced by the 'spirit of slumber', the possibility – newly advanced, as he notes, in the writings of Manasseh ben Israel – is not to be ignored.[26] The idea of the restoration of the Jews to Palestine continues with amazing persistence in the writings of Christians of all kinds down to modern times.[27] We find it in Joseph Priestley, in Isaac Newton, in William Cowper, and by the time we reach the mid-nineteenth century, the restoration idea is the theme of foreign policy for the seventh Earl of Shaftesbury. He set up the British Consulate in Jerusalem, as is well known, with a view to helping Jews to establish themselves in the Holy Land. Some Christian 'Zionists' had in mind the conversion of the Jews to Christianity as a condition of their restoration to the Holy Land. But conversion was really not of the essence; by the nineteenth century, little was heard of it.

In fact the concept of restoration has functioned even when other Christian beliefs no longer compelled assent. With the decline of dogmatic Christianity in many quarters in the nineteenth century, we hear more rather than less of the idea of the Return to Zion. The English poet Byron may not have believed in the Trinity, but he entertained the vision of the rebuilt Temple in Jerusalem! For such men it was important (whether as a conscious or unconscious motive) that the history of salvation should continue and should root itself in the living earth. And since Christianity in the era of the Industrial Revolution was not able or willing to bring this about, the task was to be entrusted to the Jewish people who had obstinately refused to abandon it.

The love of Zion exists thus for Jew and non-Jew alike; for the Jew it is the love of a man for the unrelinquished bride of his youth, whilst for the Christian it can be etherealized into Platonic love, or, to change the metaphor, he can enjoy her vicariously through the reunion of Israel and its land. He himself does not need to possess her, but he needs to see her possessed by her true bridegroom.

IV

The fundamental Christian connection with the Holy Land is through pilgrimage; the Jewish connection is through life and possession. Even in the centuries before modern Zionism, Jews came to Israel principally not as a place to visit but as a place in which to live and die. Their bones lie in the Mount of Olives, on the western bank of the Sea of Galilee and in the great valley between Safed and Meron in the north. For the Jew the hope of redemption can never become a displaced myth. For he knows no history except covenant history and no immortality except that associated with the Holy Land. To speak of a mental communion with the 'idea' of Jerusalem as a substitute for the physical Return to the Land is to depart from the normative language of Judaism.[28] Ultimately, as I have argued, those who no longer seek the implementation of the Covenant in a physical context announce that they are opting out of Jewish history. For the Jewish people is no mere community of faith; its Covenant seeks a concrete environment in a Holy Land which is also a land in which ordinary life is lived and in which the 'great day of the Lord' is due to be celebrated with the materials of this world.

For the Christian the Holy Land is a shrine; for the Jew it is a home. Christian pilgrims have been coming to the Holy Land in great numbers ever since the foundation of the state of Israel, and in still greater numbers since the city of Jerusalem and the adjoining town of Bethlehem passed under Jewish control as a result of the Six Day War of 1967. Ostensibly they come to visit and worship at the shrines, the Church of the Nativity and the Church of the Holy Sepulchre, but they cannot help vibrating emotionally (whether in approval or disapproval) at the sight of the Jew who is so evidently at home in Zion. However grudging may be the Church's acknowledgement of this, and however confused the Israelis may be about their birthright and about the political future of the 'territories' they occupy, there is no doubting their power and their presence. Some Christians will admit that it is marvellous in their eyes; others will not.

What, one wonders, was the reaction to Jewish power and presence of Pope Paul VI when he visited the Holy Land in 1964 and spent something less than one day in the territory of Israel? If it was marvellous in his eyes he gave little sign of it. He studiously avoided giving political recognition to the Israeli presence in Jerusalem or even to the state as such, and after boarding the plane for Rome he addressed his farewell message to President Shazar at Tel-Aviv! His business, as he made clear, was a pilgrimage to the Christian shrines; it was not a state visit to Israel. And yet is it a mere coincidence that in all the centuries during which a pope has sat in Peter's chair, no pope had ever made a pilgrimage to the Holy Land until the time when Jewish power and Jewish presence had transformed it from a mere shrine into a homeland? Can it be that Pope Paul was moved to make his journey by some obscure acknowledgement that, in the words of the gospel, 'salvation is of the Jews'? We shall never know, and probably the Pope did not know himself. But he cannot have failed to make the comparison between the situation then and that of the hundred years of the Latin Kingdom during which the Church ruled in the Holy Land and Jew and Moslem were banished from the City of Jerusalem.[29] There has been a change in the balance of power, and the Vatican has too keen a sense of history and of current political realities not to be aware of this.

In 1964, when the Pope made his visit, the political *status quo*, in spite of Jewish power and Jewish presence, was just tolerable.

True, the Jews had their state, but they did not control the Holy City itself, at least not the part of it that mattered. The Moslem occupation of that City, on the other hand, presented no acute problems. They made no claim to be there by virtue of biblical promises, and their presence as masters could scarcely be more obnoxious than the presence of a secular government in Italy itself, where the Church as such no longer claimed to rule. The real shock was to come three years after the Pope's pastoral tour. In 1967, to their own immense astonishment, the Jews became masters of Jerusalem. And it became clear at once, in spite of some initial gestures of compliance,[30] that this was a situation to which the Church could not easily reconcile itself. The cry for the internationalization of Jerusalem – a cry which had been little heard during the nineteen years of Jordanian occupation – went up loud and clear. For the Vatican, a triumphant Israel restored to its ancient dwelling-place in accordance with biblical promises represented too drastic a change in the spiritual balance of power. Ways and means had to be found to reverse the situation.

Again it must be insisted that mere political changes in the world, even those involving injustice, the oppression of populations, the slaughter of millions and the redrawing of territorial boundaries, all these are changes to which the Church can ultimately reconcile itself. There may be protests, words of rebuke at this or that outrage, but eventually the Church accommodates itself to changes when they occur. What is at issue in Israel since the Six Day War of 1967 is not a mere change in the political balance; it is a change in the spiritual balance, in the relative status of the Church and the Israel of the flesh. And the Church has been quicker to recognize this than have the leaders of the Jewish state. Jewish leaders find themselves unable to understand why Jewish occupation of some additional square miles of territory should be so much more heinous in the eyes of Christendom than, say, the Turkish occupation of additional territory in Cyprus, the Polish occupation of East Silesia, Jugoslavian occupation of parts of what used to be Italy or the re-ordering of political power in Lebanon to the great detriment of its Christian population. Why should the Arab refugees from Israel be so much more a moral issue for the Church than, say, the two hundred thousand Greek refugees in Cyprus, of whom little is now heard? To the astonishment of

Israel's leaders, the Vatican and the Churches did not seem to be overwhelmingly concerned at the onslaught made on the Christians in Lebanon by the extreme Moslem groups in 1975 and 1976. It seemed as though the Jewish occupation of Jerusalem was somehow more important than the fate of entire Christian communities threatened with destruction! And of course it was.

The Israeli government, committed to its own secular interpretation of history, still seeks to convince itself that the Jewish nation is a normal nation and ought to be treated as such by the so-called international community. Here is the original delusion of secular Zionism as we have defined it since the days of Herzl and the Basle Programme. The Church is wiser. It understands that what is at work is the Jewish myth, and what is at stake is a biblical reality violently exploding into the twentieth century. It is perfectly clear that this involves for the Church a crisis of identity which cannot be allayed by gestures of goodwill on the part of Israel or by concessions which leave the new reality basically unchanged. Israel tries to behave as though the issue between Israel and the Church were one of Church property, Church 'interests', diplomatic passports, convenient arrangements for pilgrims and so forth; all that is needed is a generous policy of conciliation in these areas. This sometimes leads to extravagant gestures and concessions.[31] But the Church will not be conciliated, for it knows that the problem is deeper. It is a question of who rules 'upon the throne of David, and over his kingdom, to establish it and to uphold it' in fulfilment of Isaiah's prophecy (*Isaiah* 9:7); and this is a question of spiritual power and privilege.

Of course deep down Israel knows this also but is unwilling to recognize it, for to do so would mean a radical re-assessment of the nature of Israeli peoplehood; it would mean recognizing the underlying religious character of the impulse that has brought the Jews back to Zion and facing up, also, to the revolutionary implication of this. When Mr Yasser Arafat declares his intention of erasing Israel from the map and replacing it by a 'secular democratic State', many Israelis innocently react by saying (to themselves as well as others): 'But aren't we already a secular democratic state?' – as though to rise like a phoenix from the ashes of history in order to restore the Jewish kingdom in the Holy City were the most 'secular' thing in the world, and as though to gather into it one's exiles from the four corners of the earth were the normal way of establishing a democratic society! The truth is that Israel is engaged upon an *extraordinary* enterprise; it is responding to a promise and a command, and this is a process quite other than that by which 'secular democratic states' – whatever they may be worth – are founded. What is, in fact, proceeding in the land of Israel is a *religious revolution*, which is a notion so alarming, so reactionary, so opposed to the assumptions of rationalism and liberalism, that the present rulers of Israel – the heirs, after all, of the nineteenth century Enlightenment – are unwilling to face up to it.

Godfrey of Bouillon in the eleventh century knew very well that he had come to place the Cross above the Crescent; Saladin, after driving out the Crusaders a hundred years later, knew equally well that his task was to tear down the Cross and restore the Dome of the Rock to Islam. For the Jewish soldier of 1967 the religious motive was more deeply buried, but the determination to restore the Kingdom to the God of the Hebrews was powerfully at work beneath just the same. For he was engaged not in a normal war of conquest but in a moment of covenant history, with all the terrible revolutionary force, the promise and the challenge that that implied.

In the end it does not seem to matter what the Jews believe; what matters is what they do, or rather what is done to them. As Sartre discerned, being a Jew is a matter not so much of believing certain things as of being in a certain unique, inescapable situation. The Jew, we may say, is that person who is caught in the grip of Jewish history with its traumas, its dangers and its glories. The religious Jew is merely that Jew who acknowledges and accepts this situation as a charge. Hence the Jew has really no escape from the Covenant; it is what determines his existence. Here is the existential difference between Judaism and Christianity. Salvation is part of Christianity also; but it is something the Christian is asked to believe in. He may choose not to believe in it; he may treat it as having no relevance to his personal life, allowing himself instead to be carried along by the current of secular, i.e. pagan, history. This option is ultimately not available to Jews. When paganism rules, it makes the Jews its victim; it does not accommodate the Jews to itself. For the Jew is ultimately unable to release himself from his Jewish '*dybbuk*'. His existence is defined by the moral imperatives, by the need to witness on behalf of the God of righteousness, who does not allow other gods (whether of blood or soil, or dialectical materialism) to share his lonely pantheon. The Jew will either reject paganism or it will reject him. His destiny is to move forward on a different path.

There is never any guarantee that salvation is just around the corner. Many felt after the victory of 1967 that the promised day of 'peace without end' was at hand. Then 1973 brought new perils and a new radical isolation. But the fundamental imperative remains: Israel, standing at the shore of the Red Sea, the foe pressing closely upon him on all sides, has no alternative but to go forward;[32] for Israel is governed not by despair but by hope, by the 'Hope of Israel'. In Bunyan's *Pilgrim's Progress* it is said that there is a way to Hell even from the gates of Heaven. But for the Jew, the opposite is true: there is a path to the Celestial City even from the gates of the City of Destruction. This is the implication of a famous rabbinic saying. Outside the gates of Rome, the capital of the arrogant 'fourth monarchy', the Messiah is said to sit among the beggars, binding up his wounds. He does not bandage them all at once, but only one at a time, for at any moment he may need to rise up and go forward to deliver the world from its bondage.[33]

What commands the Jewish people forward in these dark times is the 'Hope of Israel'. And that hope is now centred on the new Jewish entity in the Holy Land. If this were just a matter of Israel's own hopes for itself, it would seem, especially after Yom Kippur, somewhat faint and precarious. But the fact is that one is not alone. For the 'Hope of Israel', we are told (*Jeremiah* 14:8), is no other than Israel's divine partner! Here is a source of strength which secular Zionists have denied themselves. But they also deny themselves another source of strength, because the 'Hope of Israel', when properly understood, is one that Israel shares with the world, with the Christian world in particular, which still witnesses, however imperfectly, to its meaning and power. Manasseh ben Israel addressed his book, *Spes Israelis*, to his Christian friends with a sure insight, knowing that ultimately the 'Hope of Israel' was theirs also. And he did not go unanswered: he met with a response, hesitant and uncertain, that was to have the greatest consequences. To recognize the God of Israel in truth is to recognize him in his universal role: 'Now therefore if you will obey my voice and keep my covenant, you shall be my own treasure among all peoples; for all the earth is mine' (*Exodus* 19:5). The people of Israel are, as the prophet says, God's witnesses: 'You are my witnesses, says the Lord, and my servant whom I have chosen' (*Isaiah* 43:10). But witnesses become true witnesses only when their testimony is heard by others. This is Israel's task. The word which Israel has to speak must in the end be pronounced in the presence of the nations whose need of salvation is, after all, the ultimate theme of the Covenant.[34]

9

Who are the Palestinians?

I

WE HAVE SPOKEN of the Jewish Revolution in its political and national character. It involves the occupation of a land and the restoration therein of full Jewish peoplehood for a purpose which we have defined in terms of the Covenant. To the cynical observer this may seem to invite comparison with many other political movements which likewise talk of salvation, and base themselves on such ideologies as dialectical materialism, or the victory of the Aryan races, or Pan-Arabism, or the worship of the Emperor Hirohito. The biblical Covenant, especially for those who begin with no special feeling for the Hebrew Bible, would seem to have nothing in its favour to make the detached observer view it with greater respect and sympathy. Most revolutionary myths of the past have claimed to be the means of advancing the human race and have ended up by advancing the interests of some powerful and usually unscrupulous group of politicians. Why should the Jewish covenant myth fare better? And why bother with it at all if it involves a relatively insignificant part of the human race in comparison, say, with the religion of Mao Tse Tung which, destructive though it may be of some human values, involves the destiny and beliefs of close on a billion men and women?

At this point, therefore, it is necessary to insist on the qualitative distinction of the covenant idea and of the revolutionary movement which it has inspired, which gives them a special claim to attention in our dark and troubled times. I refer to the uncompromisingly ethical dimension of Zionism, to its commitment throughout the years of struggle on behalf of the restoration of Jewish peoplehood to the moral imperatives. Judaism does not require of its adherents a super-human ethical code; the Jewish people is obedient to a law which was given to human beings, not angels. But if the Jewish people's mission is within history, amid its dust and heat, its aim is nevertheless to redeem history by means of righteousness – righteousness in society and righteousness in political life. This is the essence of the Zionist Revolution. There are forms of inhumanity, unhappily common in our twentieth-century political experience, which Zionism and the Jewish state have religiously (the word may stand) avoided. Of course the Jews have not had the credit for this. The rule is that in pursuit of political aims all things are permitted, and people are not used to exceptions to this rule. When we view the rise of the many new states in Africa, in Asia and in the Indian sub-continent in the past few decades, we see that the normal course of their history has involved inhumanity on a massive scale, including rapine, robbery and murder. To take but two examples, one may cite the creation of Bangladesh by India after the earlier enormities practised on its population by the authorities of West Pakistan, and the brutal suppression of the Ibo people of Biafra by the ruling tribes of Nigeria at the end of the last decade. In both these cases the human suffering involved was such as to defy description. What is more, liberal people in the West, after registering initial shock and horror, have on the whole accepted all this as the normal process of history. During the Turkish invasion of Cyprus in 1974, the Greek residents of the newly conquered areas were summarily evicted and Turks brought in in their place. Had Israel managed its wars in this way there would be now no Arab residents west of the Jordan river. When the Israeli army marched into Hebron in June 1967 it was entering a town which had slaughtered a portion of its Jewish citizens and evicted the rest in 1929, and yet the Arab population was left unmolested. The most recent example of the way wars are usually managed by other peoples in the Middle East was provided by the Lebanese civil war in 1975 and 1976. Two communities were then struggling for control of the country, and in that instance, as the Lebanese observers themselves testify, beastiliness of every kind was the rule.[1]

Jews and Arabs, as so often happens to nations in history, are in competition for the same piece of land. According to common precedent there ought to be a fairly equal measure of brutality on both sides. Indeed liberalism itself seems to forbid one to think otherwise. Since men are thought to be equal, how can one group of men exhibit more vicious characteristics than another? Thus thirty-odd years after the Second World War there is current a kind of liberalism which compels people to agree that the aerial bombardment of Dresden was as heinous as the mass murders perpetrated by the S.S. in the concentration camps, or that the bombing of Hamburg was equal in criminality to the bombing of Rotterdam! It is as though crime and the reaction to crime are morally of the same order. Thus it has become fashionable to picture Winston Churchill as a monster only slightly less repulsive than Hitler. People who make equations of this kind do not usually stop for precise moral stock-taking, for it has become a shibboleth of liberalism and of the morality of the New Left that, since war is an abomination, both sides to a war are, of necessity, equally abominable.

Can one dare to suggest in these circumstances that with regard to the Jewish-Arab struggle there is a marked difference in the conduct of the struggle on both sides? At the risk of seeming illiberal, one must affirm that there is such a difference. The simple truth is that Israelis normally refrain from attacking civilians;[2] Arabs normally do not. Knowing this, Arab troops frequently shield themselves behind women and children during military operations. Many Israeli soldiers have paid with their lives for their restraint in these situations. These are facts which may seem unpalatable to the liberal conscience (which is more comfortable with the thought that all nations are equally unrighteous than with the suggestion that one nation might be more righteous than another – and if that nation is the Jewish nation, the discomfort is compounded). Any honest examination of the evidence will confirm these facts. The *Fatah* (the military arm of the Palestine Liberation Organization) *regularly* attacks civilians and regards a busload of children as a legitimate target. They make no secret of this. Israeli soldiers in pursuit of the *Fatah* into Lebanon and elsewhere *regularly* clear each target of civilians before attacking, often exposing themselves to acute danger in the process. Both Arabs and Israelis know these facts very well. They also know that there is a sharp difference between the treatment of prisoners of war on both sides. This can yield practical benefits for Israel. Arab soldiers, knowing that Jews do not normally torture or kill their prisoners, frequently surrender in the early stages of an engagement.

There are various ways of countering the disturbing implications of all this. It seems so improbable that there should be a gross moral inequality between the two sides to the Middle East conflict that many people, out of a simple sense of fairness (there may be darker motives also), ignore the evidence. The result is a spurious balancing of the moral accounts. The International Committee of the Red Cross tends towards this kind of even-handedness in its reports. But there are also more devious strategies known to the human psyche which help it to deal with such an unfair distribution of good and evil. One of them might be termed guilt-transference or guilt-substitution. The Bible phrases it 'to call evil good and good evil' (*Isaiah* 5:20). Arab publicity, aided by the propaganda machinery of the Soviet Union, has attempted with some success to project an image of the brutal Israeli soldiery as morally no better than the Nazis, and of the Arabs as their innocent victims. This is reminiscent of the medieval blood libel, under the cruel dispensation of which the victim was made guilty of the crime already meditated in the unconsciousness of the criminal, if not actually committed and the guilt successfully transferred. For whilst many thousands of Jews were killed by Christians in the Middle Ages for the simple crime of being Jews, not one single Christian was ever murdered by Jews for being a Christian, a fact the truth of which was simply not accessible to the imagination of medieval men. The analogy is not so remote from the present Arab–Israeli struggle. The blood libel is still disseminated in Arab lands and finds expression in textbooks used in Arab schools. And even at this date the infamous *Protocols of the Elders of Zion*, a nineteenth-century forgery originating in czarist Russia and purporting to describe the international Jewish conspiracy against mankind, continues to be published in Arab lands for use in anti-Israel propaganda.[3] We are not as far away from the Middle Ages as we sometimes suppose.

But there is another way of dealing with the manifest discrepancy between the moral posture of Arab and Jew. When Mr Arafat appeared before the General Assembly of the United

Nations, ostentatiously flaunting a pistol in his belt, he got a better reception than the Israeli representative who spoke later and who clearly lacked such strange accoutrements. It may be assumed that many of the delegates who applauded Mr Arafat represent states which live in deadly fear of terrorism of the kind which Mr Arafat and his organization have instigated in various parts of the world. Why, then, the applause? Here the very aggressiveness of the PLO representative is felt to lend weight to his just grievances. The argument is that the Arabs are driven to desperate courses by the wrongs they have suffered, whilst the Israelis, who are the true aggressors, are naturally more subdued. Thus the observance by Israel of standards of civilized behaviour becomes a sign of shame, whilst the defiance of those standards on the part of the Arabs becomes a sign of violated right! This peculiar logic depends on the acceptance of the thesis very loudly proclaimed by the Arabs and their numerous allies that the Jews are, in fact, aggressors. And yet oddly enough for this argument, the pattern, from the very beginning of modern Jewish settlement in Palestine, has always been one of Arab attack followed (or not followed) by Jewish retaliation. How does this square with the charge of aggression? The earliest troubles, those of 1920 and 1929, were basically pogroms perpetrated by Arabs on Jews, the first in Jerusalem and the second in Hebron, when Jews turned to the British for redress (which of course never came). Nor was there at that time any question of usurpation. Jews had lived in Jerusalem and Hebron throughout the Arab period and long before the Arab conquest, and, in fact, they had constituted a majority of the population of Jerusalem from about the middle of the nineteenth century. The later story was not essentially different. It was again a matter of Arab attack followed by Jewish counter-attack. That was the pattern in 1936 and again in 1948 when the Arab armies from Syria, Iraq, Egypt and Trans-Jordan attempted to invade the newly founded state of Israel. The Jews could honestly say in all those years: 'I am for peace, but when I speak they are for war' (*Psalm* 120:7).

II

It may be said, and often is said, that whilst the Jews were perhaps morally sensitive with regard to the Arabs, they were politically obtuse. They managed to ignore the Arabs as a political entity.[4] They did not reckon with their rights and claims. Now, whatever else the early Zionist leadership may be charged with, it certainly cannot be argued that they were politically obtuse or that they lacked a sense of legality. Ever since the Basle Programme the emphasis had been on a homeland 'secured under public *law*'. It was clear to all that such an achievement was impossible without consideration of the 'Arab problem'. The Zionist leaders desired to come to terms with the local Arabs, believing earnestly in the possibility of peaceful co-existence based on the recognition of the full human rights and dignities of the Arabs in the area. David Ben-Gurion reminded his fellow settlers in 1918 that 'Palestine is not an unpopulated country'.[5] In the years prior to the establishment of the state he sought out such Arab leaders as Musa Alami and Fuad Bey Hamzah in an attempt to negotiate with them the question of free Jewish immigration and to seek their co-operation for the joint development of the country. It was axiomatic with him, and indeed with the Zionist leadership generally, that the Arab residents in Palestine would remain there and share the benefits which the Jewish National Home might bring to the country. There was no question of eviction or usurpation. Speaking in 1924 not only for his party but clearly for the Jewish *Yishuv* as a whole, Ben-Gurion declared: 'History has decreed that we should live together with the Arabs.' He went on to say (in 1928) that 'According to my ethical point of view we do not have the right to deprive a single Arab child of his due in order to gain our aims.'[6]

This may have been a trifle high-minded in view of Arab animosities even then apparent, but it was certainly not morally insensitive or politically obtuse. Those at this time who speak of the blindness to the Arab problem of the early Zionist pioneers are, in fact, themselves guilty of blindness to an important part of early Zionist ideology. *All* the major leaders of the *Yishuv* gave earnest and continuous thought to the nature of the relationship with the indigenous Arab population of Palestine. Like Jews of all times, they were much given to moral debate and self-questioning, and this was the area in which the habit was chiefly exercised.

Chaim Weizmann was quite emphatic: 'The world will judge the Jewish state by what it will do with the Arabs.'[7] Nor did the nationalist right wing have an essentially different view. The revisionists, precursors of today's *Herut* party, worked out a plan in 1934 according to which a future Jewish state would offer 'civic equality' to Jews and Arabs, and 'where the Prime Minister is a Jew, the vice-premiership shall be offered to an Arab'.[8] No less! Vladimir (Zeev) Jabotinsky, the leader of the revisionists and political mentor of Mr Menahem Begin, expressed what was going on in the minds of the Zionist leadership as a whole when he declared in his address to the Palestine Royal Commission of 1936 that the Jews were ready to guarantee to the Arab minority in a Jewish Palestine all those rights, privileges and equalities to which the Jews had aspired in the lands of their dispersion but had so rarely obtained.[9] This seems to have been the guiding principle. Now that the Jews were to have a home of their own, they would show the world how the stranger in one's midst should be treated. Land would be bought not seized. There would be tolerance, neighbourliness, a sharing of blessings. This was not merely a pious wish but a policy. As a matter of principle land was bought from the Arab *effendi*, often at grossly inflated prices.[10] In most cases the land bought was not even being worked or farmed. The land of Rishon le Zion was a sand dune, that of the Jezreel Valley, a malaria-ridden swamp. In all these cases the full price was paid and the land freely and legally transferred. Under the terms of the Mandate of the League of Nations, it was natural to suppose that the British administration would make available tracts of government-owned land for the purpose of Jewish settlement, but in fact this was not done on any significant scale. Instead the Jews were obliged to purchase whatever land was available on the private market. When *fellahin* (or serfs) were dispossessed as a result of the sales made by their absentee landlords, they were regularly compensated by the Jewish purchasers under the 1922 Protection of Cultivators Ordinance. There can hardly have been a more fastidious process of 'occupation' or 'dispossession' than this in the history of nations. It is sometimes said that the Jews have made the Palestinian Arabs pay for Jewish suffering in the Diaspora by dispossessing them of their land. If the psychological motives of the early Zionist settlers are sifted, it will be seen that the contrary is true: they were striving to give expression to their sense of moral outrage at the treatment so often accorded to Jews in the lands of their dispersion by a kind of extra scrupulousness, by exemplary conduct in the sphere of Jewish–Arab relations.

But of course on one central principle there would be no compromise; the principle that the country would be the 'national home' of the Jewish people where, as a consequence, Jews would have a natural and inalienable right to come and live and so 'renew their days as of old'. For this is what the Zionist dream was all about. Shall this be charged to them as their 'original sin'? Should they not have had the sense to realize that this claim could not ultimately be sustained, for it clashed with the sovereign rights of another people?

Now if there was such a clash of sovereign rights it is remarkable that so many just and morally sensitive statesmen outside the Zionist party and the Jewish community were unconscious of it. Lord Robert Cecil, speaking of the Balfour Declaration of 1917, expressed the prevailing sense of justice: 'Arabia for the Arabs; Judea for the Jews; Armenia for the Armenians.' It seemed fair on any human scale. And what is more, this view was later endorsed by the whole international community. For in 1922 the Council of the League of Nations granted a Mandate to Great Britain to administer the territory of Palestine on its behalf, and in the preamble to the Mandate, formal recognition was given to 'the historical connection of the Jewish people with Palestine and to the grounds for reconstituting their national home in that country'. There can be few nation-states, if any, whose moral and legal basis has been defined in an international instrument of such authority.

Shall we say, then, that all the Western world was in conspiracy with the Jews against the Arabs? Mr Arafat would argue that Zionism was the original sin of the international community as a whole, for which it must now pay. But the odd thing about this argument is that the Arabs, too, were evidently in the conspiracy. The elementary justice of the Zionist cause was recognized in 1919 by the acknowledged leader of all the Arabs, the Emir Feisal, who later became King of Iraq. At that time he addressed his now famous letter to Judge Felix Frankfurter (then the legal representative of the Zionist Delegation at the Peace Conference in Versailles) 'wishing the Jews a most hearty welcome home'. In the agreement he contracted at that same time with Dr Chaim

Weizmann, Feisal made clear his acceptance of the Balfour Declaration and of the necessity flowing from that Declaration 'to encourage and stimulate the immigration of Jews into Palestine on a large scale'.[11] It is clear from these documents and expressions of goodwill that, in so far as there was a people whose 'home' was Palestine and who were entitled to return to that home, then that people was the Jewish people. They were, in effect, the 'Palestinians'.

III

The Emir Feisal was later to change his mind, as Arab hostility to the Jewish presence in Palestine became fiercer in the years following the First World War (and when he himself saw that he had failed to achieve his own ambitions in full), but his correspondence with Frankfurter and his agreement with Weizmann were, nevertheless, not momentary aberrations. The fact is that there had always been a certain lurking but quite definite consciousness among the Arabs of Palestine that the land really belonged to the Jews and that one day they would return to claim it.

This point was made by Ambassador Amiel E. Najar, an Israeli of Egyptian birth, in the course of an impressive statement before the Special Political Committee of the 32nd UN General Assembly on 14 November 1977. Speaking of the hundreds of thousands of Jews who fled from the Arab States to Israel in 1948, he declared:

Ces juifs venant d'Irak, de la Syrie, de l'Egypte, de la Lybie, de la Tunisie, de l'Algérie, du Maroc et du Yémen, ne sont pas venus en Israël à l'insu des Etats arabes, mais au contrarie à leur parfaite connaissance. Les juifs d'Irak et du Yémen, par example, ont été directement transportés par la voie des airs. . . .

Les Etats arabes ont ainsi reconnu à la face du monde que d'après leurs propres conceptions, le lieu de refuge naturel des juifs était la terre d'Israël.

Une expérience directe du monde arabe m'autorise à affirmer qu'il n'est pas d'arabe musulman qui ne sache dans la profondeur de sa tradition le lien biblique qui existe entre la terre d'Israël et le peuple d'Israël.*

* 'Those Jews, coming from Iraq, Syria, Egypt, Libya, Tunisia, Algeria, Morocco and Yemen, did not come to Israel without the Arab

In most cases the Arabs of Palestine had preserved the original Hebrew names of the places in which they took up residence: Azzah, Beth-lehem, Hebron, Tekoa, Samua (the biblical Eshtemoa). The erection of mosques on Jewish sacred spots such as the Temple Mount in Jerusalem or the Cave of the Patriarchs in Hebron indicated a strong desire to Islamize the countryside; but in another sense it indicated a veneration for places whose holiness rested originally on the Jewish biblical tradition and on that alone. In Jerusalem and Hebron the original Jewish construction, dating from the Second Temple, was preserved. Arab landlords have been known to justify exorbitant prices charged in land sales to Jews on the ground that they deserved payment for having acted as caretakers for the Jews over the centuries!

A certain ambivalence in the Arab attitude to the Jews can be detected. There was no question of according them political rights – they were an inferior people without political rights – but at the same time there was no doubt about the connection of the Jews with the land. It was real and it was continuous. There was no time during the whole Arab period when Jews did not reside in greater or lesser numbers in Palestine: for the Arabs they were a presence not to be put by. So far, the unsympathetic observer may conclude that there was, indeed, a recognized Jewish remnant, much as there is a recognized Red Indian remnant in North America, but that politically they had been replaced by the Palestinian Arabs, whose homeland Palestine had now become and who regarded it as such – much as the white inhabitants of North America have come to regard America as their home after replacing and largely eliminating the original Indian inhabitants. But this is precisely what did not happen. The fact is that the Arabs *never* made Palestine their homeland; they *never* created in it their own national institutions or their own proud national 'Palestinian'

States knowing it but, on the contrary, with their absolute knowledge. The Jews of Iraq and Yemen, for example, were directly transported by air. . . .

The Arab States thus acknowledged before all the world that they believed that the natural refuge of the Jews was the land of Israel.

First-hand experience of the Arab world enables me to state that there is no Arab Moslem who does not know that there is a traditional biblical link between the land of Israel and the people of Israel.' Official UN record. A/SPC/32/PV.23.

ethos. Historically until the time of the Balfour Declaration there was no clear Arab claim to a state called Palestine and there was little Palestine nationalism among the Arabs as distinct from a generalized loyalty to the Arab nation centred in Hedjaz. The Arabs of Palestine, whose numbers in the nineteenth century never exceeded half a million, did not feel themselves essentially separate from the Arabs of Syria and beyond. Certainly they fought Zionism, but they did so more often than not in the name of a 'greater Syria'.[12] The name Palestine was, as Bernard Lewis points out, a Roman usage 'to designate the territories of the former Jewish principality of Judea'. It meant everything to the Jews but little to the Arabs as a distinct historical or geographical entity:

For them there was not such a thing as a country called Palestine. The region which the British called Palestine, was merely a separated part of a larger whole. For a long time organized and articulate Arab political opinion was virtually unanimous on this point.[13]

One can go further than this. Not only did Palestine as such not constitute for the Arabs a central object of love and loyalty, but until very recent times they actively resisted the idea of a separate Arab Palestine nationhood. It will be remembered that the resolution of the United Nations of 29 November 1947 spoke of the setting up of two separate states in Palestine: a Jewish state and an Arab Palestine state. The recommendation was accepted by the Jews, rejected by the Arabs. We are accustomed to thinking of the Arab invasion of Palestine which followed as aimed at preventing the establishment of a Jewish state – as indeed it was. But it was also aimed at frustrating the plan for establishing a separate Palestinian Arab State! There was no support for such a concept in the Arab world, except in so far as it would serve to replace, and thus render null and void, any Jewish independent entity in Palestine. The Arabs of Palestine, who had risen under the egregious Haj Amin El-Husseini in the twenties and thirties in an attempt to stem the tide of Jewish immigration and settlement, claiming 'Palestine' as their own, were evidently not prepared to accept the challenge of an independent 'Palestinian state', in however substantial a part of Palestine, if this meant leaving the Jews *in situ* in the remainder. In fact it may be claimed that they feared any move such as the establishment of a separate 'Palestine' which might prejudice the larger unity of the Arab peoples.[14] And when the Arab–Jewish War of 1948 ended and the Jordanians and Egyptians found themselves in control of a large portion of Western Palestine, comprising Judea, Samaria, the Gaza coastal strip and East Jerusalem, they made no move whatever to set up a 'Palestine Arab state' in those regions. Instead, the Jordanians annexed their portion and the Egyptians left the inhabitants of the Gaza strip stateless. All this did not provoke the 'Palestinian' inhabitants to rise up against the foreign yoke during those twenty years from 1948 to 1967 in order to establish their own state in Palestine.[15]

In fact the opposition to Zionism, fierce, deep and bitter as it was, was chiefly in the name of an Arab nation whose empire stretched from the Atlantic to the Persian Gulf, rather than in the name of Palestine or the violated rights of the Palestinian people. What the Arabs objected to was a Jewish independent state planted in the middle of their great empire, a Jewish nation-state in however small a part of that great Arab world. It was intolerable that Jews should have their own land, even if it amounted to less than ten thousand square miles out of a greater Arabia comprising eventually four and a half million square miles! It was entirely unjust for Jews to presume to rule over an Arab minority of a million souls, whilst it was entirely just for the Arab masters of Syria, Iraq and Sudan to rule over many millions of Kurds, Druzes and Nilotic negroes. Here was the original sin of Zionism.

IV

It is against this background that we must judge the changes in the Arab attitude to themselves and to Palestine which have taken place in the past thirty years. During this time they, too, like the Jews and the Christians, have undergone an identity crisis, one which strangely resembles those that we have already examined. In the case of the Jews the historical tasks of Jewish peoplehood have transferred themselves to the new Jewish Israeli nation reconstituted in the small territorial area of Zion. This has been the fundamental change of the past thirty years. Similarly, it might be said that as a result of the crises of 1948, 1967 and 1973 the Arab nation has gradually delegated the historical task of opposing Zionism to the 'Palestinian people'.

The first moves in this direction were made soon after the Arab–Jewish war of 1948. Some 600,000 Arabs fled at that time from the area of the new Jewish state and sought refuge in surrounding Arab lands (the greater part of them found themselves in those parts of Palestine itself which remained outside the borders of the new Jewish state). They were victims of war – as, indeed, were the 600,000 or so Jews who fled at the same time from the Arab states of North Africa and the Middle East. The natural thing would have been for these unhappy people to have been rehabilitated in the Arab lands of their refuge, in much the same way as the Jews fleeing from Arab lands were rehabilitated in Israel. Instead of this the Arab world began to conceive a different plan, a plan to separate them artificially from the other Arabs in order to stress their separate identity. The refugees were confined to refugee camps and shanty towns in Gaza, Judea, Samaria, in Lebanon and Syria. They were deliberately, and as a matter of policy, prevented from finding employment among their Arab brethren in nearby towns and settlements. Their Palestinian identity or personality was thus not so much the expression of certain shared national aims and values, but the result of a policy of quarantine and isolation. The Palestinian Arabs were not allowed to assimilate themselves into their Arab surroundings. Their only hope for normal existence lay in the idea of a return to Palestine. A partial exception to this was provided by the Jordanian administration on the West Bank, that is to say, in the provinces of Judea and Samaria. There, too, as the visitor may see to this day, the Jordanian government had confined the refugees to their camps and had largely prevented them from infiltrating into the towns (Palestinian towns, it should be noted), but they had not prevented them from drifting away to the more distant Arab lands, especially to Kuwait and the oil sheikdoms of the Persian Gulf. Tens of thousands of the younger generation of refugees, in fact, emigrated eastwards during the years from 1948 to 1967, to find a new and productive life in other parts of the Arab world. It is hard to believe that they live there in the profound consciousness of being in 'exile'.

But they were the fortunate exceptions. The larger part of the unhappy population of the refugee camps became the nucleus of a new 'Palestine people'. The purpose of their new-found nationality was not the creation of a national existence for themselves in Gaza, Judea or Samaria, or on the east bank of the Jordan (although these are just as much a part of 'Palestine' as Jaffa or Ramlah). The purpose was to dramatize, through their suffering, the need to bring the Jewish state of Israel to an end. Pan-Arabism has made the refugees its victims, so as to convert them into a political instrument for the holy war against Israel.

For the refugees themselves this was the beginning of a profound crisis of identity rendered infinitely more acute by the Israel victory of 1967. From then on we find an enormous emphasis placed on 'Palestinian rights', 'Palestinian nationality' and the 'Palestinian Revolution'. There is an element of fantasy in all this. Of course the refugees had local patriotism: those who had fled from Acre had a feeling for Acre; those who fled from Jaffa had a feeling for Jaffa, and so forth. And of course they had common interests, arising out of their fate as refugees and their bitterness against Israel. But does this add up to a corporate nationality? And does this constitute a claim to sovereignty? On this basis any group of refugees might lay claim to the land they have left behind them. The Jews of Yemen now living in Israel have to this day strong sentiments towards the towns and villages of Yemen and strong feelings for the property they left behind in 1950 (and we may add that their ancestors had lived in Yemen even longer than the Arabs had lived in Palestine), but does this make them Yemenite nationalists? To construct a nationality and a claim to sovereignty on such a basis would be a work of fiction.

An objective study of the history of the Arab Palestinian struggle must yield the conclusion that the natural bent of the Arabs of Palestine was towards an Arab nationality and a common Arab loyalty. If they have developed instead a strongly emphasized Palestinian nationhood, this was not due primarily to cultural need and to deeply cherished memories binding them together as a people belonging to a certain land and no other. It was due rather to fantasy, to a selective reading of history and to an educational programme designed to foster such an awareness.

At this point it may be objected that whatever may be the origins of their separateness, the fact is that the refugees have come to think of themselves as a separate people, as a nation with its unique history and its own destiny, unable to assimilate into the surrounding peoples. Their peoplehood is therefore a fact and must be respected as such. This is the argument often heard from the supporters of a Palestine national homeland to be created in the provinces of Judea, Samaria, and Gaza. And although the national consensus in Israel denies this argument, it has become more and more insistently pressed upon Israel by both friends and enemies and it has penetrated the thinking of many Israelis. It is suggested that there is a symmetry between the Palestine people and the Jewish people, both of whom achieved their national self-awareness at about the same time. Both have a claim to territorial space, and it is only a pity that they 'happen' to claim the same space. What we have therefore is a kind of Greek tragedy in which two more or less equal rights are pitted against one another.

Against this argument, which has been repeated to the point of cliché, it must be insisted that there is no real symmetry between the two situations. In the case of the Palestinian Arabs we have an invented national identity – its shaping force is external rather than internal. Sartre maintained that it was only the outside pressure on the Jew which created Jewish identity. In this he was wrong. He overlooked, as we have said earlier, the positive drives of the Jewish spirit, the need for a specifically Jewish self-expression. But his formula would fit the case of the 'Palestinians'. It was precisely the pressure of their environment, both Arab and non-Arab, which has fashioned for them a special Palestinian identity. One can go further than this. The Palestine national identity was invented as a kind of antithesis, a parody of Jewish nationhood. They too would become a nation apart, bearing the promise of salvation. But that salvation would come with the subversion of the Jewish state, followed by the physical destruction of its Jewish inhabitants and the sharing of the resultant spoils in one unbelievable orgy of national restoration. This is the content of the educational programme that was set up for the generation of refugees born in the camps. It is reflected in numerous text-books and classroom illustrations. We have here a strange imitation of the doctrine of Jewish nationhood – a dark replica of the Jewish people awaiting the promise of the Return to Zion.

To balance the Zionist myth there is the anti-Zionist myth of the Palestine Liberation Movement. The Palestine Arab nation, or rather anti-nation, represents the inverted image of Israel. It thus hardly exists in its own right. If, like Israel, it too has arisen out of the historical pressures of the past thirty years, then it has arisen as the photographic negative of Zionism.[16] While Zionism came into existence in order to express the creative needs of the Jewish people, in order to build a people anew, the Palestine Arab nation has been created in order to frustrate by every means the creation of Israel. Its aim is not to build but to destroy. It is not the love of the land which inspires it but the hatred of the Jewish inhabitants of the land. From this point of view it may be claimed that Palestinian nationhood is a profoundly unnatural creation whose *raison d'être* is bound up with the rise of the Jewish national movement, the coming into existence of Israel and the felt need to bring that existence to an end.

V

The Palestine Liberation Organization (PLO), founded in Cairo in 1964, was not exactly a spontaneous creation of the Palestine people. Much of the original impetus, as is well known, came from the larger Arab states confederated in the Arab League. Its founder and first leader was Ahmed Shukeiri, who had been assistant to the Secretary General of the Arab League.[17] Of course, having been set up, it developed its own dynamic, though it was never free of the influence, indeed control, of the Arab states in which its organization was based. Thus the political and military command has been located at different times in Gaza (before the Six Day War), Cairo, Damascus and Beirut. Whilst the natural constituency of the PLO is to be found in the refugee camps in Syria and Lebanon, it is worth noting that the attitude to it of the Palestinians who are not refugees is ambiguous in the extreme. It was unsuccessful in establishing itself as a Palestinian underground movement in the towns of the West Bank, Nablus, Jerusalem, Bethlehem and Hebron, after they had been occupied by Israel in 1967,[18] and east of the Jordan the 'freedom fighters' of the PLO have been rejected by King Hussein and his people, a majority of whom are, of course, Palestinians. What all this means is that the ontological basis of the PLO cannot be taken for granted. Its appeal to the Palestinians, in particular to those not actually confined in refugee barracks, is not self-evident. The very fact of a Palestine national identity, as something specific and separable from Arab nationality, has to be constantly fought for, agonized over, proved and then proved again.

To illustrate this we can do no better than turn to the document which defines the aims and character of the Palestinian Revolution, namely the National Charter or Covenant, drawn up originally in 1964 and revised at a meeting in Cairo in July 1968. There was a further revision in 1974.[19] The very first paragraph (in the full, 1968, version) introduces us to the problematical nature of the Palestinian identity: 'Palestine is the homeland of the Arab Palestinian people; it is an indivisible part of the Arab homeland, and the Palestinian people are an integral part of the Arab nation.' Integral or separate? The Covenant performs a difficult balancing act between the two. The need to establish a Palestinian identity as something separate from general Arab nationalism and, at the same time, to transcend it in favour of the larger vision, are revealed in later paragraphs of the same document:

The Palestinian people believe in Arab unity. In order to contribute their share toward the attainment of that objective, however, they must *at the present stage of their struggle*, safeguard their Palestinian identity and develop their consciousness of that identity, and oppose any plan that may dissolve or impair it. (Paragraph 12; author's italics)

'Palestinian identity' has to be kept up, but only for 'the present stage' of the 'struggle'; the ultimate aim is 'Arab unity'. Never yet achieved in history, this unity has to be brought into existence somehow by constant invocation. The Palestinian Revolution has a critical role to play in the bringing about of this longed-for eschaton. This is made clear in a cryptic sentence in paragraph 13: 'Thus, Arab unity leads to the liberation of Palestine, the liberation of Palestine leads to Arab unity.' This seems to mean that all that prevents the achievement of 'Arab unity' is the foreign body named Israel. Once the war against Israel and Zionism has been prosecuted to a successful conclusion, 'Arab unity' will be marvellously achieved. Likewise it is the inner strength, the cohesive moral force provided by that unity, which ultimately makes possible the 'liberation of Palestine'. It is sometimes said that the Palestinians are the key to the Middle East conflict. The implication is that it is their struggle, and that once some way can be found of satisfying their desire for a home in Palestine, they and the rest of the Arab world will be content to see a Jewish and Palestinian state living side by side. This, however, is contradicted by both the spirit and letter of the Covenant. The war is ultimately one of the Arab nation as a whole, and its fore-ordained aim is 'Arab unity'. More than that, it is, astonishingly, a war for the very existence of the Arab nation as a whole: 'The destiny of the Arab nation, and indeed Arab existence itself, depend upon the destiny of the Palestinian cause.'

The Covenant is a pseudo-religious document. It contains a vision of heaven (Arab unity) and it contains a vision of hell (Zionism, the state of Israel). The successful attainment of the one depends on the elimination of the other. This is the 'harrowing of hell' which must precede the final phase of messianic fulfilment. The politicidal intent of the document may not be glossed over. No moral, social or ideological content is provided for the term 'liberation of Palestine' other than 'the elimination of Zionism' (paragraph 15). The establishment of Israel in 1947 is said to have been 'entirely illegal' (paragraph 19); the Balfour Declaration is 'null and void' (paragraph 20) for the Jews are not a nation which qualifies for statehood: 'Judaism being a religion, is not an independent nationality. Nor do Jews constitute a single nation with an identity of its own; they are citizens of the states to which they belong.' (paragraph 20)

There is thus no Jewish national identity, and consequently there can be no Jewish state. If it seems to exist, then it should not and cannot really be there. Paradoxically, whilst the Jewish state is evidently so powerful and dangerous that it poses a threat to the very existence of the Arab nation (paragraph 14), it cannot really represent an 'independent nationality' since the Jews are a non-nation, merely a religion, whose members are citizens of the states in which they happen to reside (paragraph 20). This is a paradox. But the Palestine Covenant harbours many such paradoxes. Another may be noted in the very definition of 'Palestine' as a geographical entity. In paragraph 20, the Mandate for Palestine in which the League of Nations authorized the setting up of a

Jewish National Home is said, as we have remarked, to be 'null and void', but in the second paragraph Palestine, the country which has to be liberated by and on behalf of the 'Palestine people', is defined 'according to the boundaries it had during the British Mandate'. The point is that since Palestine has no well-defined existence as a separate territorial or national entity in the Arab tradition, it cannot be geographically defined except by invoking the League of Nations Mandate, which in turn rests on the claim, therein upheld, of the Jewish people on a certain land called Palestine!

The Palestinians have thus a highly problematical identity. Their ostensible aim is self-determination and sovereignty in an Arab Palestine (paragraph 9); this aim can be achieved only by the elimination of Israel and Zionism (paragraph 15); but on the other hand, the need to liquidate Israel provides the sole basis for a Palestine national identity. There is even, as we have seen (paragraph 12), a hint that with the accomplishment of its historical role, namely, the liberation of Palestine, the Palestinian Arab people might disappear and merge itself in the larger Arab collectivity.[20] The words 'liberation, unity, progress' (paragraph 22) cannot conceal the negative character of the impulse behind the whole so-called Palestinian Revolution. It is not a dream of salvation but one essentially of destruction – the destruction of Israel in the name of a mythical 'Arab unity'. When translated into historical terms this means, at best, the integrity of the greater Arab empire as it has been reconstituted as a result of the two world wars of our century. Palestinian national identity is the instrument for serving this grander purpose, by means of the elimination of Israel. Once that has been brought about it will really have no further role to perform.

VI

We may thus conclude that we have in the Middle East crisis two Covenants standing over against one another. There is, on the one hand, the Jewish Covenant, with its dream of salvation to be achieved through the 'liberation' of the Jewish people and its return to Zion where it will refashion the ethical civilization with which it is charged: 'For out of Zion shall go forth Torah and the word of the Lord from Jerusalem.' But this purpose does not remain within the limits of a religious confession. The dream of salvation requires the political process; it operates within history by means of a land and a polity. Zionism is a revolutionary programme; it has behind it all the power, all the readiness for sacrifice, even for armed struggle, which we associate with the great revolutions of history. The Jewish people is in no position to relinquish its aims, since these constitute the very basis of its existence.

And then, on the other hand, we have the 'Palestine Covenant', a programme curiously fashioned in imitation of the Zionist Revolution. Here, too, it is proposed that a people return 'home' from 'exile' in order to 'provide the Holy Land with an atmosphere of safety and tranquility' (Palestine Covenant, paragraph 16). But its basic premise is the denial of any political rights to that people from whose connection with it the land in fact derives its holiness! The Palestine Revolution, no matter how deeply we sift it, has no higher aim, no more transcendent value, than 'Arab unity' and in the pursuit of that all things may be permitted. Aeroplanes may be pirated, school children may be terrorized, Arab villagers and workers themselves may be murdered. Indeed when the count of the victims of Arab terror attacks is made, it will be found that there have been more Arab victims than Jews. Sometimes this is the effect of chance, of a certain randomness in the sowing of destruction; in other instances buses conveying Arab workers to their places of work in Israel are made the deliberate object of attack. When neither Jews nor Palestinian Arabs offer themselves as targets for destruction the zeal of the liberators is turned against other communities, against Christians and Moslems in Lebanon or against Arab diplomats in Vienna. For, ultimately, the Palestinian Revolution is an instrument of destruction. Politicide is both an aim and a method; it is of its essence.

There is in all this, however, something even more deeply disturbing than the politicidal tendencies of the Palestinian Revolution; I refer to its *suicidal* tendencies. The notion that the Zionist creation in the tiny area of Palestine represents a threat to the very existence and life of the greater Arab people and to their enormous empire (see Palestine Covenant, paragraph 14) is a fantasy. But fantasies can take on a dangerous life when entertained with sufficient tenacity and passion. To give an example: between 1968 and 1970 the Arabs, recovering from the shock of the Six Day War but unable, as yet, to mount a full-scale attack on Israel, declared instead a War of Attrition. On the Jordanian front this took the form of the sporadic bombardment of Israeli settlements mainly in the upper Jordan valley. The attacks were carried out by the *Fatah* (the military arm of the PLO) with the full support of the Jordanian army. Israel called upon King Hussein repeatedly to curb these attacks made from his territory and called upon the *Fatah* to desist, but to no avail. The result was that the Israeli army was called in to return the fire and the Jordan valley became the scene of constant but static warfare. In mid-June 1969 the *New York Times* published a leader in which it spoke of the Middle East turning into a wasteland for *both* sides, the Arab and the Israeli, their cities and fields being gradually reduced to rubble, etc. It sounded as though that *ought* to have been true – for, after all, the Arabs were investing a great deal of moral and material capital in their bombardment of the Israel front line and in their terrorist operations in the rear. Yet the strange truth is that the real ravagement and destruction was *all* on their side. When the count was made it was revealed that not one single village on the Israeli side of the Jordan valley had been laid waste, not one settlement had been abandoned by its settlers, whereas the visitor to the area could see even with the naked eye that on the Arab side a vast area of farming land had been abandoned, and that its population of upwards of 100,000 souls had left its towns and villages and fled to the mountains. And all this because of the suicidal tactics of the Jordanian army and the *Fatah*. In 1970 the *Fatah*, having achieved such disappointing results in open warfare and through its incursions into Israel, turned its attentions to the hijacking of aircraft on international routes. At this point its activities became such an acute embarrassment to King Hussein and his government that in September he mounted a violent attack upon the 'Liberation army' and the refugee camps in which it was based. In a series of bloody engagements several thousands of the liberators were exterminated and the whole organization was expelled from the Jordanian kingdom, i.e. eastern Palestine.

The devastating effect of the War of Attrition on the Egyptian front is well known. Launched by President Nasser as a means of bringing Israel to her knees, it ended in June 1970 with the Israeli line intact and many thousands of Egyptians dead. The casualties on the Israeli side, though heavy, bore no numerical comparison with those of the Arabs.

All this is the effect of *thanatos*, a death-wish which proves to be potentially even more dangerous than the other destructive forces released in the Arab struggle against Israel. Moreover it is a force which Israel is helpless to arrest, because when the attack is launched Israel has no option but to defend herself, come what may. For Israel is fighting for life itself and, more than that, for the fountain of life, for the tree of life in the midst of the garden.

10

Epilogue

I

THE SIX DAY WAR was, as we have seen, a kind of spiritual watershed. For the Jewish people there was the 'shock of self-identification' as the meaning of Jewish existence was suddenly illuminated. And for the Palestinians, too, there was the crystallization of a new identity in their Covenant as formulated in 1968. From now on the battle was joined between two parallel but opposing ideologies, two opposing myths, two opposing Covenants, the one the dark antithesis of the other. The issue was clear. It would be for both sides a life-and-death struggle, and by no means a dispute about territories or borders.

The Yom Kippur War of 1973 marked a further, almost apocalyptic, development of the same process. For what we have witnessed since then is the seeming involvement of the world community in the confrontation between Israel and the Arab nation. The stage has been enormously enlarged as the struggle has taken on a universal character. In November 1975 the General Assembly of the United Nations adopted by a large majority a resolution condemning Zionism and thus, in effect, endorsing the assault upon Zionism and Judaism contained in the Palestine Covenant. This vote clearly denied the ideological basis for an independent Jewish state in Palestine. As the Dutch Council of Churches pointed out in its statement of 12 November 1975, the very existence of the state of Israel is attacked in this resolution. It is, in a word, politicidal. Of course the resolution in itself, in spite of the large majority of those voting in its favour, does not decide the outcome of the combat; it merely indicates where the battle line is drawn. It should be noted that at this point the Christian Church as a whole (the World Council of Churches, the United States Catholic Conference and many others) took a stand for Zionism and for Israel. Evidently the denial of Jewish nationhood is something to which the Church cannot ultimately agree. Moreover both America and a majority of the west European and Latin American countries opposed the resolution.*

What we have now, in effect, is a world-wide confrontation in which the ideological issue, though by no means clear to either side, is nevertheless a factor in the confrontation. Israel has no cause to despair at the fact that the anti-Zionist and anti-Israel vote was carried by a majority. If the numbers of combatants on either side were the deciding factor, Israel would have gone down in its war with the Arabs long ago. But on the other hand it cannot be said that the vote of those who opposed this political statement represented a clear understanding of, and identification with, Zionism, just as it cannot be said that the vote of the many nations which favoured the resolution represented a clear understanding of, and identification with, the ideology of the Palestinian Revolution. There are other factors tipping the scales. One very weighty factor is the Arab oil threat. It is perhaps this more than anything else which has served to universalize the conflict, to give it its apocalyptic dimension during the past three or four years. It has had the effect of forcing everyone to take sides, for no one can remain indifferent when their economic stability is involved.

The immediate impact of the oil embargo, when it was imposed in October 1973, was to create an atmosphere of bitter animosity towards Israel. Israel had been attacked some days earlier, but a visitor to the deliberations of the Security Council of the United Nations, not knowing this, might have concluded from the ugly temper of the delegates that the contrary had happened, namely, that Israel had fallen suddenly and treacherously upon her neighbours, thus endangering the peace of the world![1] The reason for this extraordinary attitude was, of course, the pressure of the oil

* The actual voting was 72 in favour of the Assembly's resolution (no. 3379), 35 against and 37 abstentions. Given the general anti-Israel bias of the UN, this result, in which the combined negative votes and abstentions equalled the positive votes, represented something of a moral victory for Israel – a fact rarely noted.

embargo which was making Europe and, to a lesser extent, the United States aware of how much their wealth and comfort depended on the goodwill of the Arab states. And no matter what injustice is needed to buy that goodwill there is always a temptation to pay the price. This is one important factor which tends, at this point, to cloud the moral issue.

But, of course, extortion can and does work the other way also. Many of the Asians and African states which voted with the Arabs against Israel and Zionism really hope that one day something may happen to release them from the Arab stranglehold. For them the effects of the international oil cartel, the organization of oil producing and exporting countries (OPEC), is more than a threat to their prosperity; it radically affects their very existence in a world where even a minimal subsistence depends on this source of energy which the Arabs so largely control. Grotesquely the old anti-semitic libel of the Jewish financiers who control the world (the foundation of the amazing *Protocols of the Elders of Zion* referred to in Chapter IX) is coming true in reverse, as the Arab oil moguls palpably seem to have the world's economy by the throat, whilst, by contrast, the attempt of American Jewry to apply an economic boycott to Mexico (after the latter had voted against Zionism at the United Nations) has proved pathetically ineffective. But one does not require the gift of prophecy to foresee that the oil monopoly which now seems to be so powerful a weapon for the Arabs may eventually become their undoing. In that case we would be witnessing, on an infinitely larger scale than previously, the operation of the same suicidal tendencies which have already proved so potent a force in the history of the Arab struggle against Israel.

Such considerations are for the long term. In the short term, the nations have evidently decided that, in their search for an illusory peace in the Middle East and for an illusory relief for themselves from the oil threat, the best course is to pressure Israel into political and economic concessions. The pressure upon Israel, especially from the United States, is unbelievably great; and the effect of this 'persuasion' has, from time to time, caused a certain weakening in the national resolve. It can also work the other way: In May 1977 it helped to bring about a radical political change in Israel, marked by a new determination not to yield. The 'hard-liners' had gained the ascendancy, for the time being, over the 'moderates'.

The 'moderates', whose strength is in the left-wing parties, are men of lofty ethical outlook who seek to convince themselves and others that there are many 'moderates' like themselves on the Arab side, who merely await a sign of goodwill and 'flexibility' on the part of Israel to come forward and seek an accommodation. A little here, a little there, withdrawal even to the 1949 armistice lines – this will surely bring peace nearer! The wish is father to the thought. Perhaps here we, too, have to be on our guard against the effect of the dark force of *thanatos* which can threaten the whole Zionist enterprise from within.[2] For the truth is that there is *no* corresponding movement by 'doves' among the Palestinian Arabs. There is no real movement for accommodation with Israel on the basis of a recognition of the legitimacy of a Jewish–Zionist state in Palestine, in however limited a territorial space. Quite the contrary, the revised form of the Palestine Covenant as approved in Cairo in June 1974 represents a considerable hardening. It explicitly rejects the notion of 'peace and secure boundaries' for Israel, and calls for the liberation of 'every part of the Palestinian territory'. It also indicates the new aim of liquidating the present regime in Jordan – hitherto regarded as a relatively moderate partner in the Arab war against Israel – and replacing it by a 'patriotic and democratic regime'. And, of course, let us not forget that in the year 1975 the Arab states (including the Egypt of Sadat) jointly and unanimously sponsored the anti-Zionist resolution in the United Nations Assembly, which in effect carried the holy war against Israel into the broad international arena. It left no room for a recognition by the Arabs of the legitimacy of Zionism as the basis of the state of Israel.[3]

In these circumstances the Israeli 'moderates' who counsel maximal concessions, including recognition of the Palestinians as a negotiating partner in some imaginary peace settlement, are out of touch with today's reality. More than that, they have not learned the simple lessons of the past. For the route of concession has been tried repeatedly in Zionist history without bringing peace any nearer. Again and again the Zionist leadership, and later the state of Israel, have sought an accommodation with the Arabs based on some political or territorial compromise. They have been rebuffed each time. The Jews sought peace with the Arabs as early as 1922 on the basis of a proposal for a legislative assembly which would have given the Arabs a permanent majority over the Jews in the government of the country. The Jews were ready to accept this: the Arabs refused. The Arabs could have had peace in 1947 on the basis of the United Nations partition proposal awarding them control of a solid half of western Palestine. They refused this and preferred to go to war. With the doubtful exception of the Egypt of Sadat, the Arabs are not prepared to conclude a genuine peace with the Jewish–Zionist state. This position is held with greater consistency now than ever before by the so-called 'rejection front', for they have been able to convince themselves since the Yom Kippur War that military pressure, combined with an adroit use of the oil weapon, will guarantee their ultimate victory. In these circumstances any concession made by Israel will, from the Arab point of view, simply bring the final victory nearer. And final victory means for them the disappearance of Israel.

II

The debate between the Israeli 'hard-liners' and the Israeli 'moderates' is therefore strangely irrelevant to the issue of peace or war. An Israeli hard line over concession will not push the otherwise peace-loving Arabs towards war, nor will an Israeli soft line persuade the Arabs to make peace. The opposite is just as likely to eventuate from the two positions. We have seen recently how President Sadat's peace initiative of November 1977 was addressed to the 'hard-line' administration of Mr Begin! But if the deep and painful division within Israeli public life between the 'hawks' and the 'doves' has little bearing on the attitudes and conduct of the Arab enemy, it is extremely relevant to the issue with which this study is mainly concerned: the definition of Zionism itself. For it is really, at bottom, a debate about the nature of Zionism and, more particularly, about the nature of the Jewish condition and of Jewish history.

It must be emphasized that what we have here is not the standard confrontation between 'right' and 'left'. There are many important left-wing elements in Israeli public life which take their stand in principle on an 'undivided land of Israel',[4] just as there are right-wing elements which are prepared for compromises. The real division is between those who are powerfully influenced by 'world opinion', who feel that Israel must at all costs project a liberal, progressive image, must become 'normal' and 'accepted' as the Basle Programme required, and those who are prepared to accept and even welcome the uniqueness of the Jewish destiny and the peculiar trials and burdens that go with it. Historically Zionism represents the politics of the Covenant; but it also represents, as we have seen, the struggle against the Covenant, the attempt to achieve, through nationhood, the ultimate emancipation, the final release from the burden of difference.

The 'moderates', we may say, are fundamentally unwilling to contemplate the existential uniqueness of Jewish history. They argue that since Zionism came to normalize the Jewish condition, it is intolerable that we should be involved now in a dispute of so abnormal a character that it is incapable of solution by ordinary diplomatic and political means. If other disputes between 'normal' sovereign states can be settled by negotiation, then clearly this one must also be thus settled. And if the Arabs refuse to sit down with us in order to negotiate it, then we must be at fault somewhere along the line; we must have been too 'chauvinistic', perhaps, or too 'inflexible' between 1967 and 1973. (To judge from their references to this period one would suppose that the Arabs were all that time offering to negotiate and Israel was refusing to come to terms!) To make up for this, we must now be more reasonable and make a suitable gesture in their direction. These 'moderates' are rather like the assimilated Jews of the Diaspora who, when faced with vicious anti-semitism, would turn all their anger against the Jewish community and against any Jews who, through an accidental grossness of manner or some lack of total public spiritedness, might be the 'cause' of anti-semitism!

To recognize the Arab hostility to Israel as diabolical, as a continuation of Hitler's war against the Jews, involves a recognition of the essential abnormality of the Jewish condition, and a recognition, also, that this abnormality has not ended with the establishment of a Jewish state. There are still many who are not prepared for such recognition. It will not do to tell them that the mystery of Jewish existence includes not only trial and suffering, but also exaltation, privilege and even power. They want neither the blessings of election nor its outrageous slings and arrows. They simply want to be relieved of its pressures. They are not prepared for the scandal of a biblical reality, neither the Crossing of the Red Sea nor the War with the Amalekites. From their point of view there is nothing in the problem of Israel today, just as there was nothing in the Jewish problem of the nineteenth century, which is not susceptible of a rational solution. Neither the mystery of the love of Zion nor the mystery of the Arab hatred of Israel can be allowed to interfere with 'normal' political logic, and this logic must be maintained at all costs and despite all appearances.

All this is rather like the attitude of Herzl and his friends who, in 1903, favoured the Uganda plan as a reasonable accommodation to circumstances. Uganda, for them, could provide a logical alternative to the 'holy hill of Zion'. But Herzl did not carry the day. And now, as then, we may discern in contrast to the 'Zionism of Uganda' a still-active 'Zionism of Zion'. Just as the passionate and irrational love of Zion irrupted into the Sixth Zionist Congress to upset the more rational counsels of Herzl and his friends and finally to overthrow them, so now, too, there are significant elements in the country to avow the absoluteness and transcendence of the Jewish bond with the Holy Land and the Holy City, and to affirm, even in defiance of current political trends, that history will finally justify them. If I am not mistaken, the chief representatives of an uncompromising Zionist Covenant faith at this time are the activists of the so-called *Gush Emunim* (the word *Emunim* signifies faith – faith in the tradition of the past and in the promises of the future), a powerful group drawn mainly, but not entirely, from the religious youth of the country. Though there is clearly much sympathy for them in the Likkud party, they are politically unaffiliated with either the right of left.

Since the Yom Kippur War *Gush Emunim* has come to the fore as the most revolutionary force in Israeli public life. Disdaining parliamentary representation, it prefers to make its appeal directly to the populace. In a two-day march across the countryside towards the biblical city of Shomeron (Sebastia) in occupied Samaria which was organized in April 1975, it was able to rally some 30,000 supporters. It repeated the performance in the spring of 1976 in another two-day march, this time from Bethel to Jericho. This kind of demonstration is too massive to be ignored. As a result

Emunim has become a major force in determining the pace, character and location of Jewish settlement in occupied Judea, Samaria and the Golan Heights. Its motto might be: 'For the sake of Zion I will not hold my peace' (*Isaiah* 62:1); and in this it has made an instinctive appeal to the deepest layers of national sentiment and consciousness. In August 1975 *Gush Emunim* mounted a series of mass demonstrations against the Kissinger-engineered partial agreement which involved an Israeli withdrawal from the strategic passes of Gidi and Mitla and the oil wells of western Sinai. Their argument was based not so much on the sacred character of the territories involved, as on the absurdity of surrendering vital areas to an enemy which maintained full belligerent rights. Israel was endangering its basic security and thus its ability ultimately to defend Zion itself.

Gush Emunim are commonly accused of 'mysticism' and lack of political realism. No doubt the 'Zionists of Zion' in 1903 were also thus accused, but history proved them right in the end. If *Emunim* were less practical and more 'mystical', they might argue that oil wells are not important and that all we have to do when the time comes is to pray for oil to descend from heaven to supply Israel's needs. Instead of which they argue, as believing Jews have always argued, that salvation has to be worked for as well as prayed for. This leads them in the direction of a political hard line over American 'persuasion' and Arab threats, and to a very practical emphasis on military preparedness and intensive Jewish settlement along the new borders created as a result of the Six Day War.

The thrust, therefore, of Jewish activism has changed. In the period prior to the State, the strong line was represented by such militant groups as the *Irgun* (National Military Organization) who opposed 'soft' policies on the somewhat narrow ground of national and historic rights. What we have now is a definite upsurge of what can be recognized as a covenant faith, the often muted counter-theme of political Zionism at all times. Its spokesmen are intellectually unsophisticated, innocent of political science or philosophy, but they mediate an elementary faith in Israel's uniqueness, Israel's mission and Israel's power of survival – the basic components of the Covenant. In a time of darkness and confusion all of this has an immediate and revolutionary appeal to large sections of the population. The political significance of this movement, therefore, should not be underestimated. In fact without some appreciation of its impact during the past few years, it is impossible to understand the background of the change which took place in the political life of the country in May 1977.

III

Ultimately, however, we are less concerned with political changes than with movements of the spirit. *Emunim*'s success is perhaps no more than a sign of a widely felt need for a greater inwardness in Zionism and in Israeli life. Within the religious community there has been a certain weakening of the moral fibre; it has not always set an example of dedication in every sphere of public and private life. It is time for a return to first principles. But in Israel's current crisis the main challenge is directed at the larger community of the religiously indifferent and the non-observant. Having started with high ideals of self-sacrifice and moral austerity, this secular world has now revealed a certain moral emptiness. It no longer provides a solid ground even for national self-respect and loyalty to the flag. At the time of the beginning of the state the streets were filled with singing youngsters dressed in white and blue on every national occasion of rejoicing or defiance. They were members of the youth movements affiliated with the left-wing parties in Zionism. The youth today who belong to that section of the population are often confused about their basic rights and basic purposes in the land. A group of Israeli students in a mid-western university in the United States were asked recently why they did not attempt to counter the anti-Israel propaganda of the very active Arab students on the same campus. Their answer was that they were there to study and not to engage in politics. Such an answer would have been inconceivable from a typical group of Israeli youngsters during the period of the Mandate or even in the first decade of state-building. It seems as though the very will to live, the very commitment to the *patria* itself is, for the Jew, ultimately a function of his covenant faith. Where that is lacking, national morale itself is in danger of erosion.

And there are other symptoms, too, of the complex spiritual crisis at present affecting secular Israeli society. Among those who might be expected to be the followers of A. D. Gordon there are too many office-seekers. Among the children of the socialist pioneers there is too much cheap imitation of the culture of the West, too much nihilism in literature and the arts and too much manipulation of public funds for private gain. Among the children of pious Jews from the *mellahs* (Jewish quarters) of Casablanca and Marrakesh there are too many crimes of violence, too much drug addiction. On their arrival as infants in the early fifties a secular society deprived them of their spiritual birthright and gave them shoddy goods in return. In these circumstances there is throughout the community a deep and barely articulate desire to rediscover a more authentically Jewish spirituality, to reinstate in both public and private life the category of holiness.

Mere statehood, it is clear, is not enough. It has not brought with it the promised release from external pressures, nor the promised ease of the spirit. And it is the ease of spirit which is most sorely missed. If this were merely a matter of nostalgia for old-world pieties, for the sabbath-candles on one's grandmother's table, one might treat it as a sentimental irrelevance and return to a consideration of Israel's real, i.e. political, problems. But the truth is that what is being sought in the realm of the spirit is a formula for survival. Without a fuller Zionism, one that includes in itself the mystery of holiness and the dream of salvation, it is difficult to see how the Israeli people can maintain themselves in the face of the ideological offensive currently directed against them. They will not convince others of their righteousness, of their need, if they do not first reinstate and re-affirm their understanding of that need and that righteousness.

Can such spiritual rehabilitation be achieved in our time? Were it to be left to men and women alone – including those many millions of Jews and non-Jews beyond Israel's borders who share the 'hope of Israel' – the prospect of so momentous a renewal of the spirit would be faint indeed. But what gives hope is the fact that we are driven on, even, in a manner, coerced. The crisis which we endure leaves us little alternative to faith and holiness. And perhaps this is ultimately the nature of the Covenant. We do not necessarily initiate its dialogue ourselves: it is rather a matter of a response forced out of us by the inexorability of those events through which the unseen Guardian of Israel, now as at all times, addresses his word to us.

Notes and References

1: Introduction

1 Cf. Leo Pinsker, *Auto-Emancipation*, translated by D. S. Blondheim (New York 1906), p. 12: 'The great ideas of the eighteenth and nineteenth centuries have not passed by our people without leaving a trace. We feel not only as Jews; we feel as men. As men, we, too, would fain live and be a nation like the others.'

2 See Ludwig Lewisohn, *Up-Stream* (New York 1922), and *Mid-Channel* (New York 1929), passim.

3 Chaim Weizmann, *Trial and Error* (London 1949), pp. 41–2.

4 On the background of the Basle Programme, see D. Vital, *The Origins of Zionism* (Oxford 1975), p. 368.

5 Theodor Herzl, *The Jewish State*, translated by Sylvie d'Avigdor (London 1934), p. 64.

6 Cf. Jacob Neusner, 'Zionism and the Jewish Problem', *Midstream*, XV (November 1969), p. 45.

7 Maurice Samuel, *Light on Israel* (New York 1968), chapter 1.

8 This aspect is ignored by many writers on the subject. Amos Elon, in his remarkably one-sided *The Israelis: Founders and Sons* (New York 1971), presents the history of modern Jewish settlement as brought about solely by nationalism, socialism, populism, etc., 'as in other developing countries' (p. 147). On the continuity of Jewish settlement in Palestine, see ed. Dan Bahat, *The Forgotten Generations* (Jerusalem 1975), passim.

9 Cf. some perceptive remarks of Yaacov Herzog in *A People that Dwells Alone* (London 1975), pp. 53, 128–9.

2: The Covenant

1 Herzl, *The Jewish State*, p. 78.
2 Jean-Paul Sartre, *Anti-Semite and Jew*, translated by Georges B. Becker (New York 1965), p. 137.
3 Jacques Maritain, *Antisemitism* (London 1939), p. 20.
4 Ibid.
5 Ibid., p. 19.
6 Sartre, *Anti-Semite and Jew*, p. 67 (italics added).
7 Lewisohn, *Mid-Channel*, pp. 28, 31.
8 Martin Buber, *Moses* (Oxford and London 1946), p. 112.
9 Cf. Martin Buber, 'Holy Event', in his *The Prophetic Faith* (New York 1949), p. 51.
10 Cf. J. B. Soloveichik, 'My Beloved Knocks', in his *The Man of Faith* [Hebrew] (Jerusalem 1968), pp. 86–94.
11 Martin Buber, *On Zion: The History of an Idea* (London 1973), p. 35.
12 See Harold Fisch, 'The Absent God', *Judaism*, XXI (1972), pp. 415–27.
13 Abraham Joshua Heschel, *Israel: An Echo of Eternity* (New York 1969), p. 48.
14 Cf. *The End of the Ideology Debate*, ed. Chaim I. Waxman (New York 1968), passim. Zionism is not often referred to in this debate, but the implications for Zionism are clear. See, for instance, Raymond Aron's words: 'Let us teach everyone to doubt all the models and utopias, to challenge all the prophets of redemption and the heralds of catastrophe' (ibid., p. 48). Aron, a 'de-Judaized' Jew, as he termed himself, was, however, stirred to his depths by the Six Day War (see his *De Gaulle, Israel and the Jews* (New York 1969). If Israel were to be given up to destruction, he declared, 'that would deprive me of the strength to live' (p. 69).

3: Alienation

1 Pinsker, *Auto-Emancipation*, pp. 2, 9. Shmarya Levin makes a similar observation (see *Out of Bondage* (London 1919), p. 65).
2 See 'Slavery in Freedom' (1891), in *Selected Essays of Ahad*

Ha'am, translated by Leon Simon (Cleveland and New York 1962), pp. 170–94.

3 'A New Savior' (1901), ibid., p. 252.

4 From Max Nordau's address to the Fifth Zionist Congress, quoted in Anna and Max Nordau, *Max Nordau: A Biography* (New York 1943), pp. 173–4.

5 See his address to the Second Zionist Congress, ibid., pp. 141–6.

6 Ibid., p. 151.

7 For some relevant rabbinic *dicta*, see C. G. Montefiore and H. Loewe, *A Rabbinic Anthology* (London 1938), pp. 63–4, 81.

8 For a fuller discussion of Kook's ideas, see below, chapter 5.

9 See Harold Fisch, *The Dual Image: The Figure of the Jew in English and American Literature* (New York 1971), pp. 122–3.

10 On this implication of the Holocaust experience, see Emil L. Fackenheim, *Quest for Past and Future* (Bloomington, Indiana 1968), pp. 287–90.

11 This option is urged in Eliezer Livneh's *Israel and the Crisis of Western Civilization* [Hebrew] (Tel-Aviv 1972), pp. 144, 173 and passim. I find myself in general agreement with Livneh's position, though his grasp of the nature of Judaism seems to me inadequate.

12 *Midrash, Vayiqra Rabba*, chapter 32.

13 Alienation affected the second generation of immigrants from North Africa and the Middle East. The sharp break with tradition, marked by a growing cultural and religious gap between parents and children, left the new generation 'without anchor or rudder' (S. N. Herman, *Israelis and Jews*, Philadelphia 1971, p. 199).

14 Cf. David Riesman, *The Lonely Crowd* (New York 1969), p. 25.

15 The most notorious example, however, did not involve children of oriental Jews but a large transport of some one thousand children from eastern Europe, most of them orphans, who arrived from Teheran in February 1943. Though practically all from orthodox homes, these children were, for the most part, settled in non-religious surroundings.

16 Mr Arie Lova Eliav's testimony, based on personal experience, is of particular significance. Speaking of the handling of immigrants from the oriental communities at the time of the begin-

ning of the state, he remarks, 'We pulverized the human, familial, social and traditional cement and tried to replace it with another kind, but this did not work' (*Land of the Hart*, Philadelphia 1974, p. 305).

4: Moses Hess

1 Quoted by Hess himself in *Rome and Jerusalem*, edited and translated by Meyer Waxman (New York 1943), Fifth Letter, p. 69.
2 Ibid., Preface, p. 36.
3 Ibid., First Letter, p. 43.
4 Ibid., Twelfth Letter, p. 166.
5 Ibid., Fifth Letter, p. 71.
6 Ibid., Fourth Letter, p. 58.
7 Ibid., Fifth Letter, pp. 71, 72.
8 Cf. Fourth Letter, p. 57.
9 Cf. Third and Fourth Letters, pp. 55, 65.
10 For some valuable remarks on this theme, see E. Schweid, *Judaism and the Solitary Jew* [Hebrew] (Tel-Aviv 1974), pp. 43, 47–63.
11 *Babylonian Talmud*, tractate Shevuot, folio 39a.
12 Hess, *Rome and Jerusalem*, Fourth Letter, p. 65.
13 Ibid., Sixth and Ninth Letters, pp. 85, 120.
14 Cf. Fourth Letter, p. 66.
15 See Isaiah Berlin, *The Life and Opinions of Moses Hess* (Cambridge 1959), especially pp. 13–14, 45–6.
16 Hess, *Rome and Jerusalem*, Tenth Letter, p. 132.
17 On the history of the world as a seven-thousand-year period analogous to the seven days of Creation, see *Babylonian Talmud*, tractate *Sanhedrin*, folio 97a. The idea was developed further in the sixteenth century by the famous Rabbi Judah Loew ben Bezalel of Prague (see *The Writings of the Maharal of Prague* [Hebrew], ed. A. Kariv (Jerusalem 1972), vol. I, pp. 148–9. Hess shows some affinity with the thinking of the Maharal.
18 From *Areopagitica* (see John Milton, *Complete Prose Works*, New Haven 1959, vol. II, p. 556).
19 A somewhat different view is proposed by Mary Schulman. She argues that Hess's premises are different from those of

pious Jews of his time or earlier 'because to him Jews were a nationality rather than a religious sect' (*Moses Hess: Prophet of Zionism*, New York 1963, p. ix). Who, one wonders, are the orthodox religious writers for whom Judaism was ever merely a 'religious sect' and not a 'nationality'? E. Schweid also seems to regard Hess as a spokesman of secular Zionism (*Judaism and the Solitary Jew*, p. 146). But it seems to me that a more just assessment is that of Martin Buber, who treats him as a 'religious socialist' for whom religious and political considerations are, as in classical Judaism, genuinely integrated (cf. *On Zion: The History of an Idea*, pp. 111–22).

20 Hess, *Rome and Jerusalem*, Eleventh Letter, p. 150ff.
21 Ibid., Twelfth Letter, p. 173ff.
22 Hess patronized not only Kalischer (one of the founders of the Mikveh Yisrael Agricultural College) but also Rabbi Josef Natonek, an indefatigable worker for colonization. Hess's Letters show him as much exercised with the details of fundraising for this purpose. See Edmund Silberner, *Moses Hess, Briefwechsel* (The Hague 1959), pp. 530–3, 538–40.
23 Nahum Sokolow, *Hibbath Zion: The Love for Zion* (Jerusalem 1935), p. 72.
24 Hess, *Rome and Jerusalem*, Seventh Letter, p. 101.
25 Ibid., Eleventh Letter.

5: Myth and Metaphor

1 From various essays dated between 1910 and 1920 as edited and translated by Arthur Hertzberg in *The Zionist Idea* (New York 1969), pp. 372, 381, 382.
2 Ibid., p. 381.
3 A. D. Gordon, *Selected Essays*, translated by Frances Burnce (New York 1938), p. 121.
4 Cf. Gwendolyn Bays, *The Orphic Vision: Seer Poets from Novalis to Rimbaud* (Lincoln, Nebraska 1964), passim.
5 *The Birth of Tragedy*, chapters 2, 5, 16, etc.
6 Gordon, *Selected Essays*, p. 122.
7 A. D. Gordon, *Writings* [Hebrew] (Tel-Aviv 1929), vol. IV, p. 135.

8 Quoted by Amos Elon, *The Israelis: Founders and Sons*, op. cit., p. 142. And cf. Fisch, 'The Absent God', p. 415ff.

9 Rabbi Kook was the first Ashkenazi Chief Rabbi of the new Jewish *Yishuv* in Palestine, serving in this office with great distinction from 1921 until his death.

10 On the similarities (and differences) between the two writers, see some perceptive remarks by Eliezer Schweid, *The World of A. D. Gordon* [Hebrew] (Tel-Aviv 1970), pp. 78–82.

11 *The Vision of Israel: Selected from Rabbi A. I. Kook's 'Oroth'* [Hebrew], edited by Professor Haim Lifshitz (Jerusalem 5733 [1973]), p. 48. J. Levinger considers the metaphor of organism to be an essential part of Rabbi Kook's theology (see *From Routine to Renewal* [Hebrew], Jerusalem 1973, p. 53).

12 Judah Hallevi, *Book of Kuzari*, translated by Hartwig Hirschfeld (New York 1946), pt IV, section 23, p. 200. And see below, note 18.

13 *Babylonian Talmud*, tractate *Berakhot*, folio 59.

14 *The Vision of Israel*, p. 161 (this and subsequent extracts translated by the author). To balance the account, it should be stated that A. D. Gordon's writings also show a significant recurrence of light imagery. His vision is predominantly cthonic but he is also sensitive to the 'upper' inspiration. These light images, however, are employed in relation to the cognitive process (*hakara*); less so in relation to intuitive experience (*havaya*).

15 Rabbi A. I. Kook, *Hazon HaGeula* ('The Vision of Redemption') [Hebrew] (Jerusalem 5701 [1941]), p. 124.

16 Cf. *The Vision of Israel*, p. 137.

17 Cf. *The Vision of Israel*, p. 115.

18 Israel is a vine planted in the soil and we are its tendrils (*Arfile Tohar*, 'Mists of Purity', n.d., p. 67). Cf. Judah Hallevi, *Kuzari*, pt II, section 12, pp. 77–8.

19 *The Vision of Redemption*, p. 71. It is interesting that Jacques Maritain, too, perceived Israel as a 'mystical body' in which the God of the Scriptures is present (see *Antisemitism*, p. 31).

20 These ideas are set out in the work *Nezah Yisrael* ('The Eternity of Israel'). See *The Writings of the Maharal of Prague* [Hebrew], ed. A. Kariv (Jerusalem 1972), vol. I, pp. 120–8.

21 *The Vision of Israel*, p. 141.

22 Ibid., p. 144.
23 S. H. Bergman, *Faith and Reason* (New York 1963), p. 131.
24 See his letter (1913) addressed to the Mizrachi Convention in St Louis (*Igrot Ra'yah*, 'Letters of the Rav Kook', Jerusalem 1923, vol. II, pp. 110–12).
25 Cf. Eliezer Schweid, *Judaism and the Solitary Jew*, p. 116. Kook cites Kant and Bergson and clearly knows the Jewish post-Kantians and post-Nietzscheans. In his letters he rejects the separation of the secular and the religious into autonomous realms, as in nineteenth-century German philosophy, claiming that Judaism, by contrast, insists on the fundamental unity of the Creation ('Letters', vol. II, p. 193). He shows awareness here of current trends but hardly more than that. Zvi Yaron (*The Philosophy of Rabbi Kook* [Hebrew], Jerusalem 1974, p. 105) suggests that Kook was influenced by Hegel's dialectical philosophy of history. This may be true in a general way, but the dialectical elements in Kook, including his view of history (which progresses through reverses), are cabbalistic and owe much to the *Maharal* of Prague (see above, note 20).
26 The origin of such pseudo-religious radicalism is to be sought in the seventeenth century. On this aspect of the writings of Bacon and Hobbes, see Harold Fisch, *Jerusalem and Albion* (New York 1964), especially pp. 86, 90, 225–53.
27 Cf. A. N. Whitehead, *Science and the Modern World* (Cambridge 1933), p. 54.
28 From 'Hebrew Humanism' (1942), in ed. W. Herberg, *The Writings of Martin Buber* (New York 1956), p. 296.
29 Buber, *On Zion: The History of an Idea*, p. 14.
30 Ibid., p. 77.
31 Ibid., pp. 25, 27.
32 'Hebrew Humanism', in ed. Herberg, *Writings of Buber*, p. 303.
33 Ibid., p. 304.
34 Cf. B. Kurzweil, 'Ahad-Ha'amism – The Group Will to Survive', *Judaism*, IV (1955), p. 213.
35 Cf. *On Zion*, p. 144ff.
36 For some trenchant comments on Ahad Ha'am's position, see Arthur Hertzberg's introduction to *The Zionist Idea* (New York 1973), p. 51ff.

37 Martin Buber, *The Prophetic Faith*, translated by Carlyle Witton-Davies (New York 1949), p. 170.
38 G. Scholem, *The Messianic Idea in Judaism* (New York 1971), p. 245.
39 *Kingship of God*, translated by Richard Scheimann (New York 1973), p. 145.
40 Ibid., p. 143.
41 From his introduction written in 1955, ibid., p. 58.
42 'Hebrew Humanism', in ed. Herberg, *Writings of Buber*, pp. 295, 296.
43 *On Zion*, p. 142.
44 From 'Biblical Leadership' (1928), in ed. Herberg, *Writings of Buber*, p. 230.
45 Ibid., p. 228.
46 From 'The Silent Question' (1951), in ed. Herberg, *Writings of Buber*, p. 314.
47 Ibid., p. 313.
48 Introduction, ed. Herberg, *Writings of Buber*, p. 36.
49 *On Zion*, p. 91.
50 The dangerous fascination which Shabbetai Zwi and the Sabbatian heresy had for the early Hasidim is dramatized in the legend related by Buber of the Baal Shem Tov, the founder of Hasidism, entitled 'The Temptation' (see *Tales of the Hasidim: The Early Masters* (New York 1947), p. 78.
51 Emil L. Fackenheim, 'The Commanding Voice of Auschwitz', in *God's Presence in History* (New York 1970), pp. 67–98.
52 Y. Tabenkin, Leket Sheshet HaYamim ('The Lesson of the Six Days') (Tel-Aviv 1971), p. 20.

6: The Double Calendar

1 Cf. Buber, *On Zion: The History of an Idea*, p. 142.
2 A. Koestler, *Promise and Fulfilment: Palestine 1917–1949* (London 1949), p. 316.
3 On the significance of this group, see the important essay by B. Kurzweil, 'The New Canaanites', *Judaism*, II (1953), pp. 3–15. The 'Canaanite' movement was essentially a literary and cultural phenomenon, but the term has since been applied

in a loose way to all those who deny the Jewish character of
Israeli life and nationhood.

4 Cf. *Babylonian Talmud*, tractate *Baba Metzia*, folio 59b. (See
Montefiore and Loewe, *A Rabbinic Anthology*, pp. 340–1.)

5 Ben Halpern (*The Idea of the Jewish State*, Cambridge, Mass.
1961, p. 85) very properly and accurately links the founding of
Agudat Yisrael with the approval by the Tenth Zionist Congress in 1911 of a programme of secular cultural activities. It
was this which precipitated the movement towards separatism.

6 See *Moses*, p. 75. I tried to suggest something of the miraculous
character of the Six Day War as this was generally felt at the
time in an article written just as the war came to an end (see
Harold Fisch, 'Jerusalem, Jerusalem', *Judaism*, XVI (Summer
1967), pp. 259–65).

7 *The Seventh Day: Soldiers' Talk about the Six Day War*, ed.
Avraham Shapira (New York 1970), pp. 105, 183, 228. The
last extract quoted does not appear in the English version; it is
here translated directly from the original Hebrew text (Siah
Lohamim, ed. Avraham Shapira, Tel-Aviv 1968), p. 232.

8 For further comment on this aspect of the Six Day War, see
also Milton Himmelfarb, *The Jews of Modernity* (New York
1973), pp. 355–6.

9 From a pamphlet entitled 'One Year After', reproduced in the
daily newspaper *Haaretz* [Hebrew] (Tel-Aviv 22 November
1968).

10 Reported in the daily newspaper *Haaretz* (Tel-Aviv 29 June
1967).

11 *Address by Major-General Yitzhak Rabin . . . 28th June 1967*,
The Magnes Press (Jerusalem 1967), p. 7.

12 This point was powerfully made in a letter (dated 9 October
1973) from the President of the Hebrew University, Abraham
Harman, Professor Shlomo Avineri and others, which was
widely published in the American Press. The professors also
stated that they were 'wholly convinced' that if Israel was
proving capable of repelling the attack being launched at that
moment against its very existence, it was due to the fact that
it had earlier refused to withdraw unilaterally from the territories which it had occupied in 1967. These were now proving
vital to the country's defence.

13 *Al Azhar, Academy of Islamic Research: The Fourth Conference
   of the Academy of Islamic Research, September 1968* (Cairo
   1970), pp. 330–1.
14 That was the clear conclusion of several participants at the
   conference (see pp. 103, 414). The words of Muhammad
   Azzah Darwaza are particularly noteworthy:
      It is incumbent on the Moslems to strain every nerve and
      make all efforts in order to be well equipped by all means
      to fight the Jews. The Moslems should corner the Jews
      without feeling exhausted or tired as Allah enjoins upon
      them. The Moslems should spare no effort to exterminate
      their state and deliver every place of the Moslems' homeland
      from the Jews' desecration and keep it under the control of
      the Islamic authorities as it was. Any slight indifference to
      this matter is indeed a shameful sin against religion (ibid.,
      p. 496).
15 These figures are approximate. Whilst the number of Jewish
   refugees from Arab lands (Iraq, Yemen, Syria, Libya, Tunisia,
   Egypt, Algeria and Morocco) in the years 1948–53 has been
   established with reasonable certainty, the figures relating to the
   Arab refugees from Israel have been disputed. The Arabs
   claimed at the time that they had reached 800,000. Estimates
   from other sources, including the Special Political Committee
   of the United Nations General Assembly, placed the number
   well below this. (On this topic, see Theodore Draper, 'The
   United States and Israel', *Commentary*, LIX (April 1975),
   p. 32.)

7: Who are the Jews?

1 Georges Friedmann, *The End of the Jewish People*, translated
  by Eric Mosbacher (London 1967), p. 230.
2 For some thoughtful comments on the various degrees of
  religious identification among Israel's secular majority, and on
  the underlying solidarity which exists between the religious
  and non-religious sections of the community in spite of surface
  tensions, see S. C. Leslie, *The Rift in Israel* (New York 1971),
  pp. 72–89, 145–7.
3 Herman, *Israelis and Jews*, p. 210.

4 Friedmann, *The End of the Jewish People*, p. 278.
5 Ibid., p. 279.
6 Cf. S. N. Herman, *American Students and Israel* (Ithaca, New York and London 1970), pp. 48–51. In his *Jewish Identity: A Social Psychological Perspective* (Beverly Hills, California 1977), pp. 214–18, Herman shows how these typical judgements are often based upon misunderstanding.
7 Karl Kautsky, *Are the Jews a Race?* (New York 1926), p. 244.
8 See above, chapter II, p. 15.
9 From ed. Moshe Davis, *The Yom Kippur War: Israel and the Jewish People* (New York 1974), p. 120.
10 See the *Jewish Chronicle* (London), 9 November 1956: 'All seventeen of them [the Jewish Labour MPs] supported the Opposition's censure motion against the Government. Three divisions took place on the motion, and the Jewish Labour MPs voted solidly for their party in them all.'
11 There is, of course, a respectable body of opinion on the other side. The leading spokesmen for the 'bi-polar' view of Jewish history in the post-state era, which maintains that 'Babylon' and 'Jerusalem' have complementary roles in a continuing partnership, was Simon Rawidowicz, a friend and younger disciple of the historian Simon Dubnow. A Hebrew stylist of the first rank, Rawidowicz was a curiously lonely figure in America. His books, unread by the Jews of 'Babylon', can hardly be taken as representative of a genuine affirmation of Jewish national and cultural identity on the part of the Diaspora communities of the West. See his *Babylon and Jerusalem* [Hebrew] (London and Waltham, Mass. 1957) and *Studies in Jewish Thought* (Philadelphia 1974), passim.
12 See Koestler, *Promise and Fulfilment*, p. 335.
13 Ibid.
14 Kautsky, *Are the Jews a Race?*, p. 247.
15 Koestler, *Promise and Fulfilment*, p. 331.
16 Cf. *Babylonian Talmud*, tractate *Berakhot*, folio 13.
17 Cf. Herman, *Israelis and Jews*, p. 77ff.
18 In a lecture on 'Prayer in Our Time' given at Bar-Ilan University, Israel, under the auspices of the Institute for Judaism and Contemporary Thought (July 1973). See *De'oth*, vol. IX (Jerusalem, March 1975), p. 323.

19 Cf. Hannah Arendt, *Eichmann in Jerusalem* (New York 1965), pp. 11, 12.
20 A survey by Akiva W. Deutsch, made in 1963–4, revealed significant variants from earlier stereotyped conceptions, especially among that portion of Israeli youth which identified itself as Jewish (*The Eichmann Trial in the Eyes of Israeli Youngsters*, Bar-Ilan University, Ramat-Gan 1974, pp. 49–55, 78).
21 C. Liebman, *Pressure without Sanctions: The Influence of World Jewry in Shaping Israel's Public Policy* (Cranbury, New Jersey 1976), chapter 9.
22 See above, chapter III, p. 24.
23 Published in Tel-Aviv in 1950, and produced successfully at the Cameri Theatre in Tel-Aviv in the same year.

8: Who are the Christians?

1 Cf. David Flusser, 'New Christian Understanding of Judaism', *Orot: Journal of Hebrew Literature*, 14 (World Zionist Organization, Jerusalem February 1973), p. 19.
2 There were exceptions. In addition to chiliastic sects such as the Church of the Latter Day Saints (Mormons), who came out loudly in support of Israel, there were messages of support from important Christian bodies and leaders in Israel (see the *Jerusalem Post* 15 October 1973). There was also an impressive statement by a group of leading Canadian clergymen (reproduced in *The Yom Kippur War*, ed. Davis, pp. 356–8) and by groups associated with the Council of Christians and Jews in various parts of the world. But perhaps more important than these were thousands of letters and cables of support received by the Prime Minister of Israel from individual Christians abroad during the fighting.
3 A. Roy Eckardt, *Your People, My People* (New York 1974), p. 123.
4 Ibid., p. 223.
5 Niebuhr's unequivocal support of Israel at the time of the Six Day War was expressed in his article, 'David and Goliath', *Christianity and Crisis* (26 June 1967).
6 From 'L'Église, Sa Personne et Son Personnel' (1970), quoted

by R. J. Z. Werblowsky in 'Jewish Christian Relations', *Christian News from Israel*, XXIV (Jerusalem Autumn-Winter 1973), p. 121. Maritain's position on Israel and Zionism was fully expounded in *Le Mystère d'Israel* (Paris 1965).

7 On this shameful chapter of Vatican history, see Ladislas Farago, *Aftermath: Martin Bormann and the Fourth Reich* (New York 1975), passim.

8 The phrase, occurring in a somewhat equivocal context ('some feared that the Jews . . . an élite people, etc. . . . would turn the very moving hopes they had formed over nineteen centuries . . . into a burning ambition of conquest. . . .'), was used in his famous press conference on 27 November 1967. Its implications are perceptively discussed by Raymond Aron (*De Gaulle, Israel and the Jews*, translated by John Sturrock, New York 1969), who concludes that 'the Press Conference solemnly authorized a new form of anti-semitism' (p. 19).

9 Flusser, 'New Christian Understanding of Judaism', pp. 18–19.

10 Cf. Millar Burrows, *Palestine is Our Business* (Philadelphia 1949): 'The great trouble with Zionism is the attempt to be both a religion and a nation at the same time' (p. 131).

11 Quoted by Eckardt, *Your People, My People*, pp. 118–9.

12 Cf. Burrows, *Palestine is Our Business*, p. 90.

13 Franklin H. Littell, *The Crucifixion of the Jews* (New York 1975), p. 96.

14 Ibid., pp. 98, 127, 130. A radical revaluation of Christian theology in the light of the Holocaust and the rise of Israel is also urged by Paul van Buren, *The Burden of Freedom: Americans and the God of Israel* (New York 1976), pp. 68, 83; and by Rosemary R. Ruether, *Faith and Fratricide: The Logical Roots of Anti-Semitism* (New York 1974), p. 328 and passim.

15 A. Roy Eckardt, 'Eretz Israel: A Christian Affirmation', *Midstream*, XIV (1968), p. 10.

16 A. Roy Eckardt, 'The Devil and Yom Kippur', *Midstream*, XX (1974), pp. 67–73.

17 This is the drift of the Dedication addressed in 1650 to the English revolutionary government. In his 'Humble address to His Highness the Lord Protector' of 1655, Manasseh made his appeal more emphatically.

18 Reported in the *Washington Post* (27 March and 4 April 1972).

19 For a full account of this meeting, see Joseph H. Lookstein, 'The Vatican and the Jews, 1975', *Tradition*, XV (1975), pp. 5–24.

20 Professor William G. Oxtoby, a Presbyterian minister who is strongly critical of Israel and its policies, expresses the point well. He notes the 'gratifying advances in interfaith relationships'. But the new ecumenical spirit should not obscure the factor which ultimately separates Jews and Christians, and this he says is 'the peoplehood of Israel' ('Christians and the Mideast Crisis', *Christian Century*, July 1967, reprinted in F. E. Talmage, *Disputation and Dialogue* (New York 1975), pp. 224–5).

21 This may well be the interpretation of the visit of the British Chief Rabbi Immanuel Jakobovits to the Jews of the Soviet Union in December 1975 and the remarkably helpful attitude which the Russian authorities displayed at the time.

22 Cf. W. D. Davies, *The Gospel and the Land* (Berkeley, Calif. 1974). In his detailed study Davies points to different strata of belief within the New Testament and the traditions which flowed from them. In some strata 'the need to remember the Jesus of history entailed the need to remember the Jesus of a particular land. Jesus belonged not only to time, but to space; and the space and spaces which he occupied took on significance, so that the *realia* of Judaism continued as *realia* in Christianity. History in the tradition demanded geography' (p. 366).

23 Cf. Ramsay MacMullen, *Constantine* (New York 1969), pp. 187–9.

24 Cf. R. Otto, *The Idea of the Holy* (Oxford 1923), passim.

25 Thomas Fuller, *A Pisgah-sight of Palestine* (London 1650), book 3, chapter 1, p. 355.

26 Ibid., book 5, chapters 2 and 3.

27 The best account of this that I know is that of Franz Kobler, *The Vision Was There* (The World Jewish Congress, British Section, London 1956), passim. This little book deserves to be better known.

28 I am aware that for some of the masters of early Hasidism, perhaps as a reaction to the failure of the Sabbatian Movement, the messianic elements in Judaism tended to be displaced and the emphasis was on the salvation of the individual through a

sort of spiritual 'ascent' (on this, see Sholem, *The Messianic Idea in Judaism*, pp. 194–5, 202). But Scholem himself recognizes that this was a temporary aberration.

29 See Joshua Prawer, *The Latin Kingdom of Jerusalem* (London 1972), p. 40.

30 Yaacov Herzog testifies to the extremely conciliatory attitude shown by the cardinals he met in Rome on his visit as head of the Israel Prime Minister's Office shortly after the Six Day War in June 1967 (see *A People that Dwells Alone*, p. 55).

31 One example, related by John Osterreicher, concerns the cancellation by Israel under Vatican pressure of the purchase of some disused Church property in Jerusalem, by the Hebrew University (see 'Christianity Threatened in Israel?' *Midstream* (January 1973), p. 7). There are other examples.

32 Cf. *Exodus* 14:15.

33 Cf. *Babylonian Talmud*, tractate *Sanhedrin*, folio 98a.

34 Not all Jewish theologians would agree that Jews and Christians are somehow embarked on the same journey. Eliezer Berkovits maintains that since the Holocaust we have been living in the 'post-Christian' era and that 'on the whole we have to go our own way' (*Faith After the Holocaust* (New York 1973), p. 49). This is an understandable position, but can Israel's witness be performed in a total vacuum? The term 'dialogue' may not be the most helpful as a definition of Jewish-Christian relations (see ibid., pp. 44–5), especially as the 'dialogue' seems to break down when it is most needed, e.g. at the time of the Six Day War. We would, perhaps, do better to think in terms of a drama of salvation enacted by Israel before a world-wide audience. To be properly performed, the play calls for a certain amount of audience participation; and if the audience is not always responsive, it may be because the actors have not always studied their parts as well as they should.

9: Who are the Palestinians?

1 An article by one Eliam A-Diri, published at the height of the Civil War in the Lebanese newspaper *A-Nahar*, contained a castigation of what the writer regarded as the unparalleled blood-thirstiness exhibited by all parties to the dispute (see

the translation in the Hebrew daily *Davar*, 12 December 1975).

2 The exception to this, which is regularly quoted in attacks on Zionism, is the killing of a number of civilians in the village of Dir Yassin by Jewish irregulars in 1948 – an episode of which no Israeli is proud. Even then, as one Arab observer acknowledged in 1953, 'the Jews never intended to hurt the population of the village but were forced to do so after they met hostile fire from the population which killed the Irgun commander' (quoted by Samuel Katz, *Battleground: Fact and Fantasy in Palestine*, New York 1973, p. 19).

3 Cf. Yehoshafat Harkabi's carefully documented *Arab Attitudes to Israel* (London 1972), pp. 275, 229ff., 518.

4 This is the argument of Amos Elon, *The Israelis: Founders and Sons*.

5 See David Ben-Gurion, *My Talks with Arab Leaders* (New York 1973), p. 7.

6 David Ben-Gurion, *We and Our Neighbours* [Hebrew] (Tel-Aviv 1931), pp. 72, 150.

7 Weizmann, *Trial and Error*, p. 566.

8 See Vladimir Jabotinsky, *The War and the Jew* (New York 1942), p. 215.

9 Ibid. And cf. also Ben-Gurion, *We and Our Neighbours*, p. 122.

10 Cf. M. Aumann, *Land Ownership in Palestine* (Jerusalem n.d. [1970]), passim.

11 Reproduced in Katz, *Battleground: Fact and Fantasy in Palestine*, p. 244.

12 General Louis Bols, the British military administrator, noted in 1919 that the Arab agitation at that time was in the name of an 'undivided Syria' (quoted by Weizmann, *Trial and Error*, p. 323). Arab nationalism in Palestine during this period was largely Syria-oriented (see also Yehoshua Porath, 'Political Organization under the British', in ed. Moshe Maoz, *Palestinian Arab Politics*, Jerusalem 1975, pp. 7–8). The 'Southern Syria' group included Haj Amin El-Husseini, who later became the Mufti of Jerusalem and the chief leader of the Palestine Arabs. With the collapse of the Hashemite regime in Damascus, he turned more in the direction of a Palestine Arab autonomy as a counter-weight to Zionist aspirations in Palestine. Other groups such as the Nashashibis, who were in opposition

to the Husseinis, also emphasized local patriotism. But these trends should not be exaggerated. The 'Southern Syria' notion and other forms of association based on wider Moslem or Pan-Arab loyalties continued throughout the Mandate period. As late as April 1945, the Institute of Arab-American Affairs submitted a manifesto to the UN Conference on International Organization at San Francisco, in which it stated that 'through historical continuity and associations, through a common heritage of racial culture and ideals, the people of Palestine are one with the people of neighbouring Syria. Palestine itself has been geographically and administratively, until the last war, an integral part of Syria' (paragraph 4). Pan-Arabism found its chief expression after 1945 in the newly formed Arab League, a confederation of the major Arab nations and representatives of the Palestinian Arabs. There the Palestine issue was central, but it was seen as part of a larger theme, the national struggle of all the Arabs. The idea of an independent Palestinian entity was by no means taken for granted by the League. The decisive change came with the creation of the Palestine Liberation Organization in the sixties – an organization sired, indeed, by the Arab League, but committed to the notion of a specifically Palestinian identity and a specifically Palestinian revolution.

13 Bernard Lewis, 'The Palestinians and the PLO', *Commentary*, LIX (January 1975), p. 33. By contrast Neville J. Mandel in *The Arabs and Zionism Before World War I* (Berkeley, Calif. 1976) emphasizes local patriotism as a factor in the period before 1914, leading later to Palestine Arab nationalism. But even he points out that this was just one of several strands, which must be set beside 'Ottoman loyalism' and 'pan-Arabism' (pp. 80, 226).

14 Bernard Lewis, op. cit., p. 34: 'The idea of a separate Palestinian state won little support among Palestinians who saw in this an imperialist device to divide the Arabs and thus preserve British power.'

15 Mr Arie Lova Eliav, seeking to explain why no Palestinian state was established after 1948 in the parts of Palestine liberated by the armies of the Arab states, advances the curious argument that 'the Palestine Arabs were hit so hard that they were unable to muster the strength to set up Arab Falastin in

the parts of the country that remained in their hands' (*Land of the Hart*, p. 124). If battle fatigue is the reason for the Arab failure to establish an Arab Palestine, what shall be said of the Jews after the Holocaust? If they succeeded in establishing their state, was it because they were less tired, less 'hard-hit' than the Arabs? Or was it not rather that, unlike the Arabs, they felt that the land was an altogether inseparable part of their past and their future?

16 In the use of this phrase I am anticipated by David Kama, *The Conflict* [Hebrew] (Jerusalem 1975), pp. 185–6.

17 On the circumstances surrounding the establishment of the Palestine Liberation Organization, see Y. Harkabi, 'The Palestinians in the Fifties and their Awakening. . . .', in *Palestinian Arab Politics*, ed. Maoz, pp. 81–4.

18 Mr Yasser Arafat spent some weeks in occupied Nablus after the Six Day War of 1967 and attempted to establish his base there. He was unsuccessful and left before the end of that year. Since then his organization has operated from bases outside Israeli occupied territory, with the help of small underground cells in Gaza, Nablus and elsewhere.

19 All quotations from these documents are based on the English text as published by Bernard Lewis (*Commentary*, LIX, January 1975, pp. 46–8).

20 Cf. Y. Harkabi, *Palestinians and Israel* (Jerusalem 1974), p. 59, commenting on paragraph 12 of the Palestine Covenant: 'The preservation of Palestine distinctiveness is merely a temporary necessity to be transcended in favor of Arab unity. However, there is an obvious contradiction between this intention and the previous assertion of the eternity of the Palestinian personality (cf. Article 4).' Dr Harkabi's line-by-line commentary on the Covenant is of the greatest value.

10: Epilogue

1 The attitude towards the Israelis was that of a 'lynch-mob'. Noted by Anthony Astrachan, the *Washington Post* correspondent at the UN, in 'The October War at the UN', *Midstream*, XIX (December 1973), p. 53.

2 This danger is pointed out by Y. Harkabi, *Israel's Viewpoints*

in its Conflict with the Arabs [Hebrew] (Tel-Aviv 1967), pp. 38–9.

3 The Thirteenth Palestine National Council, meeting in Cairo in March 1977, reaffirmed the Palestine Covenant as the basis for its belief and actions. Though hailed by some Western observers as moderate, the resolutions of the Council contain no hint of any readiness to recognize the legitimacy of Israel or of Zionism.

4 The Land of Israel Movement, founded in the immediate aftermath of the Six Day War, embraced all shades of political opinion. In fact the majority of those who signed its first manifesto in August 1967 were well-known left-wing personalities. The gist was that all the areas occupied by the Israel Defence Forces in the battles of 1967 were the inalienable possession of the Jewish People and could in no circumstances be ceded to Israel's enemies. On this Movement, see Rael Jean Isaac, *Israel Divided* (Baltimore 1976), pp. 45–72, 165–70; and, by the present author, 'Lobby that Stirs the Zionist Conscience', *The Times* (London), 2 September 1970.

Index

White Paper, British (1939), 102
Wiesel, Elie, 109, 181
Wordsworth, William, 55, 89

Yaron, Zvi, 177
Yemen, Jews of, 34, 37, 151, 180
Yishuv, the, 26, 103, 112, 115, 143, 176; 'old *Yishuv*', 112, 115
Yom Kippur War, 7, 18, 78, 91, 93, 94, 99, 100, 101, 102, 111, 116, 118, 136, 160, 164, 166, 179, 182, 188

Zionism, *passim*
'Zionists of Zion', 5, 22, 79, 166, 167
Zohar, the, 68
Zola, Emile, 25